T0328857

This book examines product-line diversification of large manufacturing firms. It introduces and applies methodology about
complementarities in production, marketing, distribution, and
research and development (R&D) activities. Manufacturing
firms intentionally vary production to exploit these complementarities, and Professor Scott uses evidence from U.S. manufacturing and ensuing economic performance, including
product diversification's effects on both static efficiency and the
optimality of R&D investment.

The study of hypotheses about purposive diversification and
ensuing multimarket contact of manufacturing firms yields new
perspectives on the policy debate about cooperation versus
competition among firms: Will industrial performance be better
if leading firms cooperate on research, production, and marketing? Professor Scott shows that the answers depend on circumstances that vary with different industrial environments.
His analysis offers insights about business strategy and public
policy toward business combinations in conglomerate, vertical,
and horizontal mergers, and in cooperative R&D ventures. The
author concludes by using the findings about purposive diversification and rivalry among U.S. companies to provide an
explanation of the relative success of Japanese firms in international competition.

PURPOSIVE DIVERSIFICATION
AND ECONOMIC PERFORMANCE

# Purposive diversification
# and economic performance

JOHN T. SCOTT
*Dartmouth College*

CAMBRIDGE
UNIVERSITY PRESS

CAMBRIDGE UNIVERSITY PRESS
Cambridge, New York, Melbourne, Madrid, Cape Town, Singapore, São Paulo

Cambridge University Press
The Edinburgh Building, Cambridge CB2 2RU, UK

Published in the United States of America by Cambridge University Press, New York

www.cambridge.org
Information on this title: www.cambridge.org/9780521430159

First published 1993
This digitally printed first paperback version 2005

*A catalogue record for this publication is available from the British Library*

*Library of Congress Cataloguing in Publication data*
Scott, John T., 1947–
Purposive diversification and economic performance / John T.
Scott.
p.  cm.
Includes bibliographical references and index.
ISBN 0-521-43015-1
1. Diversification in industry – United States.  I. Title.
HD2756.2.U5S37  1993
338.6 – dc20                                            92–34452
                                                                  CIP

ISBN-13 978-0-521-43015-9 hardback
ISBN-10 0-521-43015-1 hardback

ISBN-13 978-0-521-02258-3 paperback
ISBN-10 0-521-02258-4 paperback

*For Jan and Troy*

CONTENTS

## Contents viii

# LIST OF TABLES AND FIGURES

**Tables**

**Figures**

ACKNOWLEDGMENTS

The U.S. Federal Trade Commission (FTC) made this book possible by allowing me to work with the confidential Line of Business (LB) data. Of course, the views here are my own and not necessarily those of the staff of the FTC or any of its members. As certified in the disclosure avoidance procedures for each of the working papers from which my FTC LB results herein come, and as noted in the journal publications that ensued, the commission ensured that the results presented do not disclose data of any individual company. I am grateful to the FTC and to William F. Long (who at the time was the manager for the FTC LB Program) for giving me the opportunity of working with the LB data and to the FTC's George Pascoe for research assistance and computer programming that made possible many of the initial research papers on which this book is based. Joseph P. Cholka also provided assistance with computer programming. F. M. Scherer, Zvi Griliches, and Leonard W. Weiss provided some of the data that I used with the LB data, and they also provided helpful comments on early drafts. Many economists commented on the initial papers, and my thanks to them of course extends beyond the specific journal articles where their help has been individually acknowledged; their patient comments on those earlier papers made this book possible. William L. Baldwin, Richard E. Caves, Paul A. Geroski, Dennis C. Mueller, and Richard T. Shin also provided many constructive criticisms of the initial manuscript of the book. The Lewis H. Haney 1903 Endowment in Economics and The Nelson A. Rockefeller Center for the Social Sciences at Dartmouth College provided financial support. I also thank Karen Endicott, who provided countless suggestions that improved my writing, and Scott V. Parris, who as editor provided encouragement as well as much guidance throughout the project.

# INTRODUCTION: AN OVERVIEW

In the autumn of 1980, having been granted a year-long leave of absence from Dartmouth College, I arrived in Washington, D.C., at the offices of the United States Federal Trade Commission Line of Business (FTC LB) Program. As a visiting research economist, I was granted access to the program's confidential data describing in unprecedented detail the diversification of the United States' largest manufacturing firms. After roughly a decade of working, first as an in-house economist and then as an outside consultant, with the FTC's remarkable data, I decided to bring together my observations about the FTC LB reporters' diversified activities. This book is the result. In the book, I introduce and apply methodology that discerns groups of manufacturing industries that are related because of complementarities in production, marketing, distribution, and research and development (R&D) activities. Manufacturing firms purposively diversify to exploit such complementarities, and I explore hypotheses about that behavior – i.e., *purposive diversification* – and ensuing economic performance. The book studies product diversification's effects on both static allocative efficiency and the optimality of R&D investment.

The study of those hypotheses about purposive diversification yields new perspectives on the policy debate about cooperation versus competition among firms. The debate is an old one that has flared anew. Chernow (1990, p. 111) gives an interesting perspective on the debate at the beginning of the twentieth century when the firms involved were the railroads, the steelmakers, and the oil refiners. The bankers who arranged the huge combinations of previously competing firms sought to avoid "destructive competition." Now in the century's last decade, the protagonists include manufacturers of high-technology products such as semiconductors and high-definition television. The industrialists and government officials who espouse combinations seek global competitiveness. Will industrial

1

performance be better if leading firms cooperate on research, production, and marketing? The earlier debate shaped industrial structure and performance throughout the century, and the current debate will be no less important. I hope my observations contribute to an informed discussion of the relative merits of cooperation and competition.

The book is divided into four parts. In Part I, "Static Efficiency and the Diversified Firm," Chapter 1 discusses the nature of the multimarket firm and discusses motives for diversification. The chapter illustrates methodology to be used throughout the book by demonstrating that the leading manufacturers comprising the FTC LB sample purposively combine business units (also referred to as lines of business, or LBs) that share distribution channels. Thus, my methodology is first illustrated with a familiar idea: Economies of scope occur when the distribution systems for different products can share common assets. But another explanation for multimarket firms is that in their diversification the firms are seeking market power. Chapter 2 discusses theories that link diversification and ensuing multimarket contact to market power. Chapter 3 observes that if the hypothesis that multimarket contact increases market power is true, we should see firms seeking to increase multimarket contact with their mergers. The chapter then considers some evidence about such behavior.

This book introduces the idea that nonrandom coincidence of the diversified activities of manufacturers can be used to discern the underlying structure of related or close industry categories and to test hypotheses about industry behavior and performance. Chapter 4 uses the idea to show how the multimarket contact that results from firms' diversification affects resource allocation. The chapter provides evidence that for industries with high seller concentration, greater multimarket contact of their firms is associated with higher profit rates, yet in industries with less concentrated structures, profitability is lowest when multimarket contact is greatest. The chapter develops contrasting possibilities: Multimarket contact can enhance oligopolists' ability to limit production and establish supracompetitive prices, yet it can coincide with especially rapid resource flows that eliminate short-run profits in the less concentrated markets of diversified firms.

Scholars analyzing business strategy have observed that acquisitions diversifying into related industries are valued more highly by the stock market than are unrelated diversifying acquisitions; Singh and Montgomery (1987) provide important verification. Throughout this book, I introduce methodology that discerns related from unrelated groups of industry categories and show, among other things, that the performance implications of related diversification will depend on structural attributes of the industry categories involved. A firm undertaking purposive diversification will ideally seek not simply related activities, but rather related activities with conditions – such as limited competition and barriers to entry – allowing what Porter (1985) terms sustainable competitive advantage.

The hypothesis that multimarket contact can increase profitability in concentrated industries can be extended. One might hypothesize that multimarket contact is a sine qua non of successful tacit collusion among diversified manufacturers. Chapter 5 explores that hypothesis using the now classic data on U.S. manufacturing in the 1950s. The results do support the hypothesis and are consistent with the findings from the FTC LB data of the mid-1970s. In all, purposive diversification and ensuing multimarket contact, at first blush seemingly of second-order importance for the traditional resource allocation problem at the heart of industrial economics, turn out to be the keys that unlock secrets of behavior and allocative performance for diversified manufacturers.

Further, purposive diversification may drive successful technological advance. Technological successes of the Japanese have been attributed to the "fusion" of ideas generated in different but complementary industries. The technological fusion is made possible by *keiretsu,* or families of firms with ownership interests in one another (*The Economist,* 1989, pp. 5–6; Aoki, 1988, p. 250). Odagiri (1992) provides a detailed description of the various forms for *keiretsu* and other business groups in Japan, and he also observes that the *keiretsu* serve to combine complementary R&D activities (1992, pp. 98–99, p. 161). The *keiretsu* clearly effect a kind of purposive diversification of R&D. Indeed, Porter (1990) has attributed the sustainable competitive advantages of entire countries to their prowess in clusters of related industries. As documented in Part IV, public policy in the United States has moved toward promoting cooperation among firms as a means to effectively cluster complementary resources. Yet there is also a perception that the *keiretsu* linking operations in complementary industry categories may violate U.S. antitrust laws. Holstein et al. (1990, p. 107) describe that perception and note that the U.S. House Judiciary Committee asked the FTC to investigate the effects of *keiretsu* that have operations in the United States. Throughout the book I shall address the static and dynamic performance implications of diversification and cooperation; then, in the Afterword, I shall use my findings to address directly the issues that *keiretsu* have raised about private business strategy and public policy.

The book explores the implications of diversification and cooperation for technological advance and productivity as well as for static allocative and technical efficiency; however, first, it explains the need for such exploration. To do that, Part II, "Firm and Industry Effects versus Traditional Models," explores the explanatory power of simple traditional models of structure and performance that do not focus on multimarket strategies. Our initial observations in Part I that diversification and the multimarket contact resulting from diversification affect importantly the behavior of firms – together with the fact to be developed in Part III that firms within the same industry category often belong to very different multimarket groups – imply that we should find strong company effects in addition to traditional industry effects in the general linear model of business unit performance. Part II explores the extent of such company effects (also called firm effects) and observes that traditional industrial organization models explain a relatively small part of the systematic variance in LB behavior and performance. The presence of strong company effects and different patterns of multimarket operation for the firms in any particular industry category fit nicely with the Milgrom and Roberts (1990) prediction that complementarities in the production, marketing, engineering, and organizational operations of multiproduct firms will lead to a heterogeneous mix of firms with distinct clusters of characteristics.

Chapter 6 uses fixed effects to control for, among other things, differences in capital costs specific to firms and the industries in which they operate. The chapter shows that traditional structural models of concentration and barriers to entry explain only a small portion of the *systematic* variance in profitability across firms and industries. Industries and firms differ significantly, but our traditional models do not explain much of those systematic differences. There is also evidence that in the mid-1970s difficulties for capital-intensive firms undermined the traditional positive association between seller concentration and profit rates.

Chapter 7 shows that the failure of simple, traditional structural models to explain systematic differences among firms and industries obtains for R&D intensity as well as for profits. The chapter develops – with firm effects as well as the more conventional industry effects – the longstanding hypothesis that technological opportunity is far more important for understanding variance in innovative activity than are measures of rivalry. That hypothesis has found wide support beginning with Scherer's pioneering observations (1965, 1967a). Geroski (1990; 1991a, chapter 6) has supported the hypothesis using data on major innovations in the United Kingdom for the 1970s, the time period from which my United States observations were taken. Yet, in Part III, I shall hypothesize that desirable rivalry is at the heart of the substantial differences in behavior captured by firm effects. The evidence presented provides some support for the hypothesis. Rivalry stimulates diversity in research strategies, and purposive diversification effects that diversity and thereby leads to productivity growth.

The results in Part II demonstrate unequivocally that a firm's performance is not solely determined by the attributes of the industries in which it operates. By using appropriate strategies, a firm can perform better than would be predicted from the firm's set of industries. Executives are taught that differentiating business strategies can advantageously set their firms apart from the pack (see Oster, 1990, and Porter, 1985). The importance of firm effects, as shown in Part II, suggests that indeed the firm's strategies do distinguish it from others in the same industry categories. Further, evidence from several countries suggests that such distinct performance persists – there are permanent differences in profitability across firms (Mueller, 1990).

After Chapter 8 begins with a theory of R & D rivalry that provides an analytical framework for both Part III and Part IV, Part III, "Dynamic Efficiency and the Diversified Firm," explores the pronounced differences in operations among firms in the same industry category. Chapter 9 suggests that the reason for the differences may be the firms' differing patterns of purposive diversification as they seek to exploit synergies in the R & D activities of different industry categories. Indeed, after reviewing conventional studies of diversification and R & D, Scherer and Ross (1990, p. 659) note that different results are obtained in Scott (1988) when *purposive* diversification is studied. The relation between purposive diversification and R & D activity is the focus of Part III.

General Electric Company, for example, has profited from many well-documented cases of R & D spillovers among its diversified operations in lighting, medical equipment, plastics, power generation, and aircraft engines (Naj, 1990). The methodology in Chapter 9 detects such related, or close, industry categories for the FTC LB sample of manufacturers and demonstrates that the exploitation of complementarities in R & D across close manufacturing categories changes R & D effort and productivity growth. Further, as explained in Chapter 9, the finding of purposive diversification across even the very aggregative two-digit industry categories suggests that there are potential problems with estimations of intraindustry and interindustry spillovers from R & D investment when each firm's R & D investments are assigned to a primary industry category or when firms are not grouped according to their purposive diversification. In any case, my results are quite consistent with the general direction of others looking for evidence of spillovers. Bernstein (1988) and Bernstein and Nadiri (1988a, 1988b) are prominent examples.

Similarly, my findings are consistent with those of Caves and Barton (1990), who find that corporate diversification decreases technical efficiency, and with those of Lichtenberg (1990), who finds that the de-diversification movement of the 1980s increased industrial productivity. At first blush, their results are different – more diversification is associated with lower productivity. My finding that purposive diversification increases productivity growth is not a contradiction, because the back-to-basics movement of the 1980s reduced the random diversification that had increased with the conglomerate mergers in the 1960s and 1970s and increased the purposive variety. More diversification has led to lower productivity, yet productivity increases with *purposive* diversification.

Chapter 10 asks whether evidence for traditional structural models, found wanting in Chapter 7, can be found if firms are reorganized into groups based on the observed patterns of purposive diversification. Arguably, firms compete, especially in areas of R & D, in multimarket sets of related industry categories. As Chapter 10 shows, the poor explanatory power of the traditional models still obtains despite the reorganization. Yet I shall argue that rivalry among firms is nonetheless a major determinant of R & D behavior and performance. Findings of strong company effects in R & D effort and also differences among an industry's firms in terms of their purposive diversification of R & D suggest that more competition, envisioned as rivalry among larger numbers of firms, may improve dynamic performance because it increases diversity in R & D efforts. Chapter 11 develops that hypothesis; the diversity synonymous with the rivalry in Schumpeter's (1942) creative competition is the chapter's subject. The diversity of R & D effort induced by rivalry may underlie the observation in Acs and Audretsch (1988) that less concentrated industries show better innovative performance than more concentrated industries do.

Part IV, "Industrial Policy," relates the findings about diversified manufacturing firms to the debate about the effects of antitrust policy on technological change and productivity. In the United States, the 1980s brought a surge in advocacy of cooperation among previously competing firms as a way to promote technological progress and international competitiveness. In prominent policy analyses, Jorde and Teece (1988) called for further changes in antitrust law to extend those introduced in the National Cooperative Research Act of 1984 (NCRA), and Baily and Chakrabarti (1988) concluded that joint ventures would increase innovation. Such analyses emphasize the appropriability problems and the wasteful duplication of effort that can result from rivalry.

Chapter 12 uses theory and evidence about the NCRA to question the efficacy of cooperation as a means to innovation and competitiveness. Competitive pressures can drive firms to innovate even though they appropriate smaller portions of their innovations' social benefits. Further, just as flipping additional but identical coins increases the probability of at least one favorable outcome, much of what might appear to be wasteful duplication may in fact provide the numerous research trials needed to increase the probability of innovation to an appropriate level. And, as Chapter 11 emphasizes, rivalry may increase desirable diversity in R&D effort.

Chapter 13 offers more general perspectives about the shift in antitrust policy that underlies the clamor for more cooperation and less rivalry. The clamor has indeed been great. When in 1984 I tentatively discussed with the U.S. National Science Foundation (NSF) the possibility of a proposal to analyze whether or not the emerging legislation on R&D joint ventures was sensible, the NSF policy analyst helping me advised me to shift the focus of my proposed inquiry because the support for antitrust relief for joint ventures was so great. To highlight that support, he cited a California congressman who for over twenty years had represented the California congressional district containing Silicon Valley, the chairman and chief executive officer of the most prominent R&D joint venture, and the Assistant Attorney General from the U.S. Department of Justice's Antitrust Division. He suggested that rather than asking whether the new law providing such relief made sense, I instead could usefully work on determining guidelines for evaluating the R&D joint ventures formed under the new law. Those ventures, after all, would still be subject to challenge for any antitrust violations they committed, although the new law changed procedure for evaluating potential violations and lessened penalties for violations in order to encourage cooperative ventures.

Perhaps, in the spirit of the NSF policy analyst's suggestions, Chapters 12 and 13 will provide insights which will improve the evaluation of the economic effects of cooperative R&D, whether challenged or not, yet also explain the historical context in which the new law was widely and uncritically accepted. Both houses of the U.S. Congress have prepared extensions, to cover joint production efforts, of the 1984 law about cooperative R&D, and the need for the new laws and the form they should take has been earnestly debated (Brodley, 1990; Jorde and Teece, 1990; Shapiro and Willig, 1990; Adams and Brock, 1991a). Chapters 12 and 13 use my findings about purposive diversification to offer a different perspective on the debate about the effectiveness of joint ventures and also provide some greater appreciation of just how blunt are the policy tools provided by fashionable adjustments to our antitrust laws. Because current policy emphasizes cooperation in order to mitigate risks, achieve economies, lessen wasteful duplication, and appropriate returns, it necessarily sacrifices competition. Thus, Chapter 14 concludes by suggesting an unusual form of taxation that could be used to simulate the desirable effects of competition when actual competition is forgone.

The industrial policy discussed in Part IV has been formulated as a response to the declining effectiveness of U.S. manufacturers in international trade. In the Afterword, I first observe that my findings about U.S. manufacturers are broadly consistent with and complementary to findings in the literature about the manufacturers of other countries. I then use my findings about the implications of purposive diversification for static and dynamic efficiency to compare the relative success of Japan's manufacturers with what at times has been rather lackluster performance of much of U.S. industry. Interesting points of comparison are provided by the decrease in purposive diversification for the typical U.S. manufacturing firm after World War II as contrasted with Japan's *keiretsu* linking complementary activities, and the recent encouragement of joint venture activity by U.S. firms as contrasted with the more long-standing public policy in Japan through which government nurtures cooperative activity among an industry's competitors. In the Afterword, I use the findings throughout the book to offer straightforward policy prescriptions to improve industrial performance and the performance of a nation's international competitors.

# PART I

Static efficiency and the diversified firm

# 1

## The multimarket firm

Large manufacturing firms typically operate in many markets. As a result, when we analyze a market's performance as a function of its structure, we need to consider the diversification of the market's sellers and their multimarket contact. The operations of the typical firm among the largest 1000 U.S. manufacturers span several lines of business. Table 1.1 provides the frequency distribution describing the number of manufacturing lines of business (LBs – an LB is a company's operations in a particular industry) for the 437 companies in the sample used in this chapter.[1] The companies are all among the largest 1000 U.S. manufacturers and comprise the Federal Trade Commission Line of Business (FTC LB) Program sample for 1974. These large companies average a bit under eight manufacturing LBs per company.

Of course, the motives for such diversification are numerous. For just a sampling of the variety of commentary through the years, consider Penrose (1959), Gort (1962), Rumelt (1974), Berry (1975), Mueller (1987), and Montgomery and Wernerfelt (1988). Although random discrepancies in the valuation of assets (Gort, 1969) and the risk aversion of managers (Amihud and Lev, 1981) can motivate pure conglomerate diversification, the purposive pursuit of (private) efficiencies because of complementarities across industry categories motivates "related" diversification. I shall focus on the trade-off that such diversification creates between the possibilities for technical efficiencies and for market power and then investigate the ensuing overall performance effects on static and dynamic efficiency.

I shall explore the causes and effects of diversification. Diversification can yield gains to the firm if it can realize economies of scope that increase

---

The statistics used in this chapter were first presented in a paper given at the Econometric Society's Winter Meetings in Washington, D.C., 1981.

Table 1.1. *Frequency distribution showing the number of companies with a given number of manufacturing lines of business (LBs)*

| Frequency class: Number of manufacturing LBs (1) | Frequency: Number of companies (2) | Class total: Number of LBs (1) × (2) |
|---|---|---|
| 1 | 38 | 38 |
| 2 | 34 | 68 |
| 3 | 41 | 123 |
| 4 | 51 | 204 |
| 5 | 40 | 200 |
| 6 | 35 | 210 |
| 7 | 34 | 238 |
| 8 | 25 | 200 |
| 9 | 20 | 180 |
| 10 | 20 | 200 |
| 11 | 16 | 176 |
| 12 | 15 | 180 |
| 13 | 6 | 78 |
| 14 | 11 | 154 |
| 15 | 5 | 75 |
| 16–20 | 23 | 407[a] |
| 21–28 | 14 | 331[a] |
| 31–47 | 9 | 326[a] |
| Total | 437 | 3388 |

[a] Column (1) contains a range of classes to avoid disclosure of disaggregated data. The number in column (3) is the exact result of using the disaggregated data.

the revenue productivity of its resources. Such gains can be predicted either as a consequence of the structures of markets across which firms diversify (for example, requiring common inputs) or from the abilities of individual firms (abilities not fully explained by industry structures) to achieve such scope economies. Part II documents the latter basis, while Part I selectively investigates the former.

The chapters in Part I recognize that diversification can be explained by several factors. Such factors include efficiency because of economies of scope, efficiency because the multidivisional "M-form" corporate structure (Mueller, 1987, pp. 25–29) induces profitable capital redeployment, market power for several reasons (detailed specifically in Chapter 2), and the spreading of risk. The book uses the idea that firms facing similar opportunities regarding such factors will meet in a common set of markets more than would happen by chance. The implication of the idea is the major message of Part I: *Diversification accomplishes various privately efficient objectives for firms but may have the consequence of increasing the potential for collusion or cooperative-like outcomes (even when competitors compete in noncooperative games) among diversified competitors in particular markets.*

I shall focus therefore on an industry as a group of sellers supplying several markets, the markets being distinguished by their buyers or products. There are two reasons for my focus. First, economies of multimarket operation – i.e., economies of scope (Baumol et al., 1982) – may be important. It is plausible that a multimarket setting is necessary for the firm to realize technical efficiency. Coase (1937) and Williamson (1981) have explained why the price mechanism – the arms-length market mechanism – for allocating resources is replaced by conscious control within the firm. Multimarket operation, whether "horizontal" or "vertical," may be efficient because it reduces the number of market transactions. To the extent that resource flows needed in the production process are stochastic or there is fixed overhead associated with those flows, it may be efficient to put together lines of business that sell to the same industries or more generally the same customers, sell through the same distribution outlets although not necessarily to the same customers, use inputs from the same industries, use similar technologies, use similar marketing strategies, or are vertically related. In short, coordination of flows of inputs and outputs may be easier within the firm than by the market. My second reason for studying industries as groups of sellers serving several markets has been explained by Edwards (1955), Adams (1974), Scott (1982), and Bernheim and Whinston (1990), among others. Multimarket contact of sellers may affect the ability of the sellers to sustain cooperative-like performance in an uncooperative environment by affecting sellers' ability to communicate, by changing conjectural variations within markets, by changing the incentives to undercut any potential consensus with cooperative-like results, and by changing entry conditions.

Thus, to understand fully the implications of market structure and conduct for performance, firms should be considered in their multimarket setting. In this introductory chapter about the multimarket firm, I shall use a very simple and commonplace example to illustrate the idea that a firm diversifies in order to purposively exploit economic opportunity. The presence of a purposive nature for diversification underlies my method of discerning related industry categories by observing the nonrandom multimarket meetings for firms pursuing similar opportunities. In subsequent chapters I shall use the method to explore diversification's implications for economic performance. Here, though, I shall illustrate the pronounced nonrandomness of diversification by making the simple observation that actual diversification in manufacturing exploits the opportunities for shared distribution channels among business units. What is striking is not that the null hypothesis of randomness is rejected, but rather how great is the departure of actual diversification from a random assignment. The randomness hypothesis is quite far off the mark; and thus, for subsequent chapters I can expect to find strongly defined groups of related categories in which my sample of diversified firms compete.

Often multimarket operations are predominantly complementary in production or distribution – if not vertically related, then the operations typically reflect "product extensions" or "market extensions."[2] Putting together such related product lines, whether through internal growth or merger, allows the firm to make further use of marketing contacts, specialized management, and technological know-how, for example. For our introductory case, though, I shall observe that diversified firms often produce products that share the same distribution channels. The three-digit Standard Industrial Classification (SIC) wholesale categories provide the groupings of industry categories needed to test the hypothesis that diversification exploits efficiencies of shared distribution channels. To begin, I use FTC and Census sources[3] to divide the FTC manufacturing industry categories[4] among the SIC's three-digit wholesale categories. As it turns out, there are ten of these wholesale categories with ten or more FTC manufacturing industry categories assigned to them. From each of those ten groups, I randomly chose ten manufacturing categories. The resulting ten wholesale groups (each with ten manufacturing categories) provide the input for our introductory experiment.

The manufacturing categories in each of the ten groups are "close" in the sense that they share the same wholesaling channels. Notably, the ten groups do not simply mirror two-digit industry classifications. For example, a firm producing entirely within the wholesaling category for paper, paper products, and other goods sold through the same channels appears to be highly diversified in terms of two-digit industries if it produces envelopes (in SIC manufacturing group 26), greeting cards (in SIC manufacturing group 27), and pens and pencils (in SIC manufacturing group 39). Yet these manufactured products from different two-digit manufacturing categories share the same distribution channels. Or for another example, from the wholesaling category for construction materials, a firm might produce lumber (in SIC manufacturing group 24), roofing materials (in SIC manufacturing group 29), concrete (in SIC manufacturing group 32), and metal door frames (in SIC manufacturing group 34).[5]

Table 1.2. *The significance of grouping of manufacturing LBs into wholesaling categories for companies with x = 6 sampled LBs*

| $f^a$ (1) | $p(f)^b$ (2) | Observed frequency$^c$ (3) | Empirical probability$^d$ (4) |
|---|---|---|---|
| 1 | 0.00000176 | $11^e$ | $11/27 = 0.407^e$ |
| 2 | 0.00145 | | |
| 3 | 0.0481 | 7 | $7/27 = 0.259$ |
| 4 | 0.299 | $9^e$ | $9/27 = 0.333^e$ |
| 5 | 0.476 | | |
| 6 | 0.176 | 0 | $0/27 = 0.000$ |
| Total | $\sum p(f) = 1.00$ | 27 | 1.00 |

$^a$ The number of wholesale categories into which the company's sampled LBs fall.
$^b$ The probability that the company's sampled operations will fall into $f$ categories if behavior is not purposive.
$^c$ The number of companies for which the sampled lines of business fall into $f$ categories.
$^d$ Column (3)/total number of companies for which $x = 6$. Letting the random variable $Z = (1/27)\sum_{i=1}^{27} f_i$, the variance of $Z$ given the null hypothesis is $E(Z - EZ)^2 = (1/27)^2 \sum_i \sum_j E\tilde{f}_i \tilde{f}_j = \sigma_f^2/27$. Given the null hypothesis, the ratio of the absolute difference between the observed $\hat{Z}$ and the expected value of $Z$ to the standard deviation of $Z$ is 11.9. There is clearly a significant amount of grouping of lines of business into the same wholesaling categories since, using Chebyshev's inequality, the probability of a deviation from the mean equal to 11.9 times the standard deviation or more is at most 0.0071.
$^e$ Combined to comply with disclosure avoidance procedures.

Given the ten wholesaling categories, the question is whether, for the firms in the sample, there is a statistically significant amount of grouping of diversified activities into those categories. The 437 large manufacturing firms comprising the FTC Program sample for 1974 are the subject of this experiment.[6] To answer our foregoing question, we need the probability distribution giving the probability that a firm in $x$ lines of business will have those operations distributed over $f$ wholesaling categories, $f = 1$ to $x$, if in fact behavior is not purposive, i.e., random. Table 1.2 shows that distribution for companies with $x = 6$ lines of business in our test group of 100. To save space and avoid repetition, I shall report here in detail only that case, but the other cases, $x = 2, 3, \ldots$, were computed and showed essentially the same result, a result that is summarized for all cases once I have presented the $x = 6$ case in detail.

Throughout the book, I shall want to look for purposive, nonrandom behavior, and to do so I shall ask whether a firm's behavior in diversifying appears to show a statistically significant tendency to group industry categories into an arrangement suggested by a hypothesis under consideration. I reject that hypothesis if instead the firm's choice of categories to combine does not exhibit such grouping, but rather a scattering of industry categories not falling into the pattern predicted by the hypothesis. Such scattering would result if instead of trying purposively to group the categories in the way predicted, the firm was as likely to choose one category as another – at least as far as we could tell using as our base the particular grouping predicted by the hypothesis. If the probability of less than the observed amount of grouping of categories is small against the null hypothesis of random behavior, then the grouping observed is not significant and we cannot accept the hypothesis. When I apply such methodology subsequently, my hypothesis of purposive behavior refers to the general pursuit of economies or market power or both. My simple introductory example is much more specific regarding the source of the purposive behavior and oversimplifies for the sake of using a very familiar idea to begin introducing the methodology.[7]

For the distribution used in Table 1.2, let $p(f)$ denote the probability, assuming nonpurposive, random behavior, that a firm with $x$ lines of business (LBs), among the 100 in our 10 groups of 10 manufacturing categories each, will have those LBs distributed over exactly $f$ of the 10 groups. The denominator of $p(f)$ shows the total number of ways a firm could have $x$ lines of business among the 100 in the 10 groups of 10 manufacturing categories each. For example, with $x$ less than or equal to 10, all $x$ could fall into the same group or could be dispersed among the groups. The denominator of each probability is then $C_{100,x}$, where $C_{z,t}$ denotes the combination of $z$ things taken $t$ at a time. The numerator of $p(f)$ shows the number of ways that the $x$ LBs could fall into exactly $f$ of the 10 groups.

For example, against the null hypothesis that the firm is not purposively combining manufacturing categories that share distribution channels and instead behaves randomly insofar as we can discern with the grouping of manufacturing categories on the basis of shared distribution channels, the probability that a firm with $x = 3$ lines of business (in the test universe of 100 lines of business) will have those 3 LBs fall into 2 of our 10 groups is

$$p(2) = \frac{C_{10,2}(C_{10,2}C_{10,1})C_{2,1}}{C_{100,3}} = \frac{40,500}{161,700}.$$

Looking at the numerator, we see that it is the product of (1) the number of ways to get 2 different groups among the 10, and (2) for each of those paired groups, the number of ways to get 2 LBs in 1 specific group and 1 in the remaining group, and (3) the number of ways to choose which of the 2 different groups gets only 1 of the 3 LBs.

For our illustrative case of $x = 6$, the reasoning is the same, but we just have to keep track of more possibilities. For $P(2)$, the denominator is still $C_{100,x}$, and for the numerator we still have the term (1) $C_{10,2}$; however, the information captured in the second and third terms becomes more complicated in general, although the reasoning is the same. The reason for the more complicated general formula is that with higher numbers of LBs, we have more than one way to divide $x$ LBs into $f$ groups. Thus, for $p(2)$ with $x = 6$, we have 3 ways – (5, 1), (4, 2), and (3, 3) – that 6 LBs can be divided into 2 groups; and hence, we have

$$p(2) = \frac{C_{10,2}[(C_{10,5}C_{10,1})(C_{2,1}) + (C_{10,4}C_{10,2})(C_{2,1}) + (C_{10,3}C_{10,3})]}{C_{100,6}}$$

$$= \frac{1,725,300}{1,192,052,400} = .00145.$$

Table 1.2 compares the theoretical and actual distribution for multimarket grouping by shared distribution channels of a firm's LBs and computes a statistic illustrating the significance of such grouping for the firms in our sample. If behavior were not purposive for those companies with $x = 6$ lines of business in our test group of 100, 95 percent of the sample should have their 6 LBs fall into 4, 5, or 6 different multimarket groups. Yet only 33 percent of the sample firms have activities that span that many of our 10 wholesaling groups. Further, only 0.14 percent should fall into 1 or 2 wholesale groups, but in fact the actual frequency (41 percent) is close to 300 times greater than expected. The sample average number of groups falls 12 standard deviations below its expected value given the null hypothesis of random behavior. If the null hypothesis were true, conservatively using Chebyshev's inequality to calculate an upper bound, the probability of a departure from the mean that great or greater is at most 1/144. For the complete set of cases, $x = 2, 3, \ldots$, examined, there is also clearly a significant amount of grouping of manufacturing lines of business into the same wholesaling categories, since using Chebyshev's inequality, the probability of a deviation from the mean as great or greater than that observed is on average at most .0107. Large U.S. manufacturing firms evidently do attempt to diversify into industry categories that share distribution channels since, far more than would happen by chance, the typical multimarket firm operates in industries that do share such channels.

Coase (1937) directed attention toward the firm as a collection of activities for which resource allocation is coordinated by conscious planning rather than by markets. Using markets rather than internal organization must yield the firm gains since it could use open markets otherwise (Coase, 1937, p. 338). According to Coase, the gains are likely to come from reducing the cost of dealing in markets – the "cost of using the price mechanism" (1937, pp. 335–336). In this book, I shall explore that possibility, but I shall also emphasize that diversification and the multimarket contact that it creates can result in the private gain of market power for the diversifying sellers.

In our first look at diversified manufacturing firms, we have seen that they consist of manufacturing LBs that share distribution channels. That observation alone certainly fits well with Coase's view of the nature of the firm. It evidently costs less for a firm to coordinate the sharing of common assets used in the distribution of several products than it would cost to have each of several single-product firms purchasing a fraction of such assets at arm's length in the market. We shall now, however, begin to explore the market power as well as the efficiency motive for diversification. For efficiency reasons alone, firms should seek, purposively, to diversify.[8] But I shall develop a market power motive too. If there were a market power motive, we might, for example, find firms seeking symmetry with their rivals with regard to their diversified operations. In Chapter 2, I shall develop that hypothesis and others that link diversification and market power; in Chapters 3, 4, and 5, I shall test the hypotheses. Of course, as I shall emphasize throughout my study, whether market power is the goal or not, whenever firms facing similar opportunities diversify to improve private efficiency for any of a number of sometimes independent reasons, their market power may increase as a result of their diversification.

# 2

# Theories linking multimarket contact and market power

In Chapter 1, we observed that diversification can be a way to achieve economies of scope, and the pursuit of such economies could explain why, for example, diversified firms combine lines of business (LBs) that share distribution channels. However, we also noted that there are hypotheses outstanding, suggesting that diversification can create private but not necessarily social gains if it is also a means to achieve market power. In this chapter, we shall begin our exploration of that possibility by developing the hypotheses; in subsequent chapters we shall examine evidence about the hypotheses.

## 2.1 Introduction

The Celler–Kefauver Act of 1950 amended Section 7 of the Clayton Act and redirected mergers toward the conglomerate variety (Scherer, 1980, pp. 123–124). Do the ensuing conglomerate mergers reflect a redirecting of mergers for market power? Since firms' limited organizational capacity for assimilating acquisitions could no longer be focused on horizontal mergers, perhaps conglomerate mergers afforded an alternative source of market power. Yet, as Section 2.2 explains, even the activist antitrust enforcement policies of the 1960s did not address the issue fully, and recent merger enforcement has certainly ignored the possibility.

After Section 2.2 discusses the theories about market power that have been used in policy toward conglomerate mergers, Section 2.3 turns to a theory not used in such public policy – namely the theory that multimarket contact can increase market power. Section 2.4 concludes by emphasizing the complementarities among the older and newer theories about multimarket contact.

## 2.2 Theories used in policy toward conglomerate mergers

Remarkably, the U.S. Supreme Court (and indeed the lower U.S. federal courts) has not been asked to consider the principal potential source of market power from conglomerate mergers. The enforcement agencies have not argued the matter and so the Court has not been concerned that multimarket contact among sellers in a concentrated market might create market power by facilitating oligopolistic consensus. Using different theories developed by economists and argued by the antitrust enforcement agencies, the Court *has,* of course, used Section 7 of the Clayton Act to block some conglomerate mergers. Anticompetitive consequences from reciprocal dealing were hypothesized in the *Consolidated Foods–Gentry* case, 380 U.S. 592 (1965). The Court believed that a conglomerate's purchases of another firm's product could be used as leverage to convince that other firm to purchase one of the conglomerate's products, with adverse consequences for that product's market structure if the reciprocal dealing caused concentration and barriers to entry to increase.[1] A theory of predatory or disciplinary pricing was proffered in the *Procter & Gamble–Clorox* case, 386 U.S. 568 (1967). The Court stated that the presence of a conglomerate among specialized firms might make the latter more willing to follow the former because of fear that the conglomerate would discipline uncooperative rivals with low prices, covering the temporary losses from its deep pocket of financial resources from operations in other markets. In the *Clorox* case and others, the Court has considered the conglomerate merger's effects on potential competition. Conglomerate mergers could also make more likely the types of tying arrangements that increase market power (Whinston, 1990); such arrangements have been addressed in the Court's decisions under Section 1 of the Sherman Act and Section 3 of the Clayton Act.[2]

The Court, however, has never used Corwin Edwards's idea (1955) that large conglomerates, having grown interdependent in several markets, will compete less vigorously. He hypothesized that in the presence of such multimarket contact conglomerates would avoid the risk of general price warfare throughout the several markets they supplied by leading in markets where they are strong and following in markets where they are weak.[3] Edwards (1949, p. 106; 1955, pp. 342–345) put as much emphasis on increased overt collusion as on what I shall refer to as increased cooperative-like behavior among firms engaged in noncooperative rivalry. More generally, as explained in Section 2.3, multimarket contact can facilitate oligopolistic consensus, because it increases the likelihood that each firm will independently choose a strategy close to the one maximizing joint profits for the set of interdependent firms.

Despite the a priori possibilities for market power created by conglomerate mergers, the U.S. federal antitrust establishment's concern about such mergers largely vanished during the 1980s. In 1982, the Assistant Attorney General for Antitrust, William Baxter, the Reagan administration's chief antitrust enforcement official, stated that "during the 1960s, in its general hostility to conglomerate mergers, the Supreme Court cooked up a variety of esoteric and totally baseless theories about the harm caused by conglomerate mergers" (Taylor, 1982). Obviously, the Court did not invent the theories, and it is misguided at best to say that the theories are baseless. Yet the antitrust authorities persisted in expounding this view well after 1982. In 1986, then Assistant Attorney General for Antitrust Douglas Ginsburg stated that "in the case of a purely conglomerate merger . . . [as contrasted with horizontal mergers in concentrated markets] no serious anticompetitive problems arise because the firms involved in the deal, by definition, do not actually compete with one another in any relevant market. One exception to this occurs in cases where one firm is properly characterized as a potential competitor of the other . . ." (U.S. Department of Justice, March 5, 1986, p. 8). This belief is embodied in the Justice Department's *Merger Guidelines* (U.S. Department of Justice, June 14, 1984) when, once again, the chief antitrust spokesperson for the enforcement agency asserted that several theories about anticompetitive problems because of diversifying mergers are not important empirically. The 1980s views about conglomerate mergers are still held in the 1990s. In their joint statement (p. 3, April 2, 1992) accompanying the release of the 1992 *Horizontal Merger Guidelines,* the Justice Department and the Federal Trade Commission (FTC) state that "neither agency has changed its policy with respect to nonhorizontal mergers. Specific guidance on nonhorizontal mergers is provided in Section 4 of the Department's 1984 *Merger Guidelines,* read in the context of today's revisions to the treatment of horizontal mergers."

These views of the Reagan antitrust establishment notwithstanding, I shall explain why policy should be concerned about conglomerate mergers that increase the multimarket contact of sellers in concentrated markets. Theory and evidence show that the classic *horizontal* merger issue – efficiency loss because of increased monopoly power versus efficiency gain because of reduced costs – is the antitrust issue in *conglomerate* mergers, even when there is no argument about potential competitors. The present chapter and those following provide some basic research to inform policy decisions about (1) multimarket contact among sellers in an industry that is becoming more concentrated because of a horizontal merger and (2) conglomerate mergers that increase the multimarket contact of sellers in concentrated markets.

### 2.3 Market power from multimarket contact

*The hypothesis:* Multimarket contact can facilitate oligopolistic consensus; it can not only make overt collusion easier, it can also allow noncooperative rivals to achieve cooperative-like outcomes with behavior that is "independent" in the legal sense. Consider two markets, each with only two sellers. In the first and second we find seller A. In the first, we find seller B competing with seller A. In the second, seller A competes with seller C. If sellers B and C merge, even though they are not competitors, the merger creates a situation in which the tacit cooperation, the communication needed to overcome myopic behavior of a prisoner's dilemma game, is more easily attained. Since the same set of sellers now meets in two markets, there are twice as many opportunities to come to understand one another. I shall argue, therefore, that the process of reaching a consensus on price is facilitated because there is more contact. Additionally, with complementarities in production and marketing, the costs and strategies of the two sellers in each market are now more symmetric, making tacit agreement easier. These ideas about the impact of multimarket contact on market power seem at first glance to contradict one of the results in the work of Bernheim and Whinston (1990). There is no contradiction; in fact I shall show below that the ideas are highly complementary.

*The relevance of multimarket contact given symmetry:* Bernheim and Whinston begin with "an irrelevance result" – i.e., they claim to show that "when identical firms with identical constant-returns-to-scale technologies meet in identical markets, multimarket contact does not aid in sustaining collusive outcomes" (1990, p. 5). I do not think they show that at all, although their "irrelevance result" does set up contrasting asymmetric cases in which they show an interesting class of ways that multimarket contact *can* sustain collusive outcomes. It will be instructive to reproduce their result (1990, pp. 5–6).

To prove "irrelevance" given completely symmetrical firms and markets and constant returns to scale, Bernheim and Whinston build on the work of Abreu (1988). They first consider a single market. A simple trigger strategy (Friedman, 1990, p. 110, pp. 108–158) for price-setting firms with homogeneous products will support a cooperative-like equilibrium outcome if

$$(p-c)Q(p) \leq (1/(1-\delta))(1/n)(p-c)Q(p), \tag{2.1}$$

where $p$ is a price in the set $[c, p^m]$ with $p^m$ being the monopoly price, $c$ is marginal (and average) cost, $\delta$ is the discount factor, $n$ is the number of firms, and $Q(p)$ is the demand function. If inequality (2.1) holds, the monopoly price can be sustained if each firm follows the simple trigger strategy of adhering to the monopoly price until detecting that the price has been undercut and then upon discovering a defection returning to the single-period Nash (Bertrand) noncooperative equilibrium forever. The left-hand side shows each firm's perception of its profits from cheating by undercutting the cooperative-like price by a very tiny amount. The deviating firm gets essentially $(p-c)Q(p)$ in the first period, but forever after firms revert to the punishment mode – the most severe punishment is best since it will be the most effective at deterring cheating – of the Nash equilibrium for the single-period game. The right-hand side of inequality (2.1) shows each firm's perception of the value of maintaining the collusive price. The firm reckons that the present discounted value of getting $x = (1/n)(p-c)Q(p)$ – its share of the monopoly profits forever – is $(x+\delta x+\delta^2 x+\delta^3 x+\cdots) = (1/(1-\delta))x$. Thus, dividing both sides of inequality (2.1) by the monopoly profits and rearranging, we have the condition for the monopoly price to be supported by the simple trigger strategy:

$$n \le (1/(1-\delta)), \tag{2.2}$$

or equivalently,

$$\delta \ge 1-(1/n). \tag{2.3}$$

For example, if $n = 2$, then $\delta$ must be $\ge 1/2$ if the joint profit–maximizing price is to be sustainable.

Now, what is the situation with multiple markets – say, two markets denoted by $k = A, B$? Bernheim and Whinston begin with Abreu's observation that for optimal equilibria for firms designing trigger strategies across the two markets, a deviation will be punished in both markets. Thus, for the two markets, the cooperative-like outcome is sustainable if for the $i$th firm with share $\lambda_i$

$$\sum_{k=A,B} [(1/(1-\delta))\lambda_{ik}(p_k-c)Q(p_k)-(p_k-c)Q(p_k)] \ge 0. \tag{2.4}$$

Summing inequality (2.4) over the $n$ firms gives

$$\sum_{k=A,B} \{(p_k-c)Q(p_k)[(1/(1-\delta))-n]\} \ge 0. \tag{2.5}$$

Thus, Bernheim and Whinston have shown that in the multimarket setting, for the simple trigger strategy to sustain the monopoly equilibrium it must be that $[(1/(1-\delta))-n] \ge 0$, but then they have shown that the necessary condition is precisely inequality (2.2) or its equivalent (2.3). For $n = 2$, they go on to say (p. 6, italics in original):

Thus, if $\delta < 1/2$, it is again impossible to sustain any prices above $c$, so multimarket contact replicates the single-market outcome in *both* markets. If $\delta \geq 1/2$, on the other hand, then a completely monopolistic outcome is possible even without multimarket contact. Thus, in this simple model, multimarket contact does not facilitate collusive behavior.

I do not find this to be a proof that multimarket contact is irrelevant even under the stringent assumptions of this "simple" model. It is instead a proof that the same set of trigger strategy equilibria are attainable with multimarket contact as without it. With continuous prices, there are innumerable simple trigger strategy equilibria, although the monopoly price provides a nice focal point for one. However, there are innumerable ways to devise more complicated strategies supporting monopolistic equilibria once we think in terms of more general extended folk theorems (Friedman, 1990). In even the simplest trigger strategy equilibria in repeated games with discounting, the punishment mode might last for various numbers of periods and then sellers would revert to the monopoly price. Friedman's (1990, pp. 124–125) discussion of "grim trigger strategies" as contrasted with those that incorporate "finite reversion" documents the point. Further, the single-period Nash noncooperative equilibrium is also a Nash equilibrium in the supergame. Kreps (1990, pp. 98–99) comments as follows when discussing the simple trigger strategy in the context of the prisoner's dilemma and the ability to sustain cooperative-like behavior as a noncooperative equilibrium:

This is but one Nash equilibrium in this context, however. It is also equilibrium behaviour for each player to act non-cooperatively at all times. More interestingly, it is Nash equilibrium behavior for each player to alternate co-operation and non-cooperation. . . . And so on.

I shall claim, then, that multimarket contact can increase market power in precisely those cases in which Bernheim and Whinston (1990) conclude that multimarket contact is irrelevant, because the contact can help firms choose which equilibrium to play. Their proof that multimarket contact is irrelevant given symmetry is really a proof that the set of trigger strategy equilibria that yield cooperative-like results in a noncooperative multi-period game is invariant to the extent of multimarket contact. Of course there is a plethora of such equilibria, and multimarket contact can help the sellers learn which equilibrium strategy combination to play, because they have more opportunities to learn how to "cooperate." As Kreps (1990, pp. 34–35) says: "In certain situations, participants do seem to 'know' or at least have a good idea how to act. From where does this knowledge come? If we imagine two (or more) individuals interacting repeatedly, then *modi vivendi* may develop between (or among) them through a process of trial and error." As Kreps develops the idea (see chapter 6 especially), the players in a noncooperative game can learn how to play the game through experience. One is reminded of Fellner's (1949) discussion of a few sellers, each testing various strategies to discover the reactions of its rivals. Eventually Fellner's rivals reached an accord and it was as if a bargain had been struck even though there was no direct bargaining. When the set of Nash noncooperative equilibria is large, the experience from playing the game in several markets may allow sellers to reach such an accord that has a cooperative-like outcome. Or as Kreps (1990, p. 141) puts it in his more general context, "some *modus vivendi* for coordination will arise." Quoting Kreps (1990, p. 101, italic in original):

The point is that in some games with multiple equilibria, players still "know" what to do. This knowledge comes from both directly relevant past experience and a sense of how individuals act generally. And *formal mathematical game theory has said little or nothing about where these expectations come from, how and why they persist, or when and why we might expect them to arise.*

*Multimarket contact and asymmetry:* When Bernheim and Whinston relax their symmetry assumptions, variants of their model yield several "relevance" results. Their basic argument is that multimarket contact allows conglomerates meeting in multiple markets to transfer the ability to coordinate behavior in one market to another by pooling their incentive constraints across markets. Suppose that in one market where just the conglomerates compete, $\delta$ is greater than the critical level supporting the cooperative-like price level – i.e., the profitable noncooperative trigger strategy equilibrium. Then there is slack in the incentive constraint. Now, imagine another market where the conglomerates compete with several other firms and where $n$ is so large that the trigger strategy cannot work because each firm's share of the cooperative-like profits is too small to prevent defection from the cooperative-like price. The conglomerates can *restrict* their output and share in this other market so that the other firms' shares increase enough to give them the incentive to maintain the "collusive" price *and* the expected profits for the conglomerates are nonetheless still higher with the "collusive" price than with defections because they consider their pooled profits in the two markets together – cheating would lose their profits in both markets. Just as different $n$'s across markets can imply a gain from pooling incentive constraints with multimarket contact, different $\delta$'s across markets can have the same effect.

Bernheim and Whinston's results seem to me somehow less likely to be a significant source of multimarket contact's effects than the experience or practice story that I have tied to thoughts from Kreps and Fellner, or the Chamberlinian story that I shall develop below. Admittedly, there is evidence suggesting at first glance that the Bernheim and Whinston scenarios may actually occur. Scott and Pascoe (1984) estimate significantly different $\delta$'s across markets for multimarket firms, and of course different markets have different numbers of firms. Thus, the basic conditions for the Bernheim and Whinston asymmetry effects for multimarket contact are surely present. Further, there is evidence for one of the effects implicit in the story about behavior when $n$ varies across markets. Bernheim and Whinston observe (1990, p. 8):

> . . . contrary to conventional wisdom, the purchase of market B firms by "powerful" market A firms would lead to a decline in these firms' market shares – indeed, the conglomerate firms achieve a collusive outcome precisely through the contraction of their shares.

Mueller (1987, pp. 50–51) reviews a considerable amount of evidence suggesting that the market shares of target firms acquired in conglomerate mergers actually decline after the acquisition. Reporting on his earlier studies Mueller observes that he

> . . . examined the market shares of companies acquired in conglomerate mergers between 1950 and 1972 and pairs of companies engaged in horizontal mergers during the same years. The changes in market shares for these firms between 1950 and 1972 were compared with those of nonmerging companies in the same industries. The companies acquired through conglomerate mergers or involved in horizontal mergers were found to have experienced significant losses in market shares following the mergers relative to nonmerging companies. For example, while the average nonacquired company had a 1972 market share that was 88.5 percent of its 1950 value, the average company acquired through a conglomerate merger had a 1972 market share of only 18 percent of its 1950 value.

However, Mueller (1987) and others (Ravenscraft and Scherer, 1987; Porter, 1987) have shown that the shrinking shares appear to have been the result of inability to run the newly acquired companies effectively. Therefore, it seems unlikely that the shares were deliberately reduced as a way to change incentives in the acquired firms' markets. Indeed, even if the shrinking shares reflected the restriction of output in order to raise price, the restriction would probably reflect the conventional logic that if the firms exercise increased market power, they will have to restrict output to raise price. The conventional logic seems more compelling here than the story about fine-tuning incentive constraints.

The Bernheim and Whinston effects tend to require behavior that somehow seems unlikely. It is for me, at least, somewhat difficult to imagine a conglomerate acquisition with the purpose of shrinking market share to allow a simple trigger strategy to sustain a supracompetitive price. That story and the others spun by Bernheim and Whinston are nonetheless intriguing; their empirical relevance remains an open question. In any case, if the experience story or the Chamberlinian symmetry story to be developed next are empirically important, then multimarket contact may lessen static allocative efficiency through an increase in market power. We should, however, always keep in mind that the structural condition – the diversification that increased multimarket contact – underlying the behavior that increases market power may be accompanied by technical efficiencies that could increase total economic surplus by more than the new market power decreases it.

*Three complementary views:* We have, in fact, at least three distinct yet complementary approaches to understanding how multimarket contact can increase market power. First, in the context of multiperiod games with symmetry for the sellers, multimarket contact can facilitate achieving a *modus vivendi* for coordination that allows the sellers to play a favorable (from their perspective) noncooperative equilibrium in the multiperiod game. After all, the Nash noncooperative equilibrium for the single-period game is an equilibrium in the multiperiod game even when incentives are right for sustaining a supracompetitive price with an appropriate trigger strategy. Multimarket contact can create the experience with playing the game that allows a profitable *modus vivendi* for coordination. Second, as Bernheim and Whinston show, given asymmetries in the numbers of firms in the markets, in the discount factors, and so forth, multimarket contact can, by means of the pooling of the conglomerates' incentive constraints across the markets in which they meet, allow the attaining of "cooperative" outcomes in noncooperative games where the incentive to cheat would undermine those outcomes in the absence of the multimarket contact and the behavior it induces. Third, multimarket contact can increase the symmetry of sellers' situations within a market and thus make possible Chamberlin's (1929) thoroughly cooperative-like solution achieved in a thoroughly independent way.

*Multimarket contact and Chamberlin's solution:* Interestingly, Chamberlin's solution to the oligopolists' problem is not attainable by game theory because Chamberlin's theory relied on the conjecture of simultaneous moves. As Friedman (1990, p. 156) observes after defining the concept of noncooperative equilibrium: "Simultaneous deviations are thus not relevant for determining if a strategy combination is an equilibrium." Obviously this statement follows by definition, not logic! Sellers can certainly conjecture that before a market clears their moves will be matched. Chamberlin thought about that possibility in the context of the price and output decision by the firms. However, it is useful to think about his approach in terms of investment generally construed.

Thus, following Chamberlin, when mergers increase multimarket contact among sellers competing in concentrated markets, they make more likely each firm's independent choice of the solution-maximizing joint profits, because symmetry increases. Consider a game of indeterminate length, and let $N$ denote the net market value of the stockholders' wealth for an investment $z$ in, for examples, plant and equipment, research and development (R&D), or advertising. Given a monopoly, necessary and sufficient conditions for equilibrium for the industry are $N'(z) = 0$ and $N''(z) < 0$, where ' and '' denote respectively first and second derivatives. If there were instead $s$ firms, each would attempt to maximize the net market value $N_i$ of its own investment $z_i$.

If each firm believes that its own long-run strategy will be matched by every other firm and symmetry will prevail among the $s$ firms, each maximizes $N_i(z_i)$, which equals $(1/s)N(sz_i)$ if, for the division of the industry's investment among $s$ firms, there are constant returns to scale. Since for each individual firm the maximum $N_i$ occurs at $z_i$ such that $N_i'(z_i) = (1/s)N'(sz_i)s = N'(sz_i) = 0$, then total investment $sz_i$ for the $s$ firms in equilibrium must be identical with the monopolist's investment $z$ in equilibrium. If symmetrically situated, each firm independently chooses the joint profit–maximizing investment – at the individual net value-maximizing solution, $\sum z_i = sz_i = z$ such that $N'(z) = 0$.[4]

Simple symmetry is a special case of a more general proposition: If each firm believes that its rivals will adjust their strategies in ways that cause its own share $y_i$ of investment to remain the same regardless of its own investment, then each firm will again choose the joint profit–maximizing solution independently. Now, $N_i(z_i) = y_i N(\sum z_j) = y_i N(z_i/y_i)$, where $y_i = (z_i/\sum z_j)$ is constant. Thus, $N_i'(z_i) = y_i N'(z_i/y_i)(1/y_i) = N'(z_i/y_i) = 0$, and again total investment $\sum z_i$ (which equals $z_i/y_i$ for any $i$) for the $s$ firms in equilibrium must be identical with the monopolist's investment $z$ in equilibrium. If each firm believes that its share of investment will remain the same regardless of its investment decision, each firm independently chooses the joint profit–maximizing investment – at the individual net value-maximizing solution, $\sum z_i = z$ such that $N'(z) = 0$.[5]

This more general case entails symmetry through time *and* symmetry in the diversified operations undertaken by the firms, but not cross-sectional symmetry in shares. Symmetry in the *types* of investments of the firms, even though not in the *sizes* of their investments, may ensure similar cost structures and an approximation to constant returns to scale in the observed range of investments.

Thus, joint net value maximization is possible if sellers are few enough for all to maintain conjectures recognizing their mutual interdependence instead of the simple competitor's assumption that the parameters of its environment will not change as a consequence of its own strategies. If, for marginal net value of investment schedules, the private value of investment is a fraction of the social value, joint net value maximization implies underinvestment from a social standpoint. Yet for private gain, in order to make independent net value–maximizing solutions more likely, concentrated, diversified sellers may undertake conglomerate mergers that increase symmetry in their *types* of investments.

Applying Chamberlin's idea, then, we see that multimarket contact can facilitate oligopolistic consensus because having grown interdependent and symmetrically situated, each firm may believe that its strategic plays will be matched by rivals so that each firm's share of the market's net value is always preserved. Given the firms' investments, the joint profit-maximizing solution in terms of their output in each period could then obtain even with independent behavior – i.e., each firm maximizes its own profits given its own costs and constant-share demand curve and chooses to produce its share of the monopoly output. If the firms hold Chamberlin's conjecture (that all prices will be matched and hence market shares preserved before the market clears), then the monopoly result holds even without recourse to formal multiperiod games in which monopoly-like solutions can be sustained when the number of firms is small enough and the interest rate small enough so that a trigger strategy can be devised where the individual firm's incentive to reduce price to get an immediate extra profit is not as attractive as adhering to the monopoly price and having a share of the monopoly profits indefinitely. If the Chamberlinian conjecture of simultaneous deviations is not considered to be an appropriate characterization of the way the sellers think about their situation, then we have no theoretical alternative to the multiple equilibria of the multiperiod game solutions. Even then, as we have seen above, multi-market contact can be important. If multiperiod games are the appropriate way to view the situation, multimarket contact can be important because it provides a setting where sellers can gain the experience necessary to avoid unprofitable equilibria and to choose the best of the equilibria that yield cooperative-like results.

Thinking about the symmetry issue in Chamberlin's terms leads in a different direction from Bernheim and Whinston's ideas. They find a role for multimarket contact only when there are asymmetries. In terms of our discussion of Chamberlin's idea, sellers' multimarket diversity unaccompanied by multimarket contact can reduce market power in any given market. Without multimarket contact, coordination is likely to break down because independent decisions would imply different preferred prices for the diversified firms. The diversity of the manufacturers' operations causes intramarket diversity in their costs and even demands. Customers may prefer to buy from a particular type of multimarket seller, and, given cross-price elasticities, a multimarket seller may want to coordinate prices across markets. With different demands and costs, the sellers would typically want different prices.

Thus, most real world games are like the battle of the sexes – the players prefer somewhat different strategy combinations, any of which would be Nash equilibria (Kreps, 1990, pp. 39–40). If diversified oligopolists are in the same markets, they are more likely to prefer the same strategy combinations, so there is less to negotiate – fewer equilibria to choose among. Thus, in addition to the Bernheim and Whinston set of ideas that find a role for multimarket contact in asymmetries, even with symmetry multimarket contact can increase market power not only by giving practice in several markets that helps select which equilibrium to play in any particular market when there is the usual plethora of equilibria, but additionally by reducing battle-of-the-sexes disagreements. Any such disagreements that remain are more likely to be solved by some sort of convention given the sellers' experiences of dealing with one another across several markets. Indeed Kreps (1990, pp. 100–102) uses the battle-of-the-sexes game to illustrate how such conventions could help players "decide" who would obtain his or her preferred equilibrium. With some asymmetries for multimarket firms, the convention could be precisely as Edwards suggested – the strongest firm in a particular market would lead; the weaker firms would follow.

Stigler's (1988) basic insight about oligopoly theory – that price cutting is less likely the more likely its detection – fits well with Chamberlin's theory because it gives conditions for which price matching and share preservation will be likely. Stigler's insight bolsters the argument that multimarket contact will increase the ability of diversified oligopolists to reach a consensus on a high price.[6] First, because multimarket contact increases the number of common buyers with whom the sellers deal, it raises the probability that price cutting by a firm hoping to increase its market share at the expense of its rivals will be detected. Because of the transactions costs of dealing with multiple sellers, a multimarket buyer tempted by a price cut in one market may defect to the cheating seller in all markets. As the probability of detection increases, undercutting the consensus becomes less profitable, since price cuts, once detected, will be matched, and the price-cutting firm will not in fact experience an increase in its share of the market. Second, as Bernheim and Whinston (1990, p. 9) observe:

> . . . firms may be able to respond more quickly to deviations from collusive agreements in some markets than in others. Actions may be directly observable and immediately punishable in some markets, while in others, defections may be detected and punishment initiated only with a lag or some statistical uncertainty. . . . Multimarket contact can create potential

gains by allowing firms to shift enforcement power from a market in which responses are rapid to one in which they are sluggish.

Thus, multimarket contact makes independent choice of compatible supracompetitive prices more likely because it makes more likely independent choices of similar prices and raises the probability that a price-cutting firm will not increase its market share.

### 2.4 Conclusion

The integration in this chapter of new game theoretic models with more traditional views yields a useful synthesis of theory supporting the hypothesis that multimarket contact increases market power. I have left unresolved the issue about whether the results of how businesspeople think are more closely approximated by the Chamberlinian short-cut (for analyzing why cheating from the "cooperative" result is inadvisable) or instead by a multiperiod game scenario following the rules of game theory regarding what constitutes a noncooperative equilibrium. However, the resolution is not necessary for our purposes since either approach to understanding the behavior of multimarket oligopolists yields the prediction that multimarket contact will increase market power. With that hypothesis in mind, we turn now to evidence linking multimarket contact and market power.

# 3

## Diversifying mergers and strategic congruence

Chapter 2 explained that one way conglomerate mergers could create market power is by increasing multimarket contact and symmetry among a market's firms. Chapter 2 showed that multimarket contact can theoretically increase the stability of cooperative-like behavior among the rivalrous firms in any given market in which the firms meet. Further, as emphasized in Chapter 1, if the various motives for diversification rest on industry-specific properties, then the extension of diversification will tend to increase multimarket contact with the potential for increasing cooperative-like behavior (whether or not bolstering such behavior was primary among the firm's objectives). This chapter tests the hypothesis that mergers serve to increase multimarket contact and symmetry.

### 3.1 Overview

Section 3.2 measures the contact and symmetry created by two large conglomerate mergers just after the passage of the Celler–Kefauver Act and illustrates the change in market structure expected if a merger were designed to increase market power. Of course, the diversification and ensuing symmetry could be a response to any sort of synergy based on industry characteristics. As explained in Chapter 2, gains in potential for cooperative-like behavior from increased multimarket contact could in principle induce diversification, but as Chapter 1 has explained, there are strong "innocent" explanations for diversification that can make it impossible to show that much diversification is on balance because of such potential. Thus, one could say that changes in market structure induced by conglomerate mergers may show the likelihood that diversification was "purposive" but do not establish the purpose to be increased

This chapter revises part of the material in Scott (1989a).

parallelism among rivals per se. However, with the case of Pullman, Inc. and also the case of National Distillers Products Corporation, both discussed below, the timing of the acquisitions suggests that they may well have been aimed at generating market power. As explained in Chapter 2, mergers to increase multimarket contact may have been especially likely after the passage of the Celler–Kefauver Act in 1950. The new law foreclosed more conventional ways to increase market power.

Section 3.3 uses a sample of the large conglomerate mergers tracked by the Federal Trade Commission (FTC) to ask if such mergers have increased contact and symmetry. Section 3.4 concludes that, just as with horizontal mergers, economic welfare analysis of conglomerate mergers requires weighing efficiency losses from market power against efficiency gains from lower costs, even when potential competition is not a factor.

### 3.2 Case studies of large conglomerate mergers and symmetry

I introduce a measure of congruence to ask whether a conglomerate acquisition changes market structure in the way expected if the merger were designed to increase market power. Each firm in an industry chooses among a set of potential strategies and thereby affects the extent of symmetry among the industry's firms and the likelihood of the joint profit-maximizing solution. Congruence increases with the number of the industry's firms making the same choice. The question then becomes: Does the conglomerate merger increase congruence – an aspect of market structure – for some subset of the industry categories in which the acquiring and acquired firms compete? The answer is yes if congruence increases significantly against the null hypothesis of no purposive attempt to increase symmetry via the merger; otherwise, the answer is no.

Thus, the extent of congruence achieved could be high or low. If an industry has five firms, congruence is greatest when all five firms choose the same strategy. Congruence is least when none of the firms have matching strategies. Letting $x$ denote the number of distinct firms – distinct in the sense that they choose different strategies, $x$ ranges from 1 through 5 as the industry's congruence varies from high to low. When $x$ is 1, all five firms have the same strategy. If $x$ were 2, either four firms choose the same strategy and one differs from those four, or one group of three compatible firms and another group of two constitute the outcome. Thus, when $x = 2$, the general patterns for sets of distinct firms are 4 and 1 or 3 and 2. When $x = 3$, the patterns are 3, 1, and 1; or 2, 2, and 1. When $x = 5$, the only general pattern is 1, 1, 1, 1, and 1. Each of the five firms is distinct – chooses a distinct strategy.

Let $C$ denote the number of firms. Let $Z$ be the number of ways each firm could choose a strategy among a set important for supporting joint profit maximization. The industry, given $C$ and $Z$, can have $Z^C$ possible outcomes.

Let $y$ be the number of ways that each particular general pattern for sets of distinct firms could occur. Let the set of integers, ordered from largest to smallest, denoting any such general pattern be

$$q = \{q_{11}, q_{12}, \ldots, q_{1Q1}, q_{21}, q_{22}, \ldots, q_{2Q2}, \ldots, q_{v1}, q_{v2}, \ldots, q_{vQv}\},$$

where there are $Q1$ instances of the largest integer, $Q2$ of the second, and so on until $Qv$ instances of the smallest integer. The $\sum_{ij} q_{ij}$ is equal to $C$, the number of firms associated with the industry. And, for any general pattern, there are $v$ distinct integers and

$$x = \sum_{h=1}^{v} Qh$$

distinct firms.

Then, with $\Omega_{s,t}$ denoting the combination of $s$ things taken $t$ at a time, the number of occurrences $y$ for any given general pattern will be, since $q_{ij} = q_{ik} = q_i$:

$$y = \prod_{n=1}^{v} \left[ \Omega_{Z - \sum_{i<n} Q_i, Q_n} \cdot \Omega_{C - \sum_{i<n}(Q_i \cdot q_i), Q_n \cdot q_n} \cdot \prod_{i=1}^{Qn} \Omega_{q_n \cdot i, q_n} \right]$$

The mergers discussed below provide examples for the congruence of the diversification profiles of the competing firms; applications to other forms of congruence are discussed in subsequent chapters.

In the year following the passage of the Celler–Kefauver Act, the FTC's large merger series (U.S. FTC, 1980) reports two conglomerate mergers (product extension mergers in both cases) for which both the acquiring and the acquired firm are in the FTC's corporate patterns data for 1950 (U.S. FTC, 1972). For the 1000 largest U.S. manufacturers, the corporate patterns data give a complete breakdown of each firm's value of shipments by five-digit product classes and, therefore, allow, among the firms covered by the data, a complete understanding of a merger's consequences for the symmetry of competitors' operations. The large merger series records only those acquisitions of $10 million or more, and the corporate patterns data cover just the leading 1000 manufacturers in 1950; hence, the corporate patterns data become less and less useful as the time from 1950 to a merger's date of completion increases. Smaller acquisitions or divestitures cannot be traced accurately, and firms diverge in unknown ways from their 1950 diversification profiles. New data for lines of business, such as the FTC gathered for the mid-1970s in its now abandoned Line of Business (LB) Program, are needed to evaluate subsequent mergers.

The two cases available for 1951, however, provide interesting examples. In the first case, Pullman, Inc. acquired Trailmobile Company. Pullman's

Table 3.1. *Manufacturing areas$^a$ of the producers
of new cars for passenger trains, before and after
Pullman's 1951 acquisition of Trailmobile*

|  | Before | After |
|---|---|---|
| Pullman, Inc.$^b$ | {1, 2} | {1, 2, 3} |
| The Budd Company | {1, 2, 3} | {1, 2, 3} |
| American Car & Foundry Company | {1, 2, 3} | {1, 2, 3} |

$^a$ Areas: 1 = various metal inputs – basic metal products, fabri-
cated metal parts and machinery; 2 = railroad cars; 3 = various
stages of truck manufacturing.
$^b$ Pullman also had somewhat more than 1% of its receipts from
R&D on aircraft engines, but far less than 1% of its shipments'
value came from aircraft-related manufacture.

primary product was new cars for passenger trains. In that product, its
competitors among the top 1000 manufacturers were The Budd Company and American Car & Foundry Company. Excluding lines of business where the sales of manufactured goods contributed less than 1 percent
to the value of shipments, we can describe the diversified operations of
the three companies as shown in Table 3.1. Before Pullman's acquisition
of Trailmobile, Pullman produced various metal inputs and railroad cars.
The acquisition resulted in all three competitors producing various metal
inputs, railroad cars, and various stages of truck manufacture.

For a strategic move with respect to a firm's diversification profile, there
are $Z \le C + 1$ strategies the firm could choose via an acquisition or a dives-
titure. For the merger of Pullman and Trailmobile, $Z = 3$; after the conglomerate acquisition, Pullman's profile could look essentially the same
(if the acquisition were in product classes not previously occupied by Pullman yet falling in a general area, such as various metal inputs, in which
Pullman did operate), could be like the identical profiles of its two competitors, or could be a new one. Thus, we have the case where the number
of competitors $C$ equals 3 and the number of strategic postures $Z$ equals 3.

Table 3.2 illustrates the distribution of possible outcomes for congruence. Against the null hypothesis that the three competitors' choices
of areas and Pullman's acquisition of Trailmobile were random choices
among the $Z$ strategies, the increase in congruence measured by the fall
in $x$ from 2 to 1 increases the probability of less congruence from 0.22 to
0.89. Thus, it is highly likely that the strategic diversification profiles and
Pullman's acquisition were not random diversification and, instead, were

Table 3.2. *The extent of congruence:*
$C = 3; Z = 3$

| $x^a$ | General patterns[b] | Occurrences[c] $= y$ |
|---|---|---|
| 1 | 3 | 3 |
| 2 | 2, 1 | 18 |
| 3 | 1, 1, 1 | 6 |
| | $\sum y = 27 = Z^C = (3)^3$ | |

[a] $x$ denotes the number of distinct firms.
[b] The general patterns for sets of distinct firms consistent with $x$ are shown as integers ordered from largest to smallest with each integer being the number of firms with a particular strategy.
[c] The number of ways that each particular general pattern could occur is shown in this column.

purposive attempts to increase symmetry among the producers of Pullman's primary product. One could construct cases where even additional congruence was insignificant in the sense that the probability of less congruence was still quite low against the null hypothesis. Here the merger resulted in significant congruence.

In the second case, National Distillers Products Corporation acquired United States Industrial Chemicals, Inc. National Distillers' primary product was bottled liquors. In that product, its competitors among the top 1000 manufacturers were Joseph E. Seagram & Sons, Inc.; Schenley Industries, Inc.; Hiram Walker & Sons, Inc.; Publicker Industries, Inc.; Brown-Forman Distillers Corporation; Glenmore Distilleries Company; The American Distilling Company; and Standard Brands, Inc. In this case, all of the firms' activities are sufficiently focused that I do not need to exclude LBs to have a subset of operations common to some of the competitors and, arguably, to have the group of operations that affect decisions regarding bottled liquors. Table 3.3 describes the diversified operations of the nine companies.

Thus, for this merger, $Z = 6$; after the conglomerate acquisition, National's profile could look essentially the same, could be like one of the four profiles of its eight competitors, or could be a new one. Thus, we have the case where the number of competitors $C$ equals 9 and the number of strategic postures $Z$ equals 6.

Table 3.4 illustrates the distribution of possible outcomes for congruence. Against the null hypothesis that the competitors' choices of areas

3 Diversifying mergers and strategic congruence

Table 3.3. *Manufacturing areas[a] of the producers of bottled liquors, before and after National Distillers Products Corporation's 1951 acquisition of United States Industrial Chemicals, Inc.*

|  | Before | After |
|---|---|---|
| National Distillers Products Corporation | {1, 2, 3, 4} | {1, 2, 3, 4, 5} |
| Joseph E. Seagram & Sons, Inc. | {1, 2, 4} | {1, 2, 4} |
| Schenley Industries, Inc. | {1, 2, 4} | {1, 2, 4} |
| Hiram Walker & Sons, Inc. | {1, 2, 4} | {1, 2, 4} |
| Publicker Industries, Inc. | {1, 2, 4} | {1, 2, 4} |
| Brown-Forman Distillers Corporation | {1, 2} | {1, 2} |
| Glenmore Distilleries Company | {1, 2, 4} | {1, 2, 4} |
| The American Distilling Company | {1, 3} | {1, 3} |
| Standard Brands, Inc.[b] | {1, 2, 3, 4, 5} | {1, 2, 3, 4, 5} |

[a] Areas: 1 = beverages and related products; 2 = wood products (in every case, exclusively or primarily tight cooperage and cooperage stock); 3 = miscellaneous foods and related products (e.g., flavoring syrups and concentrates); 4 = various chemicals and allied products (e.g., carbon dioxide and industrial ethyl alcohol); 5 = grain mill products.
[b] I have classified salad dressings (about 0.1 of 1 percent of Standard Brands' value of shipments) with Standard Brands' numerous miscellaneous foods.

Table 3.4. *The extent of congruence:* $C = 9$; $Z = 6$

| $x^a$ | General patterns[b] | Occurrences[c] = $y$ |
|---|---|---|
| 1 | 9 | 6 |
| 2 | {8, 1}, {7, 2}, {6, 3}, {5, 4} | 7650 |
| 3 | {7, 1, 1}, {6, 2, 1}, {5, 3, 1}, {5, 2, 2}, {4, 4, 1}, {4, 3, 2}, {3, 3, 3} | 363,000 |
| 4 | {6, 1, 1, 1}, {5, 2, 1, 1}, {4, 3, 1, 1}, {4, 2, 2, 1}, {3, 3, 2, 1}, {3, 2, 2, 2} | 2,797,200 |
| 5 | {5, 1, 1, 1, 1}, {4, 2, 1, 1, 1}, {3, 3, 1, 1, 1}, {3, 2, 2, 1, 1}, {2, 2, 2, 2, 1} | 5,004,720 |
| 6 | {4, 1, 1, 1, 1, 1}, {3, 2, 1, 1, 1, 1}, {2, 2, 2, 1, 1, 1} | 1,905,120 |

$$\sum y = 10,077,696 = Z^C = (6)^9$$

[a] $x$ denotes the number of distinct firms.
[b] The general patterns for sets of distinct firms consistent with $x$ are shown as integers ordered from largest to smallest with each integer being the number of firms with a particular strategy.
[c] The number of ways that each set of general patterns could occur is shown in this column.

and National Distillers' acquisition of U.S. Industrial Chemicals were random choices among the $Z$ strategies, the increase in congruence measured by the fall in $x$ from 5 to 4 increases the probability of less congruence from 0.189 to 0.686. Thus, the acquisition is unlikely to reflect random diversification, but rather, appears to be a purposive increase in congruence among the producers of bottled liquors.

### 3.3 Symmetry creation in a sample of large conglomerate mergers

This section combines information about the large conglomerate mergers tracked by the FTC with information from the FTC's LB Program to ask whether large conglomerate mergers frequently increase multimarket contact and symmetry. In Chapter 9 we shall examine the FTC LB 1974–76 sample and identify sets of FTC four-digit manufacturing industry categories that were evidently purposively joined by firms in order to pursue complementarities in research and development (R&D) investments. However, as we shall see, numerous FTC LB sample firms operated in the various industry categories without combining them. Did the conglomerate mergers tracked by the FTC subsequent to 1976 increase symmetry and multimarket contact by combining the same categories that the purposively diversified firms had previously combined?

For each of the large product extension or pure conglomerate mergers (U.S. FTC, 1980) in 1977–78, for which both the acquired and acquiring firms' primary industry categories were in manufacturing, I translated the primary four- (and occasionally three-) digit Standard Industrial Classification (SIC) codes into the appropriate codes for FTC four-digit industries (U.S. FTC, 1985). This allows us to evaluate the extent to which the mergers were joining four-digit categories that were already joined by purposively diversified firms in the FTC LB sample. By observing the significant multimarket meetings of the FTC LB firms, Chapter 9 identifies groups of industries with complementary activities. Among the 127 groups of complementary industry categories identified in Chapter 9, there are 935 distinct pairs of four-digit FTC industry categories.[1] For the sample of 95 large conglomerate mergers, 26 mergers created pairs of primary industry categories that were identical to pairs among the 935. There are 261 FTC four-digit manufacturing categories; hence, the paired categories observed in the 95 cases could potentially have been among 33,930 different pairs of categories.

Are the pairs of categories created by the conglomerate mergers congruent with – i.e., do they overlap to a significant extent – the pairs of categories previously brought together by the firms in the LB sample? Let the pairs of industry categories brought together by mergers number $k$, and let the number of previously existing pairs be $g$. Let the total number of possible pairs of industry categories be $m$.

Table 3.5. *Probability $p(f)$ that $f$ of the 95 pairs coincide with pairs among the 935*[a]

| | |
|---|---|
| $p(0) = 7.00621 \times 10^{-2}$ | $p(6) = 3.15495 \times 10^{-2}$ |
| $p(1) = 0.189151$ | $p(7) = 1.13243 \times 10^{-2}$ |
| $p(2) = 0.252367$ | $p(8) = 3.51279 \times 10^{-3}$ |
| $p(3) = 0.22184$ | $p(9) = 9.56519 \times 10^{-4}$ |
| $p(4) = 0.144522$ | $p(10) = 2.3146 \times 10^{-4}$ |
| $p(5) = 7.44207 \times 10^{-2}$ | $\vdots$ |
| | $p(95) = 5.38616 \times 10^{-151}$ |

[a] The complete distribution, showing $p(f)$ for $f = 0, 1, 2, ..., 95$, is available on request.

Then where $p(f)$ is the probability that $f$ of the $k$ sets coincide with $f$ of the $g$ sets, we have, given random choice of the $k$ sets,

$$p(f) = [(\Omega_{g,f})(\Omega_{m-g,k-f})]/(\Omega_{m,k}),$$

where $\Omega_{s,t}$ denotes the combination of $s$ things taken $t$ at a time and where $p(0) + p(1) + p(2) + \cdots + p(k) = 1$. The formula for $p(f)$ results because $\Omega_{g,f}$ is the number of ways to get $f$ of the $g$ sets; $\Omega_{m-g,k-f}$ is the number of ways to get $k - f$ of the non-$g$ sets; and $\Omega_{m,k}$ is the number of ways to draw $k$ sets. With the distribution for $f$, I can ask if the overlap of the $k$ and $g$ sets is significant. Since 26 of the 95 sets observed for the conglomerate mergers are identical to sets among the 935 found for the FTC LB sample, if the mergers combine industry categories randomly, the probability of an equal or greater number of congruent sets is $\sum_{f=26}^{95} p(f)$. As shown in Table 3.5, that probability is far less than 0.001, and I infer that the mergers were, to a significant extent, purposively increasing multimarket contact and symmetry.

### 3.4 Interpreting strategic congruence

In this chapter, we have seen that conglomerate mergers have, in the cases examined, increased multimarket contact and symmetry among industries' firms. The implications for economic performance are complex. Multimarket contact is coincident with diversification, which may lower production, distribution, marketing, and R&D costs. Markets may work better when firms are diversified and provide intrafirm solutions for transactions that would be less effectively conducted at arm's length in markets (Teece, 1980). Hence, markets may work better when multimarket contact is high. Yet the resulting symmetry among competing sellers can increase market power at the same time that the multimarket development of sellers can increase operating efficiency.

Most leading U.S. manufacturing firms *are* highly diversified, and it makes little sense to think of their behavior in one industry without reference to how they are situated in others. Industry effects do explain a large and significant portion of the variance in line of business performance (Scott, 1984; Schmalensee, 1985; Scott and Pascoe, 1986). The interaction of an industry's seller concentration and its barriers to mobility with the multimarket congruence of the industry's sellers, across the set of other industries affecting their decisions, may be an extraordinarily important factor behind the estimated industry effects.

A priori, the diversification resulting from conglomerate mergers could increase static allocative efficiency by improving information about profitable opportunities and improving the ability to redeploy resources into those profitable activities, but decrease static allocative efficiency by increasing multimarket contact and thereby promoting oligopolistic consensus. We shall explore these possibilities next in Chapter 4. Further, in Chapter 4, we shall make some initial observations about the possibility that diversification could increase technical efficiency by combining activities with complementarities in production and distribution, but decrease technical efficiency by increasing multimarket contact, which in some circumstances induces wasteful Nash noncooperative equilibria in promotional activities. In Part III, we shall consider the possibility that diversification can increase dynamic efficiency by combining activities with complementarities in innovative investment, but decrease dynamic efficiency when ensuing multimarket contact results in privately optimal changes in innovative investment that move the investment farther from the socially optimal level and pattern. Thus, we shall see that conglomerate mergers have important consequences that should be considered by public policy; yet, antitrust enforcement agencies routinely exclude conglomerate mergers from their scrutiny.

When the a priori possibilities for the effects of multimarket contact resulting from diversification are studied in Chapters 4 and 5, the evidence supports the presence of sensible, profitable diversifying behavior. However, the findings of Mueller (1987) and Ravenscraft and Scherer (1987) show that the potential for profitability has not been realized by U.S. conglomerate mergers. Of course, although that is inconsistent with their purpose of the rational pursuit of increased profits, it does not mean that large conglomerate mergers were not purposive. Risk aversion and other managerial motives could well have been involved. The profitability of "purposive diversification" as I define it and in my samples may not imply the profitability of conglomerate mergers for several reasons. The mergers in the Mueller and Ravenscraft and Scherer samples possibly did not typically effect purposive diversification of the type that my procedure discerns; or possibly internal growth effected much of the purposive diversification in my samples; or possibly Mueller's version of managerialism has driven the mergers despite transactions costs that overwhelm the potential efficiencies.

Mueller observes that some managers may use mergers to increase the size and growth of their firms even though profits are not increased. Given that a management undertakes such mergers, however, Mueller notes that it may not merely throw darts at the back of the *Wall Street Journal* to select targets, although profits ex post may suggest that procedure.[2] Some more intelligent purposive strategy might inform the selection of acquisitions, given the prior decision to diversify and grow. The high premiums paid and other transactions costs could make most mergers unprofitable; an intelligent strategy would make them less unprofitable. Finally, conglomerate mergers that increase congruence should increase observed profits only when the congruent sellers occupy concentrated markets protected by barriers to mobility; otherwise, profits are expected to fall as profitable opportunities are exploited more quickly (Scott, 1982). Firms may individually undertake the mergers to increase their own efficiency, yet find that in the new equilibrium profits have fallen.

Conglomerate mergers should be scrutinized under Section 7 of the Clayton Act, because when mergers increase multimarket contact among sellers competing in concentrated markets, they make more likely each firm's independent choice of a strategy that results in an outcome close to the joint profit–maximizing solution. Further, multimarket contact is coincident with diversification, which may lower costs. Taken together, the market power and cost-reducing hypotheses imply that an analysis of the economics of a conglomerate merger case requires weighing any welfare loss from increased market power against any welfare gain from lower costs. Antitrust policy should not continue to ignore that important task.

Now, purposive diversification that induces symmetry could reflect solely an efficiency motive. The behavior may not indicate the deliberate pursuit of symmetry itself and market power, but instead the pursuit of efficiencies with the result of increased symmetry as a by-product. But next, in Chapter 4, we shall observe the performance of lines of business as a function of multimarket contact and additionally the extent of seller concentration. If multimarket contact has a different effect depending on the level of seller concentration, the possibility that market power results from multimarket contact will be more convincing.

# 4

# Multimarket contact and resource allocation

For the economy to work well, resources should flow freely from one industry to another in response to changing demands and costs. The capital market can allocate resources by means of the entry and exit of firms. But entry can be by new firms *or* existing ones through diversification. Chapter 1 observes that a multimarket firm may use its own internal organization to allocate resources more efficiently than the arm's-length market mechanism could do. For example, Williamson (1970) and Weston (1970) stress advantages of internal capital transfers over the market.[1] Because of such advantages, Gort (1962, p. 4) and Rumelt (1974, p. 2) state that multimarket operation of firms will speed redeployment of resources in response to profitable opportunities. They would be right *if* multimarket operation were not coincident with multimarket contact.

## 4.1 A priori impact of multimarket grouping

While diversified companies may have advantages that would facilitate the movement of capital, as explained in Chapter 2 they have enhanced opportunity for coordination if they meet in several markets. Multimarket groups are groups of diversified firms whose activities span the same markets to a significant extent. Multimarket grouping of sellers could reduce the flow of resources, thereby inhibiting a socially desirable competitive process, *if* it proceeded until the diversified sellers recognized their mutual dependence and coordinated a reduction in competition, tacitly or otherwise.

In short, where sellers have grown large through diversification, resources may not be efficiently reallocated among markets in response to changing conditions because interdependent groups of sellers recognize

Chapter 4 is a revision of Scott (1982).

that that reduces their profits. Even then, in a frictionless world, sellers other than those in the multimarket group could move resources into profitable areas. I reject such a frictionless world given evidence such as Mueller's (1977b) and the general theory of barriers to mobility (Caves and Porter, 1977). The interdependent sellers who meet in several markets are the very ones who would have been most likely to enter given new profitable opportunities. Capacity expansion given such opportunities should be less rapid than if the multimarket interdependence did not exist.

With market concentration, not only the philosophy embodied in the Jeffersonian ideal – the preservation of small, independent businesses as a social and political goal of democracy – but also concerns about economic efficiency provide grounds for an antitrust policy. With aggregate concentration, are the concerns of public policy about only the Jeffersonian ideal, or are there meaningful issues of economic efficiency? This chapter introduces methodology for measuring the significance of grouping and shows that when significant and coincident with high seller concentration, multimarket grouping – typically a by-product of high aggregate concentration – does have economic implications. That coincidence *and* high profits occur together in both the Federal Trade Commission Line of Business (FTC LB) sample examined in this chapter and in the sample for 1950 examined in Chapter 5. One could argue that the coexistence of high seller concentration and multimarket contact implies the conjecture of economies of both scale and scope. The question is whether the high profits result from coordinated behavior or lower costs or both. The evidence suggests that they are the result of "economies" of multimarket operation and barriers to the mobility of resources from outside the *interdependent* groups of sellers. Profits are *lower* for lines of business where multimarket contact is high but seller concentration is low, but *higher* when both contact and concentration are high than when concentration alone is high.

### 4.2 Previous studies and a new methodology

The earliest arguments (see Scherer, 1980, chapter 12) that multimarket firms caused static allocative inefficiency did not receive wide acceptance or empirical support. In contrast to the fairly wide consensus among economists that horizontal mergers that substantially increase market concentration do lessen competition and allocative efficiency, little consensus (excepting possibly arguments about potential entry) exists regarding the effects of mergers that increase multimarket contacts.[2] Scherer and Ross (1990) relegate discussion of multimarket contact to a section about "The Social Scene" where they treat a "set of influences [that] lies beyond the reach of conventional economic analysis" (Scherer and Ross, 1990, p. 311). The strongest case against conglomerate mergers has been evidence that multimarket mergers do not result in efficiencies, coupled with an extra-economic appeal to the social and political philosophy of the Jeffersonian ideal (Mueller, 1977a, 1981; Ravenscraft and Scherer, 1987).

The lack of compelling theoretical argument and empirical evidence about the effects of multimarket contact has begun to give way to new theoretical treatments (Feinberg, 1984; Woodward, 1989; Bernheim and Whinston, 1990) and empirical treatments (Scott, 1982; Rhoades and Heggestad, 1985; Mester, 1985; Evans and Kessides, 1991; Kim and Singal, 1991). Prior to Scott (1982) there *had* been formal statistical tests of Edwards's hypothesis (1955, and his testimony cited in Scherer, 1980, p. 340) about "spheres of influence." He hypothesized that when sellers meet in several markets, their recognition of the interdependence of their operations may blunt the vigor of their competition with each other. Yet there was no overwhelming statistical support for the hypothesis.[3] Scott (1982), working with data from the mid-1970s when industries' demands and costs were shifting substantially, argued that interdependence of sellers across markets affects the movement of resources from one industry to another during periods of changing demands or costs.[4]

In Scott (1982), I suggested a new method of assessing multimarket contact. Despite the theoretical possibility that conglomerate mergers and resulting multimarket contact can lessen competition, evidence was not convincing. There is a conceptual problem. How much contact is a lot? The 437 firms examined in this chapter had diversified into 259 manufacturing categories. Some contact will accompany diversification, even when neither economies nor market power are sought. The focus of my inquiry is the contact above that expected by chance meetings. The task is to formulate how contact would look if it were purely the result of chance and how it would differ from contact resulting from opportunities for efficiency in, for example, marketing and research and development (R&D) or the pursuit of market power.

My main hypothesis is that the smaller the number of contacts relative to the number of markets in which the sellers operate, the less likely the sellers' recognition of mutual interdependence within a multimarket group. Furthermore, as the number of other lines of business in which each of a market's sellers operates increases, the objective inferential significance of any given amount of multimarket contact decreases, because the contact is more likely to have occurred by chance rather than because of marketing or technological contiguity of the markets where meeting occurred. Therefore, to explore the extent and effect of multimarket contact, I begin by asking whether observed contact is different from what would have occurred by chance. Section 4.3 shows the class of probability distributions required to answer the question and describes the sampling procedure and the resulting observations used. Section 4.4 describes multimarket contact among the largest U.S. manufacturers and shows that economies of multimarket operations in marketing and R&D must be weighed against the welfare inefficiency implied by the results documented in Section 4.5.

### 4.3 An index of the size of multimarket contact

The operations of the typical firm among the largest 1000 U.S. manufacturers span several lines of business. This chapter works with the 437 firms (all among the largest 1000 U.S. manufacturers) comprising the FTC's LB Program sample in 1974.[5] These firms are studied in Chapter 1, and Table 1.1 shows their diversification. How great is multimarket contact among these sellers? Assuming sellers diversify randomly, I develop the probability distribution over the number of contacts. Contact is then greater, the greater the probability of observing less contact, given the null hypothesis of random diversification.

For example, suppose $n$ manufacturing categories into which our population of firms has diversified. Firms 1 and 2 are found operating in a market together. Firm 1 operates in $s$ LBs while firm 2 operates in $t \leq s$. What then is the probability distribution over the number of ways this pair of firms can meet in other markets? Letting $C_{x,y}$ denote the number of combinations of $x$ things taken $y$ at a time, the probability of $f$ meetings in other markets is

$$p(f) = (C_{t-1,f})(C_{n-t,s-1-f})/(C_{n-1,s-1})$$

where $\sum_{f=0}^{t-1} p(f) = 1$. For my sample, $n = 259$. Table 4.1 shows the probability distributions over $f$ for two pairs of $s$ and $t$ values.

My first measure of contact is its "probabilistic size," that is, the probability of observing less contact. I denote this measure as PMMC. For example, from Table 4.1, if the firms in the first pair meet once in a market other than the market in which we originally find them as competitors, then PMMC = 0.8558. Supposing the firms of pair 2 meet in two other markets, their PMMC will be less even though the absolute number of times they meet in other markets is greater.[6]

I then choose a pair of firms from each manufacturing category in which at least two firms reported in 1974 to the FTC's LB Program. Each firm in the category has an equal chance of being chosen as one of the firms constituting the pair. I then compute the probability distribution over $f$ for each pair of firms and the actual number of times, ICMSR, each pair met in manufacturing categories other than the one from which they were drawn.

Table 4.1. *Probability $p(f)$ of multimarket contact,*
$n = 259$

| Pair 1 $s = 14$, $t = 4$ | Pair 2 $s = 47$, $t = 8$ |
|---|---|
| $p(0) = .8557943$ | $p(0) = .2484260$ |
| $p(1) = .1373497$ | $p(1) = .3883164$ |
| $p(2) = .006754903$ | $p(2) = .2532498$ |
| $p(3) = .0001010938$ | $p(3) = .08928679$ |
| | $p(4) = .01837001$ |
| | $p(5) = .002204401$ |
| | $p(6) = .0001427811$ |
| | $p(7) = .000003848548$ |

*Note:* $\sum_{f=0}^{t-1} p(f)$ differs very slightly from 1 because of rounding to seven digits. To the six significant digits, the sums are 1.

## 4.4 The extent of multimarket contact and multimarket economies

Firms reporting to the LB Program in 1974 divided their operations among 259 of the 261 manufacturing categories classified by the FTC. Of those 259 categories, there were 246 for which "interesting," nondegenerate probability distributions of the type illustrated in Table 4.1 could be formed given the null hypothesis of random diversification.[7] Table 4.2 shows there were 51 pairs of firms for which the amount of multimarket contact, ICMSR, was significant in the sense that it would occur by chance less than once in every hundred cases if the null hypothesis were true. Relaxing the standard of statistical significance, 91 of the 246 pairs exhibited contact significant at the 0.10 level.

Clearly multimarket contact among large U.S. manufacturers is far more than would occur by chance. In other words, there is significant multimarket contact among sellers. Indeed, the amount of absolute contact is understated, in the raw contact measures underlying Table 4.2, because it is based on a population of fewer than 500 firms and because it does not take account of multiregional contacts within industry categories. Although by conventional standards of statistical significance and also in terms of economic significance there is quite a lot of multimarket contact, it is also remarkable that so many of the industries have pairs of firms that do not meet significantly in other markets. In the Afterword, I relate such lack of contact to the conglomerate diversification in the 1960s and 1970s and compare the situation in the mid-1970s with the situation in 1950.

Table 4.2. *Number of random pairs for which the probability of ICMSR ≥ observed ICMSR, given the null hypothesis, is p*

| Probability | Number | Probability | Number |
|---|---|---|---|
| $0 < p \leq .01$ | 51 | $.40 < p \leq .50$ | 5 |
| $.01 < p \leq .05$ | 27 | $.50 < p \leq .60$ | 4 |
| $.05 < p \leq .10$ | 13 | $.60 < p \leq .70$ | 5 |
| $.10 < p \leq .20$ | 26 | $.70 < p \leq .80$ | 2 |
| $.20 < p \leq .30$ | 24 | $.80 < p \leq .90$ | 0 |
| $.30 < p \leq .40$ | 12 | $.90 < p \leq 1.00$ | 77 |

*Note:* Of the 261 possible cases, there were no FTC LB reporting firms in 2, only 1 in 2, and 11 degenerate cases (i.e., at least one of the pair produced in only one industry category so that the probability of meetings in other markets was zero). Hence the total number of observations is 246.

Tables 4.3 and 4.4 suggest that any allocative inefficiency resulting from multimarket contact must be weighed against the potential for "economies" of multimarket operation. Two possibilities for such economies are in the areas of marketing and innovative investment. Tables 4.3 and 4.4 explore two aspects of economies. Table 4.3 pursues the possibility that to take advantage of managerial talents or other skills, firms are attracted to markets that are similar. In such cases there could be synergistic effects which shift the production-possibilities frontier or simply reduce excess capacity.

To explore this possibility, for those pairs of firms where contact was significant, I ask whether there appears to be something special distinguishing the markets where the contact occurred from markets in general. Table 4.3 explores the contiguity of those markets with respect to marketing and innovation opportunities[8] by asking whether the observed value of each firm's advertising intensity and R&D intensity is significantly different for those markets than for an archetypal conglomerate firm.

Manufacturing industry categories, equal in number to the number of such categories in which a given pair of firms met, were chosen randomly. Then for each such randomly selected category, one of the firms operating therein was chosen randomly, and the observation of its advertising or company-financed R&D traceable to this industry category was used as the observation for the "conglomerate's" line of business. The observations for the manufacturing categories where contact occurred are then significantly different from those for a conglomerate if $b_1$ in the following regression is significantly different from zero. The ordinary least squares

Table 4.3. *Significance of differences between observed advertising and R&D intensities for firms having significant multimarket contacts and those intensities for "conglomerates"*

| Significance level (two tails)[a] | Traceable advertising intensity | | Traceable company-financed R&D intensity | |
|---|---|---|---|---|
| | + | − | + | − |
| $p \leq .05$ | 2 | 4 | 11 | 7 |
| $.05 < p \leq .10$ | 2 | 6 | 5 | 10 |
| $.10 < p \leq .15$ | 0 | 3 | 5 | 5 |
| $.15 < p \leq .20$ | 5 | 11 | 4 | 2 |
| $.20 < p \leq .25$ | 3 | 8 | 5 | 6 |
| $.25 < p \leq .30$ | 3 | 11 | 4 | 4 |
| "Insignificant" | 13 | 31 | 20 | 14 |

*Note:* There were 51 pairs of firms for which contact occurred more frequently than would have happened by chance given a significance level of 0.01. (See Table 4.2.) Thus 102 cases are examined in this table.

The entries show for the various levels of significance the number of cases for which the observed value of the firm's advertising intensity or R&D intensity for the industry categories where contact occurred is significantly different from their observed value for the matched sample of randomly selected firms in randomly selected industry categories. The "+" columns show cases where the firm's advertising intensity or R&D intensity was greater in the industry categories where contact occurred; the "−" columns indicate cases where those variables were less.
[a] The probability $p$ of an absolute difference greater than that observed if, in fact, there was no difference. This is based on the $t$-statistic for the coefficient of the dummy variable described in the text.

regression used in each of the 102 cases had the form $y = b_0 + b_1 D + e$, where $b_1$ is the fitted coefficient for the dummy variable that takes the value of 1 for the observations of one of the actual firms (in one of the pairs drawn from each manufacturing category) in the manufacturing categories where contact occurred and takes the value of 0 for observations for the conglomerate.

Table 4.3 supports the conjecture that the markets in which contact occurred have similarities one would not expect from a random selection of markets. Given random selection, one would expect about 31 cases to show a significance level of 0.30 or higher; but 58 cases reached that significance level for advertising intensity and 68 did for R&D intensity.

Table 4.4. *Number of significant contact pairs for which the observed value of advertising (traceable) intensity or company-financed R&D (traceable) intensity is significantly different from its predicted value*

| Significance level (two tails)[a] | Advertising intensity | | R&D intensity | |
|---|---|---|---|---|
| | + | − | + | − |
| $p \leq .05$ | 0 | 13 | 3 | 17 |
| $.05 < p \leq .10$ | 0 | 3 | 0 | 7 |
| $.10 < p \leq .15$ | 0 | 3 | 0 | 4 |
| $.15 < p \leq .30$ | 6 | 15 | 6 | 10 |
| $.30 < p$ | 29 | 33 | 27 | 28 |

*Note:* See notes to Table 4.3. The firm's intensity variables for the set of industry categories in which contact occurred are compared with the sales-weighted average for each of those industry categories. The results presented appear to be insensitive to the distinction between expenses that the firms can trace to specific lines of business and those nontraceable expenses that are allocated to lines of business. When the 13 cases for which advertising (traceable) intensity was significantly less than predicted at the 0.05 level were reexamined using total advertising (traceable plus nontraceable) intensity, 11 were again in the category of significantly (0.05 level) lower intensity, 1 in the category of lower intensity but 0.30 level, while 1 was in the insignificantly higher intensity category.
[a] See note "*a*" of Table 4.3.

Table 4.4 examines a different aspect of economies of multimarket operation in the contact markets. Given that the firm is in a set of related markets, does it actually perform differently from what would be expected in *those* markets? Less advertising than predicted on the basis of all observations could imply economies of multimarket operation. Or, more advertising than predicted could imply a Cournot–Nash wasteful competition outcome of a prisoner's dilemma advertising game as firms having diversified into similar markets meet other firms with similar histories. Table 4.4 uses a procedure identical to that used in Table 4.3 *except* that predicted values for manufacturing categories where contact occurred replace the "conglomerate" values in the regression equation. The predicted value for a manufacturing industry category equals the sales-weighted average of the intensity variables for its LBs. Table 4.4 suggests "economies" of multimarket operation for some sets of the markets where contact occurred. If observations were random, one would "expect" 2.55 cases in each cell. Instead, there are 0 and 3 in the two "+" cells, and 13 and 17 in the two "−" cells. Far more than would have occurred by chance, we find the advertising and R&D intensities for LBs where significant contact occurred to be significantly less than the typical intensities for those industries.

Note that the "economies" observed may be the result of interdependence. This possibility is explored later. The tests in Tables 4.3 and 4.4 do not exhaust search for "economies" of multimarket operation but suggest that they are likely.

### 4.5 Profits and multimarket contact

The year of our observations, 1974, was one of inflation in the United States. The relation between seller concentration and profits tends to disappear in such years (Weiss, 1974), probably because of the difficulty of finding a new oligopolistic consensus on price. But coordination of restraint in expanding capacity in response to new profitable opportunity might be expected to cause higher profits for markets where high multimarket contact and high seller concentration coincide. Given an original consensus price in a concentrated market, inflation may render it obsolete yet sellers may balk at moving the price upward quickly for fear of rocking the boat. Salop (1986) has described such transition difficulties for oligopolists. Leading the market price upward subjects a firm to being undercut by rivals who may profitably drag their feet about matching the increase. And if an increase must be rescinded, a misinterpreted cut could trigger a round of price cuts.

But the same sort of oligopolistic trepidation may make it easier for sellers to avoid adjusting upward capacity in markets where changes in relative demand or costs have resulted in quasi-rents. Hence one expects that profits are higher in markets where high seller concentration and high multimarket contact coincide. The firms in these markets may be technically efficient, but if resources move freely, their profits, other things being equal, should be no more than those of other firms. My hypothesis is that firms in markets where both seller concentration and multimarket contact are high will recognize their interdependence and not compete away their own profits. Even during periods when coordination would be difficult for diversified sellers who did not meet significantly in other markets, the advantages described in Chapter 2 may allow sellers with high multimarket contact to avoid profit-eroding expansion of output. For this to show in the statistics, some immobility of resources from outside to within these industries must be present.

Tables 4.5 and 4.6 show that higher profit is what we find for high-contact high-concentration firms in our sample. Note that profits are *lower* if multimarket contact alone is high, suggesting that multimarket firms in competitive markets quickly deploy resources to compete away

Table 4.5. *Expected value of a company's profits[a] in a line of business,[b] in 1974*

| Multimarket contact measure, PMMC | Four-firm seller concentration ratio, CR4 | | |
|---|---|---|---|
| | Low | Median = 38.95 | High |
| High | 4.2%[c] | | 8.2%[d] |
| Median = 0.7820 | | | |
| Low | 5.5%[e] | | 5.9%[c] |

[a] Operating income divided by sales, $\pi$.

[b] Using the 492-observation random sample underlying Table 4.2. The equation with $t$-statistics in parentheses below the coefficients is

$$\pi = 0.055 + 0.0038DCR4 - 0.013DPMMC + 0.036(DCR4 \times DPMMC),$$
$$(5.2) \quad (0.23) \quad (-0.79) \quad (1.5)$$

where $D$ denotes a dummy variable taking the value of 1.0 when the underlying variable is greater than its median. The product of the two dummy variables equaled 1.0 144 times. The percentage of variance explained was 1.3%. The $F$-ratio for the significance of the regression as a whole = 2.14; significant at the 0.093 level. There were 488 degrees of freedom.

[c] Insignificantly different from 5.5%.

[d] Significantly different from 5.5% at the 0.093 level. See note $b$.

[e] Significantly different from zero at the 0.00005 level for a one-tailed test.

any excess profits that materialize in response to demand or costs changes. The relation exists in the simplest experiment without other controls (Table 4.5) *and* in the multiple variable specifications of Table 4.6.

Equation (1) in Table 4.6 controls for several other variables. The measures of contact have been described in detail above. The ratio of operating income to sales is the dependent variable in profitability equations. An LB's operating income is sales minus materials, payroll, advertising, other selling expenses, and general and administrative expenses. There are of course potential problems with such data, but balanced assessments (Scherer et al., 1987; Mueller, 1990, pp. 8–14) in the literature find the information useful for studies like the one here.

Leonard Weiss developed the following control variables. He developed the concepts for the controls and then with George Pascoe gathered the data and integrated it with the FTC LB data. I am indebted to them for sharing the variables with me.

The four-firm seller concentration ratios have been adjusted to correct for heterogeneity and openness of markets as defined. The adjustments reflect noncompeting subproducts, interindustry competition, regional

Table 4.6. *Regression of company profits[a] in a line of business,[b] in 1974, on multimarket contact and other structural variables*

|  | Equation (1) | Equation (2) |
|---|---|---|
| Intercept | 0.0060 (0.20) | 0.0040 (0.13) |
| DPMMC[c] | −0.017 (−1.1) | −0.019 (−1.1) |
| DCR4[c] | −0.015 (−0.84) | −0.017 (−0.97) |
| DPMMC × DCR4 | 0.045 (1.9)[d] | 0.043 (1.9)[e] |
| Minimum efficient scale | 0.46 (2.1)[d] | 0.34 (1.5) |
| Advertising intensity | −0.088 (−0.58) | −0.083 (−0.54) |
| Growth in demand | 0.044 (3.0)[d] | 0.046 (3.1)[d] |
| Geographic market size | $-0.019 \times 10^{-3}$ (−1.1) | $-0.021 \times 10^{-3}$ (−1.2) |
| Assets/sales | −0.0096 (−0.69) | −0.0082 (−0.59) |
| Share |  | 0.11 (1.8)[e] |
| $R^2$ | 0.044 (2.7)[d] | 0.051 (2.8)[d] |

*Note:* $t$-ratios are in parentheses next to the coefficients. The $F$-ratios for the significance of the equation as a whole are next to the $R^2$s.

[a] As a proportion, operating income divided by sales.

[b] Using the 492-observation random sample underlying Table 4.2, 12 had missing values. Thus there are 471 degrees of freedom for equation 1; 470 for equation 2.

[c] DPMMC and DCR4 are dummy variables that take the value of 1 when PMMC and seller concentration, CR4, are greater than their median values. Their product equals 1 in 144 of the 492 cases. It equals 1 in 142 of the 480 complete observations used in the regressions above.

[d] Significant for a two-tailed test at the 0.05 level or higher.

[e] Significant for a two-tailed test at the 0.10 level or higher.

markets, and imports. Description of the adjustments is in Weiss and Pascoe (1986). Profits are expected to increase, other things being equal, with seller concentration.

The radius in miles within which 80 percent of shipments occurred is the measure of the geographic market's size. Since the seller concentration ratio has been adjusted for geographically limited markets, this market-size variable adds a measure of diversity of costs and of buyers. Greater diversity makes a consensus on price difficult. A negative sign is expected.

The measure of minimum efficient scale is the ratio of midpoint plant shipments to industry shipments. It is expected to measure economies of scale as a barrier to entry and to have a positive impact on profits.

The advertising-to-sales ratio provides a correction of assets/sales for the accounting practice of expensing intangibles and controls for the possibility that barriers to entry are associated with product differentiation. This variable is expected to have a positive impact.

Growth in an industry's demand is measured by the rate of growth in shipments for the industry. The variable is 1976 shipments (from 1976 *Annual Survey of Manufactures*) divided by 1972 shipments (from the 1972 *Census of Manufactures*). Growth is expected to have a positive impact on profits.

The assets/sales ratio is to control for a normal rate of return. A positive coefficient is expected. Scott and Pascoe (1984) attempt a finer control for the required rate of return and find that the attempt does not have an appreciable effect on the estimation of other effects; thus, the simpler methodology conventionally used, and used here, appears to be appropriate. In subsequent chapters, we shall control for differences in capital costs, among other things, across both firms and industries by estimating fixed effects.

Equation (2) in Table 4.6 adds each firm's market share to control for Demsetz (1973)–Mancke (1974) superiority (talent or luck) explanations.[9] In both specifications, the interaction of multimarket contact and seller concentration is significant at the 0.10 level for a two-tailed test. Although the superiority hypothesis receives support given the *t*-ratio of 1.8, the relation between profits and coincidence of seller concentration and multimarket contact remains.[10]

The dichotomous treatment of seller concentration and multimarket contact is appropriate in a Chamberlinian world where a critical concentration level is hypothesized and where the sample is divided into two parts because a priori theory gives no guidance. But a continuous specification is of interest to test robustness. Such a specification was tested and the relation that exists for the dichotomous specification remained and was significant (at the 0.10 level for a two-tailed test). The superiority hypothesis received somewhat stronger support (significant at the 0.05 level) in the continuous specification, and minimum efficient scale was also somewhat more significant.

Moving from low to high concentration given high multimarket contact has a large effect on profits. Equation 1 in Table 4.6 shows that coincidence of high seller concentration and multimarket contact added about 3.0 percentage points to the expected profit rate (thus, for example, profits on sales would be about 8.0 percent rather than 5.0 percent), other things being equal. Using the covariance matrix estimated for the parameters, the *t*-statistic for the linear combination of coefficients of *DCR*4 and *DPMMC* × *DCR*4, where weights are 1, is 1.8. Since for 1974 the sample average of the profit variable (operating income on sales) was 6.9 percent for the FTC LB manufacturing sample (U.S. FTC, 1981a, p. 11), the 3.0-percentage-point impact of concentration conditional on multimarket contact is quite large. I shall argue that we have rather good support for both of the conjectures described earlier – the Gort–Rumelt conjecture and the conjecture of Edwards. But first I comment on the difference between my positive results and the largely negative ones reported by others.

In my opinion, the main reason I detect an impact of multimarket contact is the probability-related measure of contact. "Raw contact" (ICMSR) alone (i.e., entered in place of PMMC into the specifications) is not significant. It does perform similarly to PMMC regarding sign and is almost significant *if* entered conditionally on high PMMC – that is, if entered as ZICMSR, which takes the value 0 if PMMC is less than its median value but the value ICMSR when PMMC exceeds its median value.

A priori reasoning supports such a finding. The probability concept features "grouping" – activities spanning significantly the same set of markets. In those cases it seems more likely that a coherent set of strategies can be formed. There is a coherent set of markets on which the interdependent firms can focus. Perhaps it helps to view my approach as a sophisticated "scaling" technique. Compare firms A and B with firms C and D. A and B each produce in 40 industry categories, while C and D each produce in 6. Firms A and B meet in 6 industry categories other than the one from which they were drawn, while C and D meet in 5. My notion is that 5 is greater than 6 in the relevant sense.

The probability measure gives the "volume" of intertwined activity in the sense that it measures how full of contacts the space of firms' activities is. Thinking more generally about the theoretical arguments developed in Chapter 2, one could then say that firms C and D have activities so "intertwined" in the sense of spanning the same markets that it should be much easier to coordinate strategies. Firms A and B are less likely to have a coherent set of markets where interdependence and integrated strategies can take hold. Note further that it is not just economies of multimarket operation that imply nonrandomness of behavior. If there were a search for market power through multimarket operation, then we might find what Richard E. Caves has called "a mutual exchange of hostages."[11] That would imply a nonrandom pattern in meetings as well. Evidence presented in Chapter 3 supports the idea that firms use mergers to effect such a concurrent holding of hostages. Thus, I think there is viable theoretical rationale why "significant" multimarket contact matters. It reflects significant behavior – the search for either economies or market power.

### 4.6 Conclusions

The rate of profits on sales was, other things being equal, about 3.0 percentage points higher in 1974 for LBs where seller concentration and multimarket contact were both higher than their median values than for LBs where only multimarket contact was high. That is a large, economically significant effect. Further, the interaction of multimarket contact and seller concentration explains 1.3 percent of the variance in the very noisy LB data (somewhat more even than is explained by the highly touted market share variable). I attribute this fact to the coincidence of "economies" of multimarket operation *and* barriers to the mobility of resources from outside to within the markets where significant contact *and* recognized interdependence occurred. High multimarket contact alone is associated overall with *lower* profits (supporting the Gort–Rumelt conjecture). Only when both contact and concentration are high are profits and multimarket contact both "expected" to be high. True, lower values for measures of nonprice competition such as advertising and R&D are possibly the result of interdependence[12] rather than economies.

I emphasize that *even* if the lower expenditures on advertising and R&D reflect solely nonpecuniary economies of multimarket operation, excess profits would *not* be observed. Output expansion would dissipate them. Price greater than economic cost is necessary for the profitability results above. Evidently interdependence and barriers to mobility are sufficiently great to allow excess profits to remain. The results imply that multimarket contact does have an impact on performance. Conditional on low seller concentration, it is associated with lower profits, supporting the conjectures of Gort and Rumelt. But conditional on high concentration, it is associated with higher profits, supporting Edwards's conjecture. An important task for future research is to develop case studies that will provide examples of how oligopolistic coordination actually works in a multimarket setting. Adams (1974) provides an important and suggestive beginning.

Chapter 4 has adduced evidence that multimarket contact can enhance the ability of oligopolists to reach a profitable consensus. There is some inkling that in the FTC LB sample such a consensus *requires* multimarket contact, but the data are indeed special. The mid-1970s were surely unusual times because manufacturing industries' costs and demands were so variable. In Chapter 5, we shall use another sample to pursue the possibility that multimarket contact is a sine qua non of consensus among diversified oligopolists. We therefore turn our attention now, as we did in Chapter 3, to data from the 1950s.

# 5

## The market power of diversified oligopolists

As we have seen in Chapter 2, current antitrust policy ignores multimarket contact. Yet, as Chapter 2 explains, multimarket contact among firms may increase their ability to exercise market power (i.e., to raise price above competitive levels) without engaging in collusion that would violate U.S. antitrust laws. Multimarket contact can increase market power because such contact may allow oligopolists to effect a noncompetitive price with decisions made individually.

### 5.1 The hypothesis

One could even argue that multimarket contact may at times be *necessary* if a profitable oligopolistic consensus among diversified firms is to be reached. Chapter 2 explains that disagreements of the battle-of-the-sexes sort might otherwise intrude. As Section 5.2 details below, Bain's classical observations about market structure and performance were conditioned on high multimarket contact among the leading firms in each of the industries that he sampled. Thus, the classical work linking monopolistic pricing with oligopoly is consistent with the view that multimarket contact may be necessary for consensus among diversified oligopolists. This chapter analyzes Bain's sample, then tests the hypothesis that multimarket contact among diversified oligopolists is necessary for their market power because without the contact they will be unable tacitly to agree on a supracompetitive price.

### 5.2 Bain's sample

*A different interpretation of Bain's result:* Sellers' recognition of mutual dependence within markets is the typical focus of empirical models of

This chapter is a revision of Scott (1991b).

oliopolistic market power; conjectural variations and strategic games reflect sellers' interdependence. Yet contacts *across markets* can change conjectures and strategies *within markets* and thereby restrict output and increase prices and profits.[1] Bain's seminal work (1956) has been interpreted as support for the price-raising effect of sellers' recognition of their mutual dependence *within* a market. My hypothesis, however, is that Bain's effect – of concentration and barriers to entry, on profits – resulted because of multimarket contact among the firms in his sample.

I expect diversified sellers' concentration to have its strongest effect on profits earned within an industry when multimarket contact among the sellers is high. With high seller concentration, sellers recognize their mutual dependence, and, as explained in Chapter 2, the multimarket contact can enhance their ability to reach a consensus causing high prices and excess profits. With low seller concentration, however, the necessary recognition of mutual dependence is absent. In such cases sellers' diversification across many industries simply increases their awareness of profitable opportunities and their ability to deploy resources exploiting those opportunities but competing away economic profits especially rapidly.[2] Thus, with a sample including concentrated and unconcentrated markets, but with each market exhibiting high multimarket contact among its diversified sellers, the effect of concentration on profits will be especially pronounced, because the multimarket contact makes possible the supracompetitive profits in the concentrated markets and even helps eliminate excess profits in the unconcentrated markets. Bain used just such a sample.

After introducing methodology, I demonstrate the high multimarket contact throughout Bain's sample. I then present a test showing that the effect of multimarket contact on performance is not an esoteric possibility; instead, multimarket contact underlies Bain's seminal observation of the effect of seller concentration on profits. In concluding the chapter, I discuss an important alternative to my interpretation and note the implications for future research.

*Methodology:* Multimarket operations can reflect a firm's attempts to create both multimarket contact to strengthen oligopolistic consensus and diversification to realize economies of scope. If indeed a firm's multimarket operations reflect such purposive behavior rather than simply random valuation discrepancies or purely conglomerate behavior stimulated by "managerialism,"[3] then firms producing the same primary product would meet in other markets more than would happen by chance. Such significant nonrandom contact among firms in a market would occur as they each tried to exploit similar opportunities.

With the criterion for multimarket contact being *significant* nonrandom contact among the firms sampled in each market, we discover that Bain's sample is the special type, described above, that should accentuate the concentration-profits relationship. In particular, Bain's sample is a cross section of firms that not only were leaders in their primary markets but also met to a significant extent in other markets. This special cross section of firms generates his observation of the nexus among concentration, barriers to entry, and profits.

Bain studied only the leading firms in each of his industries, because he believed that the hypothesis linking seller concentration and barriers to entry to profit rates would most likely be confirmed by observing "the profit rates of the dominant firms alone" (1956, p. 191). He observed that adding the smaller firms' profit rates could obscure the relationship because the smaller firms were more likely to have "inefficiently small plants or firm scales or . . . smaller product-differentiation advantages over entrants" (1956, p. 191). Thus, Bain's study focuses on the leading firms alone – just two leading firms in each of 8 of his 20 industries, with 4 leading firms in each of his remaining 12 industries (1956, pp. 192–194).

To show the significance of the multimarket contact among the firms in Bain's sample, I examined every possible within-market pairing of his sampled firms. When would the multimarket contact of a pair of market leaders be significant? To develop the probability distribution for such contact given the null hypothesis of random behavior, we begin with the fact that there were $n = 147$ three-digit manufacturing industries into which Bain's sample of firms could have diversified.[4] Each pair of Bain's market leaders operated in a three-digit industry associated with the market in which Bain observed the two firms. Let the first firm of each pair be the one that operated in the larger number, $s$, of three-digit industries; the second operated in $t \leq s$. Given the null hypothesis, we can then determine the probability distribution over the number of ways this pair of firms can meet in industries other than the one in which Bain observed them as leaders.

Letting $C_{x,y}$ denote the number of combinations of $x$ things taken $y$ at a time, the probability, for our pair, of $f$ meetings in other markets is

$$p(f) = (C_{t-1,f})(C_{n-t,s-1-f})/(C_{n-1,s-1}),$$

where $\sum_{f=0}^{t-1} p(f) = 1$. The formula for $p(f)$ results because the first combination is the number of ways to choose $f$ nonprimary markets for the first firm from the $t-1$ occupied by the second firm, the second combination is the number of ways to choose the remaining $s-1-f$ markets for the first firm that are not among the $t$ markets occupied by the second, while the third combination gives the total number of ways to choose the nonprimary markets for the first firm.

Now with the foregoing methodology we can see that multimarket contact was extraordinarily high for Bain's market leaders. Bain studied 20 industries, and as explained next, for all 18 of his industries for which multimarket contact measures can be formed, multimarket contact was significant, and the null hypothesis of random contact must be rejected.

*A new look at Bain's sample:* Using the preceding distribution for $p(f)$, multimarket contact for Bain's firms was, in all of his industries for which the experiment can be conducted,[5] significant at the 10 percent level or higher. That is, if the firms *were* behaving randomly, the observed contact for each case was great in the sense that the probability of less contact was at least 90 percent. Most of the cases are much more significant than that; the null hypothesis is rejected, and we conclude that contact resulted from purposive diversification. A table showing the extent of the multimarket contact for the firms that Bain sampled in each industry is available on request. For 11 of the industry categories among the 18 for which multimarket contact measures can be formed, Bain sampled 4 leading firms rather than just 2 as he did in the remaining 7 categories. Using the probability PMMC that a given pair of firms will meet less than they actually do given the null hypothesis of random diversification, multimarket contact is significant throughout the sample for the 18 industry sets of diversified firms.

For example, in 1950 General Motors produced in 32 of the FTC's three-digit industries. Chrysler produced in 9. These firms are the leaders Bain chose in the automobile industry (three-digit industry 371, in part). They met in 7 other three-digit industries: 289 (miscellaneous chemical products), 339 (forge shop products, wire products, miscellaneous primary metal products), 343 (heating equipment, except electric), 351 (engines and turbines), 354 (metalworking machinery), 356 (general industrial machinery), and 358 (service-industry and household machines). PMMC for this example is 0.9999.

To the extent that the multimarket operations result from vertical integration, the competing firms may not meet as sellers in the other markets. Nonetheless, they would meet in the sense of having a common network of operations, costs, and generally interdependent interests spanning several markets. Note that purposive diversification need not be *for the purpose* of facilitating multimarket contact and recognition of mutual dependence; yet, even if vertical, it does have these effects.

The significant multimarket contact of Bain's leaders is not typical of large manufacturing firms in general. To show that Bain's sample consists of firms with unusually high multimarket contact, I examined the population of the 1000 largest U.S. manufacturing firms. From the complete set of product classes used by the FTC (1972) to classify the production of the 1000 largest manufacturing firms in 1950, I chose 100 at random. I then chose randomly a pair of firms from each product class of two or more producers. There were 89 pairs for which a nondegenerate probability distribution $p(f)$ could be formed. Of those, only 54 exhibited significant contact, in three-digit industries other than the one from which they were drawn, at the 0.10 level or higher. Although a representative sample would then show only 54 percent of the firms with significant multimarket contact, 87.5 percent of the possible within-industry pairings showed such contact for Bain's complete sample of firms in 20 industries – including the 7 degenerate pairings for which PMMC could not be formed and for which multimarket contact is then automatically registered as insignificant.[6] For the 73 pairings for which PMMC could be formed, 95.9 percent showed significant multimarket contact. Two of the three exceptions had PMMC values over 0.80 but less than 0.90. Two of the three occurred in one industry, with the other four possible pairings significant, and were generated by the fourth largest firm. The remaining exception also involved a fourth largest firm among four sampled by Bain, and for its industry the other 5 of the 6 possible pairings showed significant multimarket contact. In the random sample, from the 1000 largest manufacturers, 18 of the 89 nondegenerate pairs never met in other industries, while for Bain's sample, the firms in only 1 of the 73 pairs with nondegenerate $p(f)$ distributions never met in other industries. Thus, for his entire set of 20 industries, 90 percent exhibited significant multimarket contact; of the industries in which he sampled *diversified* firms, 100 percent had significant multimarket contact.

In concluding our new look at Bain's sample, we should note that the diversified leading pairs *alone* generate Bain's result. Thus, there is no chance that the handful of exceptional cases without significant multimarket contact were needed for his result. Bain (1956) found that profitability was highest for firms in concentrated industries protected by very high barriers to entry. Using his data (1956, p. 45, pp. 192–194, for the leading pair of sampled firms in each of the 18 industries for which the multimarket contact measure could be formed), his result does obtain for the subset of leaders. As in Bain's full sample at the industry level (1956, p. 196), the distinction between "substantial" and "moderate to low" barriers made no difference.[7] The entire impact of barriers to entry on profit rates at the firm level is captured by the distinction between industries with "very high" entry barriers and all other industries.

*Conclusion about Bain's sample:* I have discovered that Bain's test of the structure–profits relation was conditioned on a significant amount of multimarket contact for the leaders of the industries he examined. His work, which has been interpreted as support for mutual dependence recognized *within* markets, was in fact based on a sample for which contacts *across* markets were great and arguably conditioned the conjectural variations and strategic postures *within* markets. As explained above, the structure–profits relation should be especially strong in such a sample.

The multimarket contact of sellers may affect behavior and performance in markets. Sellers who meet often in other markets will have an enhanced ability to communicate. The multimarket contact creates symmetry in demands and costs that promotes common strategic interests, provides more experience and opportunity for coordination, and thereby makes coordination easier. Contact, whether within a market or across several, may increase the ability to reach a consensus, conditional of course on sufficient market concentration. For diversified manufacturing firms, multimarket contact may be a sine qua non of the concentration–profits relation.[8]

### 5.3 Empirical tests

To test the hypothesis that multimarket contact is necessary for oligopolistic consensus among diversified firms, we need a sample that, unlike Bain's, includes not only observations of oligopolies with high multimarket contact among the firms, but additionally observations of oligopolies with low multimarket contact among the firms. Does price-raising consensus fail in the latter cases but succeed in the former? To answer the question, we first need the necessary sample. Second, we need the multimarket contact measures for the leaders of each industry. Third, we must construct Bain's profitability measures for the new sample. Fourth, we can then ask if economically and statistically significant supracompetitive profits occur only for the cases where oligopolists have high multimarket contact.

First, to expand Bain's sample of U.S. manufacturing industries and their leaders in 1950, I began with Shepherd's (1982) categorization of the competitive conditions in U.S. industries in 1939, 1958, and 1980. To classify each four-digit 1950 manufacturing industry, I studied Shepherd's categorizations, the 1950 Corporate Patterns data (U.S. FTC, 1972), the *Census of Manufactures: Concentration Ratios in Manufacturing,* the *Standard Industrial Classification Manual,* Bain (1956), and Mann (1966). I required that usable industries have in the FTC Corporate Patterns 1950 data (U.S. FTC, 1972, which provides the detailed breakdown across industry categories of each reporting firm's shipments) at least the FTC sample's leading firm for the industry and a second firm that was the largest of the remaining leading firms which could be used with the leader to compute a multimarket contact measure. I required leading firms in both the sense that their sales in the industry were substantial and that they were among the top four firms reporting in the industry. Just as in Bain's original sample, the firms observed in my experiment must have had the industry in question as their primary industry (their largest line of business). However, since I want to test whether multimarket contact is necessary for a consensus among *diversified,* oligopolistic firms, the firms must also be diversified. The criteria I have used in constructing the sample are necessarily somewhat arbitrary, but also commonsensical. For a firm to be considered diversified, I have required that it produce in at least 3 LBs and have no more than 95 percent of its shipments in the primary industry. With these guidelines and the benefit of Shepherd's work and the FTC's Corporate Patterns data, I have been able to assemble a much larger sample of oligopolies than Bain did, and my sample's oligopolies do exhibit different amounts of multimarket contact. Industries that were clearly dominant firm cases (in the sense that the dominant firm model quite probably applied) were excluded; oligopolies with diversified leaders constitute the sample. A table showing my sample of diversified oligopolistic firms from 35 industries is available from me on request.

Second, to compute the measure of multimarket contact, I used the Corporate Patterns data (U.S. FTC, 1972) and the method described in Section 5.2, except that I computed the measure at about the four-digit as well as the three-digit level (there are some cases that were appropriately more or less aggregative). The calculations with the four-digit industries tell essentially the same story as those using three-digit industries, but the three-digit cases are more readily shown in an example such as the General Motors/Chrysler case developed above, while industries based on four-digit categories are arguably more meaningful as markets. Hence, although for expositional purposes above I used the three-digit level, for my hypothesis test I have developed the more computationally burdensome four-digit case. A table available from me on request shows these multimarket contact measures, computed as in Section 5.2 except that now $n$, the number of industry categories into which my firms could have diversified, equals 418. The use of the more numerous four-digit categories of course tends to make any meetings appear more significant; yet despite that tendency, we have 10 of the 35 industries with the probability of less contact, PMMC, being less than 0.95, and five of the industries have that probability less than 0.90.

Third, for each firm I constructed Bain's measure of profitability using *Moody's Manual* (1951). I calculated, as a percentage, $\pi$, each firm's average annual profit rate on equity (after income taxes) for 1949–50. Weighted least squares allows use of information available about the reliability of the whole company profitability data, but the procedure did not have an appreciable effect on the estimation below, so the ordinary least squares results are presented.[9] Nonetheless, errors in observations of profit because of accounting procedures and the use of whole company data probably result in heteroskedasticity. As a result, although the estimated coefficients are unbiased and consistent, the estimates of their standard errors are inconsistent and thus their $t$-ratios yield misleading inferences. The evidence suggests that heteroskedasticity exists in some of the models below, even though my a priori formal structure for the differences in the disturbances' variances appears unimportant empirically. Thus, White's (1980) method of computing consistent estimates of the standard errors in the presence of heteroskedasticity, but no formal model of its structure, is used, and the resulting $t$-ratios are shown as $t^*$ below those calculated by ordinary least squares.

Fourth, to ask whether profitable oligopolistic consensus appears to hold for diversified oligopolists only when their multimarket contact is high, we can observe whether and to what extent a change in multimarket contact affects the profitability of an oligopolistic industry's leading firms when those firms are diversified.[10] The data suggest that without significant multimarket contact the firms cannot expect to successfully coordinate a high profit outcome.

For the 64 diversified firms with profit data in the expanded sample of 35 oligopolistic industries, the relationship between profit rate $\pi$ and multimarket contact is shown in the following equation, with DMMC being a dummy variable taking the value 1 if PMMC $\geq 0.95$ (i.e., multimarket contact is significant at the 5 percent level) and taking the value 0 otherwise.

$$\pi = 11.68 + 5.44\,(\text{DMMC})$$
$$(t = 9.38) \qquad (t = 3.75)$$
$$(t^* = 11.48) \qquad (t^* = 4.25)$$

$R^2 = 0.18$, adjusted $R^2 = 0.17$, degrees of freedom $= 62$.

Thus, the predicted profit rate for diversified oligopolists with high multimarket contact is 17.12 percent, while the profit rate for the oligopolists without significant multimarket contact is expected to be 11.68 percent.[11] The continuous form of the measure of multimarket contact has much lower explanatory power, suggesting, in conjunction with the effect of the discontinuous measure, that multimarket contact must reach a certain threshold of significance before it affects profits.[12]

There is some evidence consistent with the profit-reducing diversification of managerialism (Mueller, 1987). For although multimarket contact appears to be a sine qua non of profitable oligopolistic interdependence, the most extreme cases of significant multimarket contact are associated with somewhat lower profits than the other significant multimarket contact cases. That refinement in the predicted relationship between multimarket contact and profitability conditional on oligopoly with diversified firms is shown in the following fitted equation, where either both DMMC and its product with PMMC are 0, or DMMC is 1 and its product with PMMC ranges from 0.95 to 1.0.

$$\pi = 11.68 + 179.80\,(\text{DMMC}) - 174.64\,(\text{DMMC})(\text{PMMC})$$
$$(t = 9.50) \qquad (t = 1.66) \qquad\qquad (t = -1.61)$$
$$(t^* = 11.48) \qquad (t^* = 6.96) \qquad\qquad (t^* = -6.67)$$

$R^2 = 0.22$, adjusted $R^2 = 0.19$, degrees of freedom $= 61$.

A diversified oligopolist's profit rate is significantly higher when multimarket contact is significant, but within the set of significant multimarket contact cases, profits decline from 25.57 to 16.84 percent as PMMC rises from 0.95 to its maximum of 1.0. Although the decline is large and significant statistically, the profit rate remains well above the 11.68 percent rate expected for diversified oligopolists without significant multimarket contact.

The same relationship holds in Bain's sample of diversified oligopolists. For the 20 observations of his sample for which he considered barriers to entry to be at least substantial and for which the four-firm seller concentration exceeds or equals 50 percent, we have the following relation, where, as we have emphasized above, PMMC is restricted to range from 0.90 to 1.0.

$$\pi = 93.99 - 78.70\,(\text{PMMC})$$
$$(t = 3.03) \qquad (t = -2.50)$$
$$(t^* = 5.89) \qquad (t^* = -4.66)$$

$R^2 = 0.26$, adjusted $R^2 = 0.22$, degrees of freedom $= 18$.

Thus, for the diversified oligopolists in Bain's sample, all of which exhibited significant multimarket contact, expected profit rates ranged from 23.16 to 15.29 percent. The average profit rate for the remaining 16 firms in the markets with lower concentration or lower barriers or both was 11.02 percent; the relation between $\pi$ and PMMC was thoroughly insignificant for that sample, with PMMC's coefficient having a $t = -0.23$ ($t^* = -0.60$) and with the relation's $R^2 = 0.0036$ and its adjusted $R^2 = -0.07$.

Why would the greater profitability associated with significant multimarket contact among diversified oligopolists decline with greater contact? Lower profit rates (relative to other cases of significant multimarket contact) may result if managers pursuing their own interests diversify when it is not in their shareholders' interests. Managers of competing oligopolistic firms may even match each other's unprofitable (to the shareholders) diversification because similar diversification patterns satisfy the managers' personal utility-enhancing goals (Mueller, 1987, pp. 34–35), such as the desire to reduce unsystematic risk that could threaten the managers' company-specific investment in human capital. Further, Paul Geroski has suggested that perhaps "too much contact" lessens managers' interest or ability to focus on a particular market; that is, a kind of bounded rationality may be at work.[13] Thus, some of the extreme cases of multimarket contact may not only induce symmetry, making oligopolistic consensus profitable, but also reflect unprofitable diversification.

### 5.4 Discussion

The research here is basic research, seeking knowledge of how markets work simply for the sake of better understanding. Yet I believe the work has important implications for public policy. With the information currently available, one cannot be sure that the profits observed do not just reflect cost efficiencies arising from economies of scope. However, the evidence provides some support for (or at the very least is consistent with) the hypothesis that multimarket contact is necessary for a profitable consensus among diversified oligopolists. In the results of Section 5.3, when multimarket contact of diversified oligopolists was low, profits averaged roughly what they were for the essentially competitive industries in the classic samples of Bain and Mann. But given significant multimarket contact, the diversified oligopolists' profits were much higher on average – significantly higher statistically and in actual magnitude.

If my hypothesis is correct, when assessing conventional enforcement policy toward horizontal mergers we should actually worry less about a merger that increases an industry's concentration whenever the oligopolists in that industry are diversified yet have little multimarket contact with one another, but we should worry more about a merger if it increases concentration for an oligopoly where the sellers do meet significantly in other markets. Thus, in the 1992 *Horizontal Merger Guidelines* (U.S. Department of Justice and U.S. Federal Trade Commission, 1992), the effect of multimarket contact would be considered when examining "factors in addition to market concentration relevant" to "the potential adverse competitive effects of mergers" (p. 33); in particular, "Market conditions may be conducive to or hinder reaching terms of coordination...."

[R]eaching terms of coordination may be limited or impeded by firm heterogeneity, for example, differences in vertical integration or the production of another product that tends to be used together with the relevant product" (p. 37). Additional development of the *Guidelines* to emphasize the importance of multimarket contact in the context of horizontal mergers could be added here and at other points in the *Guidelines* where the competitive consequences of horizontal mergers, given various market conditions, are discussed. Regarding conglomerate mergers, we should worry about their price-raising effects if they increase the multimarket contact of concentrated sellers. The evidence above suggests that with both types of mergers, the price-raising effects of a merger are more likely when multimarket contact is high.[14]

In this concluding chapter of Part I, we have seen that multimarket contact may be necessary for effective oligopolistic consensus in a concentrated industry when the industry's firms are diversified. One interpretation of the evidence is that without multimarket contact coordination breaks down because the diversified sellers have different costs and demands, and hence would not independently choose the same price, and because price cuts are less easily detected and matched. Given that interpretation, the evidence suggests that Bain's observation of the nexus among profits, concentration, and barriers resulted from the multimarket contact of the firms in his sample. As a perceptive referee urged, I must acknowledge, however, that the same factors that give rise to certain first-mover types of entry barriers – product-differentiation barriers and absolute-cost barriers resting on research and innovations – also induce diversification and consequent multimarket contact. Therefore, the correlation of profits and purposive diversification may be because of multimarket contact or because of underlying barriers to entry reflected in the diversification and consequent contact. Future research could investigate directly, in an expanded sample, the effect of purposive diversification jointly with the concentration and entry-barrier variables that Bain used. One could distinguish between research and development and advertising-based entry barriers and the others (especially production scale economies barriers) that do not give rise to diversification.

These results are outside the bounds of standard models and afford a set of results transcending the usual industry results. Moreover, as we shall see in subsequent chapters, the groups of industry categories pertinent for understanding the behavior of diversified firms are sometimes different even for firms in the same industry. Some firms in industry $x$ are also in $y$ and $z$, but others combine $x$ with $s$ and $t$. If hypotheses about multimarket contact are important, firm as well as industry effects should be discernible in business unit performance, and traditional models should explain only part of the systematic differences across firms and industries. One industry effect is the extent of multimarket contact in an industry. One firm effect is the particular multimarket span of a particular firm.[15] In Part II we shall document firm and industry effects and the relatively small part of those effects that can be explained by traditional models.

# PART II

**Firm and industry effects versus traditional models**

# 6

## Profitability effects

This chapter shows that company (or firm) effects significantly influence business-line profitability with industry effects controlled. A fundamental question underlying this book is whether (privately) efficient diversification could be because of firm-specific advantages that are not totally resolvable into industry-level effects. The chapters of Parts II and III taken together imply that firm effects in profitability and R&D exist and that differences in the types of purposive diversification chosen by competing manufacturers with different firm-specific capabilities may underlie the differences in profitability and in R&D effort and performance across firms.

### 6.1 Introduction

The mutual interdependence recognized by sellers in a concentrated market protected from entry implies behavior that differs from that predicted by the model of pure competition which takes as given large numbers of sellers or free entry.[1] For example, in such a concentrated market the equilibrium price is expected to exceed marginal cost, and resource allocation is therefore expected to be inefficient. Yet empirical verification of the a priori behavioral significance of variance in markets' structures is controversial. This chapter cannot resolve all controversy,[2] but within the general linear model, it provides insights about the importance of traditional models of structure and profitability, firm effects, and the effect of capital intensity on oligopolistic coordination. Purposive diversification provides a potential explanation for the unexplained *systematic* variance that is documented.

The statistical work uses the Federal Trade Commission Line of Business (FTC LB) data which have been described by the FTC (U.S. FTC,

Chapter 6 is a revision of Scott and Pascoe (1986).

71

1981a, 1981b, 1982) and by researchers such as Martin (1983). The results developed here are compared with the traditional model used in Scott and Pascoe (1984), and the sample used there is used here.

### 6.2 Statistical model

The LB profits for a given firm depend on industry, firm, and LB characteristics. We can specify a general linear model that can be used to approximate the relationship. The following discussion explains the dimensions of the FTC's LB observations and introduces the model used to analyze them in this chapter.

Observing $I$ industries and $N$ firms, we posit a true model linear in the parameters although not linear in the variables:

$$p = \mathbf{X}b + e \tag{6.1}$$

where $p$ is the vector of observations on LB profitability, our dependent variable, and where $\mathbf{X}$ is the matrix including the observations on each of the explanatory variables. The vector of coefficients in the true model is denoted by $b$, and $e$ is a homoskedastic random error with an expected value of zero that is distributed normally and independently of the variables in $\mathbf{X}$.[3]

Some explanatory variables characterize the industries, others the firms, while others are neither industrywide nor firmwide, but characterizations of LBs. Partition $\mathbf{X}$ so the $F$ variables characterizing industries are first, followed by the $\mathbf{G}$ vectors of firm characterizations, and finally the $\mathbf{H}$ remaining vectors. Then,

$$p = [\mathbf{R}\,\mathbf{S}\,\mathbf{T}] \begin{bmatrix} b_{\mathbf{R}} \\ b_{\mathbf{S}} \\ b_{\mathbf{T}} \end{bmatrix} + e \tag{6.2}$$

where $\mathbf{R}$ is the set of column vectors $\mathbf{r}_f$, $f = 1$ to $F$, $\mathbf{S}$ is the set of column vectors $\mathbf{s}_g$, $g = 1$ to $\mathbf{G}$, $\mathbf{T}$ is the set of column vectors $\mathbf{t}_h$, $h = 1$ to $\mathbf{H}$, and the $b$'s are conformable vectors of coefficients.

A set $\mathbf{A}$ of $I$ "dummy variables" forms a basis of vectors that can generate the observations on the industry variables. Similarly, a set $\mathbf{D}$ of $N$ dummy variables spans the vector space of observations on the firm variables. Then denoting by $r_{fi}$ the observation on the $i$th of $I$ industries for the $f$th of $F$ variables characterizing industries, and denoting by $s_{gn}$ the observation on the $n$th of $N$ firms for the $g$th of $\mathbf{G}$ variables characterizing firms, the model (6.2) can be rewritten equivalently as

$$p = [\mathbf{A}\,\mathbf{D}\,\mathbf{T}]c + e \tag{6.3}$$

where the transpose of $c$ is

$[\Sigma_f b_{Rf} r_{f1}, ..., \Sigma_f b_{Rf} r_{fI}, \Sigma_g b_{Sg} s_{g1}, ..., \Sigma_g b_{Sg} s_{gN}, b_{T1}, ..., b_{TH}].$

From (6.3), if the true model did not include the set of vectors **T**, i.e., if apart from random error it included only firmwide and industrywide characterizations, the regression of the variable $p$ on **A** and **D**, less one dummy variable or with an intercept and less one firm and one industry dummy variable, would provide the explanatory power (as measured by the coefficient of determination) of the true model, even though we did not know the true variables but knew only that the true model was linear in the parameters and that the only variables important were firmwide and industrywide characterizations.[4] The explanatory power of the estimated model with dummy variables is based on the fact that the dummy variable model actually fitted has explanatory power equivalent to a true model (6.3) for which the coefficient of the dummy variable for the $i$th industry (or $n$th firm) is the weighted sum of the entire set of coefficients for the true variables characterizing industries (or firms), with the weight of each coefficient being the value its associated variable takes for the $i$th industry (or $n$th company). In general, we cannot exclude the possibility of the **T** matrix – especially because, as noted subsequently, LB effects are likely a priori. Further, the basis vectors spanning the vector space **T** will usually exhaust our sample space given the nonexperimental data with which we work. Thus, if there *are* variables in the **T** matrix, we must in practice know them to ascertain the true model's explanatory power.

Summarizing, the two models, (6.1) and (6.3), the latter being estimated by dropping variables as necessary, yield the same statistics for the whole model. In practice, models are actually estimated with only a proper subset of the set of true variables and are thus nested within the true model. If we knew **T** did not enter the true specification, the explanatory power of the true model could be found by regressing $p$ on **A** and **D** with the necessary deletion of dummy variables. The explanatory power of the subset of variables actually examined in models attempting to find the true coefficients $b$ in (6.1) could be compared to that of the true model. Since included variables can pick up the effect of excluded ones, being conservative we would have to say that we have only an upper bound on the explanatory power of our hypothesized variables relative to the true (and unknown) set. The fact that we cannot in practice use a basis for the vectors **T** also implies that our estimate of relative explanatory power is, to be conservative, an upper bound. But if we find that we are explaining only a small portion of the variance explained by the true model, we know we have much to learn.

Now, with our model, we show that firm and industry effects appear significant, and additionally, traditional models account for only a small part of the systematic variance. Also, the matrix **T** cannot be dismissed. Since the true **T** is unknown and its vectors may be correlated with those in **R** and **S**, firm and industry effects may not be significant even though they appear to be. **R** and **S** may pick up effects of unknown elements of **T**. We demonstrate the importance of the matrix **T** by focusing on the effect of its inclusion on the interpretation of seller concentration's effect on profitability.

### 6.3 The variables[5]

*The dependent variable:* The dependent variable, $p$, measures profitability and is defined as the assets-weighted average *ratio*[6] of LB operating income to LB assets over the 3 years (1974, 1975, and 1976) in our sample.

*Variables characterizing industries:* The variables providing industrywide characterizations – the vectors of **R** – include the following: ACR is the adjusted four-firm seller concentration ratio (as a proportion); MES measures minimum efficient scale; IMP measures import competition; DS measures the geographic size of the markets served by the industry; GR measures the growth of market demand; $k$ measures the cost of capital appropriate for the industry. All industrywide variables other than $k$ characterize FTC four-digit industries, while $k$ is for FTC (and equivalently SIC) two-digit industries.

Weiss adjusted the seller concentration ratios, ACRs, to correct for heterogeneity and openness of markets as defined. Weiss and Pascoe (1982) describe the adjustments made to reflect noncompeting subproducts, interindustry competition, regional markets, and imports. As explained below, in our sample we expect the sign of the coefficient for ACR to depend on whether capital intensity is high or low.

The measure of minimum efficient scale, MES, is (based on the 1972 *Census of Manufactures*) the average plant size of the largest plants (accounting for at least half of industry output) divided by industry output.

The ratio of imports to domestic output plus imports less exports is the measure of import competition, IMP. As the variable increases, competitive pressures should increase; and hence, profitability should fall.

Weiss also provides a measure of the geographic market's size. DS is the radius in miles within which 80 percent of shipments occurred. Since Weiss has already adjusted the seller concentration ratio for geographically limited markets, he expects additional contribution of this variable to measure diversity of costs and buyers. Greater diversity is expected to make consensus on price difficult; hence, a negative sign is expected.

The rate of growth in shipments for the industry measures growth in demand, GR. The variable is 1976 shipments (from 1976 *Annual Survey of Manufactures*) divided by 1972 shipments (from the 1972 *Census of*

*Manufactures*). Growth is expected to have a positive impact on profits. But the relation is complex, as we discuss later.

Finally, the cost-of-capital estimate, $k$, is provided in two forms in Scott and Pascoe (1984). We have $k_e$, an errors-in-variables estimate, and $k_o$, an ordinary-least-squares estimate. As seen below, the results are qualitatively insensitive to the choice between the two variables. Further, the model was estimated with the cost of capital subtracted from the profitability measure; i.e., the regressions were reestimated using deviations of profitability from $k$ as the dependent variable, and the conclusions based on the more general unconstrained model remain the same.

*Firm-specific variables:* The variables providing firmwide characterizations – the vectors of **S** – are two. DIV measures diversification inversely by the sum of the squared shares of each of the firm's activities in the total operations of the firm. LEV measures the firm's leverage by the ratio of the firm's debt to its equity. The coefficient on LEV proves significantly less than zero, suggesting a disequilibrium result for which firms in trouble were heavy borrowers. The inverse measure of diversification, DIV, has a significant negative coefficient, implying, other things being equal, that less diversified firms are less profitable. Wilson (1992) reports a similar finding. The ideas developed in Part I of this book suggest that the effect of diversification here in its simple, conventional form could reflect market power resulting from multimarket operations, economies of multimarket operation, or both. Because the observation of profitability is for the business unit rather than the firm, it is less likely that the correlation reflects a tendency for more profitable firms to diversify.

*LB variables:* We shall focus on three variables – the vectors of **T** – that provide neither firmwide nor industrywide characterizations. SHR denotes, over the period of the sample, each company's average share of the particular industry from which a given profitability observation comes. ADVS measures for each LB the average ratio of LB advertising to LB sales, over the sample period. The third variable, AS/S × ACR, is the product of ACR and the weighted-average ratio of LB assets to LB sales, over the sample period. Subsequently, we introduce other vectors, $t_n$, in the form of interactions among variables already defined, but the variables introduced at this point are the ones used in the "traditional" model of Scott and Pascoe (1984), and we focus on them before generalizing the model.

### 6.4 The "traditional model," with known elements of the R, S, and T matrices

*Current interpretation and an alternative:* The FTC LB data are of great interest because, among other things, the information holds the promise

of resolving whether seller concentration in U.S. manufacturing industries facilitates sellers' coordination of production to effect supranormal
profits. Using LB data for the 1970s, researchers have provided evidence
challenging the traditional role of seller concentration as a determinant
of profitability across industries. Using the PIMS data of the Strategic
Planning Institute, Gale and Branch (1982) reach the conclusion that market share rather than concentration is the primary structural determinant
of profitability. Further, they interpret the evidence as implying that oligopolistic coordination cannot be expected to improve profit rates ap-
preciably. Results (e.g., Ravenscraft, 1983) using the FTC LB data for
the mid-1970s have been consistent with the PIMS results showing that a
firm's share of a market and not a market's concentration appears to be
the important determinant of the firm's profitability in an LB. One interpretation is that mutual dependence recognized among oligopolistic sellers
is not important; but rather, the key is superiority (see Demsetz, 1973) –
better products, better management, lower costs – or luck (see Mancke,
1974), or a dominant firm (see Shepherd, 1972, and Salop and Scheffman,
1983).

Thus, the current interpretation of the data largely rejects the traditional hypothesis that seller concentration causes static allocative inefficiency by means of the effect of mutual dependence recognized by an
industry's sellers. However, (1) the turbulence of the economy during the
mid-1970s suggests that breakdown in oligopolistic consensus was likely
in industries with high fixed costs (see Scherer, chapter 7, 1980, pp. 206–
212). Capital intensity should therefore make "more fragile pricing discipline" (Scherer, 1980, p. 212). Further, (2) one expects the profitability,
defined as the rate of return on assets, of a given degree of market power
to diminish, other things being equal, with capital intensity. Consider
two firms facing identical demand curves and with identical marginal and
average costs in equilibrium. The two firms have identical market power,
but suppose one has a larger proportion of assets to sales, sales being
identical for both. The firm with the larger assets to sales ratio will of
course show a smaller excess profit/assets.

Thus we expect the rate of change in profits with respect to seller concentration to be a decreasing function of capital intensity and even to be
negative beyond some critical point because "price warfare" may imply
subnormal returns. In less turbulent times, the relation might never turn
negative but asymptotically go to zero. To Long and Ravenscraft (1984)
and Martin (1984), the nonlinearity resulting from point (2) above suggests that a measure of profitability on sales would be superior to a measure of profitability on asssets. However, that conclusion need not follow,
because an alternative approach is to use a functional form that is linear in

Table 6.1. *Traditional model with p as the dependent variable*

| | | |
|---|---|---|
| **R** *matrix* | | |
| $k_o$ | 0.18 (1.9)$^c$ | |
| $k_e$ | | 0.16 (1.1) |
| ACR | 0.16 (6.9)$^a$ | 0.16 (6.9)$^a$ |
| MES | 0.40 (3.0)$^b$ | 0.40 (3.0)$^b$ |
| GR | 0.092 (11)$^a$ | 0.091 (11)$^a$ |
| IMP | −0.085 (−2.0)$^c$ | −0.084 (−1.9)$^c$ |
| DS | −0.000032 (−5.0)$^a$ | −0.000033 (−5.2)$^a$ |
| | | |
| **S** *matrix* | | |
| DIV | −0.088 (−4.7)$^a$ | −0.087 (−4.7)$^a$ |
| LEV | −0.019 (−4.7)$^a$ | −0.019 (−4.7)$^a$ |
| | | |
| **T** *matrix* | | |
| ACR × (AS/S) | −0.27 (−14)$^a$ | −0.27 (−14)$^a$ |
| SHR | 0.14 (3.7)$^a$ | 0.14 (3.7)$^a$ |
| ADVS | 0.20 (2.3)$^c$ | 0.19 (2.2)$^c$ |
| | | |
| Intercept | 0.035 (1.9)$^c$ | 0.042 (2.2)$^c$ |
| *F*-ratio | 38$^a$ | 38$^a$ |
| *R*-square | 0.13 | 0.13 |
| Degrees of freedom | 2759 | 2759 |

*Note:* The *t*-ratios are in parentheses beside the coefficients.
$^a$ Significant at 0.0001 for a one-tailed test.
$^b$ Significant at 0.01 for a one-tailed test.
$^c$ Significant at 0.05 for a one-tailed test.
$^d$ Significant at 0.10 for a one-tailed test.

the parameters estimated even though nonlinear in the variables. Further, the control for capital costs is more direct given our dependent variable.

*An alternative result:* Using the LB data for the 376 companies for which all data were available,[7] the effect of seller concentration for the years 1974 through 1976 is found to be a decreasing function of capital intensity. With $p$ denoting the measure (operating income to assets) of LB profitability, and ACR denoting the adjusted concentration ratio as a proportion (e.g., the mean is 0.39), and AS/S denoting LB assets/LB sales, as seen in Table 6.1, the significant relation is $\partial p/\partial \text{ACR} = 0.16 - 0.27(\text{AS/S})$. Figure 6.1 illustrates the relation. AS/S is not included independently because a priori, given the other controls, the coefficient on AS/S is expected to go to zero as ACR approaches zero.

The highly significant relation depicted in Figure 6.1 confirms the prediction above. And, among other things, share has been held constant. To

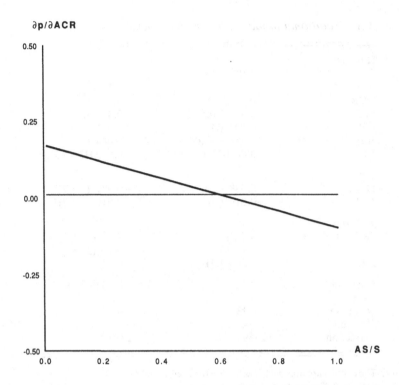

Figure 6.1   Capital intensity and the effect of seller concentration on profits.

provide some perspective, in 1976 industry average assets to sales ratios using pure LB data range from 0.176 to 2.04 with the ratio for 80 of the FTC's four-digit industries for which data on this item were available falling below the critical level of 0.59 for which $\partial p/\partial ACR$ is zero (U.S. FTC, 1982, pp. 16-35). Clearly, these disaggregated data at the FTC are consistent with the hypothesis that seller concentration increases profit by means of oligopolistic coordination. The results show that, for the period during which the LB data were collected, equilibrium is not long-run; and therefore, we cannot assume that the coefficients on our variables would apply during less turbulent times. Nonetheless, the results are consistent with what is expected for imperfect markets during a period of turbulence.

*Other possibilities:* We cannot here resolve the question of whether seller concentration, other things being equal, causes static allocative inefficiency. The hypothesis and the functional form used here is but one possibility. Dennis Mueller (personal correspondence) has found results similar to those of Gale and Branch (1982) and Ravenscraft (1983). Most importantly, he finds those results for the period 1950–72. The turbulence of the 1970s would not be a factor in that sample. He finds a negative impact of concentration that he suspects may be the result of nonprice rivalry. Further, other factors such as unionization may dissipate rents. Richard Caves has noted that a basis for low profitability *at times* in a capital-intensive industry is the building of an oversize plant too soon, resulting in excess capacity that can be eliminated only over time. Long and Ravenscraft (1984) and Martin (1984) prefer a specification using operating income to sales as the dependent variable. If one uses that dependent variable and controls for capital costs with the product of $k$ and AS/S, one finds the relations reported in Table 6.1 *except* that the coefficient on ACR is insignificantly different from zero. In other words, the significant decline in $\partial p/\partial$ACR as capital intensity increases remains, but the relation begins at the origin instead of above it. If the alternative hypothesis about coordination breaking down were "wrong," the significant negative coefficient on (ACR)(AS/S) would not be found in the specification using the dependent variable preferred by Long and Ravenscraft and Martin; yet we do find it. The specification using assets rather than sales in the denominator of the dependent variable is arguably better because it allows a more direct control for capital costs. However, the result using the operating income to sales specification does have a straightforward interpretation. The inability to respond flexibly to cost and demand changes can imply the normal return found in the operating income/sales specification, while the "price warfare" leading to the negative effect and subnormal returns occurs when capital intensity is high. Finally, the most important possibility is that Figure 6.1's result would not hold up in the larger, "complete" model that controls for all firm and industry effects. As the next section shows, the result does survive examination of the more complete model.

## 6.5 Comparison of the "traditional" model with the "complete" model

Table 6.2 shows the models that fit firm-specific effects and the vectors in **R** and **T** (i.e., the vectors not nested within the firm-specific effects), industry effects and the vectors in **S** and **T** (i.e., the vectors not nested within the industry effects), and finally both firm-specific and industry effects and the vectors in **T** (i.e., vectors of characterizations neither industry- nor firmwide). By comparing the reduction in the sum of squared residuals as we go from the traditional model in Table 6.1 to each of the models in Table 6.2, we can obtain a lower bound on how much

Table 6.2. *Firm and industry effects with p as the dependent variable*

| | | | | |
|---|---|---|---|---|
| **R** *matrix* | | | | |
| $k_o$ | 0.12 (1.1) | | | |
| $k_e$ | | 0.09 (0.55) | | |
| ACR | 0.18 (7.0)ᵃ | 0.18 (7.0)ᵃ | | |
| MES | 0.43 (3.0)ᵇ | 0.43 (3.0)ᵇ | | |
| GR | 0.10 (11)ᵃ | 0.10 (10)ᵃ | | |
| IMP | −0.11 (−2.3)ᵇ | −0.11 (−2.3)ᵇ | | |
| DS | −0.000035 (−5.0)ᵃ | −0.000035 (−5.2)ᵃ | | |
| 256 industry effects | | | Fitted first $F=2.81^a$ | Fitted last $F=2.96^a$ |
| **S** *matrix* | | | | |
| DIV | | | −0.079 (−4.1)ᵃ | |
| LEV | | | −0.018 (−4.4)ᵃ | |
| 375 firm effects | Fitted first $F=1.65^a$ | Fitted first $F=1.65^a$ | | Fitted last $F=1.50^a$ |
| **T** *matrix* | | | | |
| ACR × (AS/S) | −0.30 (−13)ᵃ | −0.30 (−13)ᵃ | −0.34 (−15)ᵃ | −0.37 (−14)ᵃ |
| SHR | 0.16 (3.8)ᵃ | 0.16 (3.8)ᵃ | 0.17 (3.9)ᵃ | 0.17 (3.7)ᵇ |
| ADVS | 0.12 (1.1) | 0.12 (1.1) | −0.029 (−0.24) | −0.056 (−0.41) |
| Intercept | z | z | z | z |
| F-ratio | 2.5ᵃ | 2.5ᵃ | 3.8ᵃ | 2.5ᵃ |
| R-square | 0.29 | 0.29 | 0.28 | 0.43 |
| Degrees of freedom | 2386 | 2386 | 2509 | 2136 |

*Notes:* The procedure for fitting effects finds the unique sum of squares for the effects, but not their unique estimated values. Thus, in column 1, with 376 firms, 375 dummies and an intercept are fitted, and the sum of squares for the 375 firm effects is found. The *t*-ratios are in parentheses beside the coefficients. *F*'s for effects "fitted last" were computed using additional regressions as in Scott (1984, p. 244).
ᵃ Significant at 0.0001 for a one-tailed test.
ᵇ Significant at 0.01 for a one-tailed test.
ᶜ Significant at 0.05 for a one-tailed test.
ᵈ Significant at 0.10 for a one-tailed test.

we have to learn about firmwide and industrywide characterizations that are important for profitability.

Comparing Table 6.1's "traditional" specification with Table 6.2, we find that unidentified firmwide variables explain at least[8] 55 percent of the variance explainable given the specifications of columns 1 and 2. Our restricted model assumes that all variables other than those in our simple model have coefficients of zero. As seen above, that restricted model is nested within the fixed-effects model. We can, adjusting for degrees of freedom, compare the reduction in the residual sum of squares as we move from the restricted to the unrestricted model with the residual sum of squares for the unrestricted model. The *F*-value for this comparison is

1.4 with 373 and 2386 degrees of freedom. Comparing Table 6.1's "traditional" specification with column 3 of Table 6.2, we find that unidentified industrywide variables explain at least 54 percent of the explainable variance given column 3's specification. The associated $F$-value is 2.1 with 250 and 2509 degrees of freedom. Finally, comparing the "traditional" model with the specification in the fourth column of Table 6.2, we find that unidentified firm and industry effects together account for at least 70 percent of the explainable variance in the "complete" model. Comparing the reduction in the sum of squared residuals with the sum of squares for the unrestricted model, we find an $F$-value of 1.8 with 623 and 2136 degrees of freedom. Paul Geroski suggests the interpretation that the unidentified industry effects may reflect barriers to entry that are different in each industry and not captured by the conventional industry variables included in the specification. He observes also that the firm effects might similarly reflect mobility barriers.[9] Another interpretation, not inconsistent with Geroski's, is that the unidentified effects reflect the purposive diversification of industries' sellers. Interindustry variance in profitability may reflect differences across industries in the extent to which the firms diversify purposively. Firm effects may reflect different patterns of purposive diversification even for firms in the same industry.

### 6.6 Robustness of the model within two-digit industries and a complete interactive specification
Conceivably, other conditional effects in the data would swamp the effect on which we have focused. This section shows that the effect of seller concentration conditional on capital intensity is robust to an interactive specification that considers all variables to have a different impact in a market where sellers are few. In an unconcentrated market, growth, for example, is expected to have a positive effect on profitability because of a disequilibrium in which capacity is not appropriate for demand. But as Bradburd and Caves (1982) explain, other possibilities intrude in imperfect markets.

Perhaps the most informative way to develop the complete interactive specification is in the context of fitting the industry effects at the two-digit level of aggregation. By doing this we can include four-digit level, industrywide characterizations, such as ACR and GR, simultaneously with the industry dummies. We can thereby explore the effect within two-digit industries of the variance in our industrywide variables.[10] Table 6.3 presents that model with and without the specification for which the effects of variables depend on the level of other variables. Note that although the model holds up within two-digit industries, it clearly deteriorates when all interactions are included. However, the significance of the interaction

Table 6.3. *Structure-performance within two-digit industries, with and without additional interactions, with p as the dependent variable*

| | | |
|---|---|---|
| **R** *matrix* | | |
| ACR | 0.18 (6.3)[a] | 0.18 (1.6)[d] |
| MES | 0.44 (3.0)[b] | 0.057 (0.13) |
| GR | 0.082 (7.3)[a] | 0.087 (2.9)[b] |
| IMP | −0.075 (−1.6)[d] | 0.060 (0.46) |
| DS | −0.000024 (−3.2)[b] | −0.000030 (−1.4)[d] |
| ACR × DS | | 0.000015 (0.31) |
| ACR × IMP | | −0.33 (−0.96) |
| ACR × GR | | −0.012 (−0.18) |
| ACR × MES | | 0.64 (0.90) |
| 19 two-digit industry effects | Fitted last $F=3.73^a$ | Fitted last $F=3.39^a$ |
| **S** *matrix* | | |
| 375 firm effects | Fitted last $F=1.53^a$ | Fitted last $F=1.52^a$ |
| **T** *matrix* | | |
| ACR × (AS/S) | −0.32 (−14)[a] | −0.32 (−14)[a] |
| SHR | 0.16 (3.8)[a] | 0.11 (0.75) |
| ADVS | 0.015 (0.14) | −0.087 (−0.24) |
| ACR × SHR | | 0.079 (0.36) |
| ACR × ADVS | | 0.22 (0.30) |
| Intercept | z | z |
| F-ratio | 2.65[a] | 2.61[a] |
| R-square | 0.31 | 0.31 |
| Degrees of freedom | 2368 | 2362 |

*Note:* Notes for Table 6.3 are exactly as for Table 6.2.

of seller concentration with capital intensity remains. The model holds within two-digit industries and with firm effects controlled, and the original form – with only the ACR × (AS/S) interaction – is best.

### 6.7 Conclusions

By emphasizing effects that go beyond "firm effects" and "industry effects," this chapter has provided three insights. First, significant effects on profitability are not captured by firmwide or industrywide variables independently of one another. The effect of an industry's seller concentration on behavior and ultimately on profitability probably has been misinterpreted because it has not been conditioned on a seller's capital intensity. Control for firm and industry effects,[11] to explore the robustness of the result about concentration and capital intensity, provides the second and third insights. The second is that there are significant firm effects on profitability.[12] The third insight comes when we compare the explanatory power of a conventional model of structure and performance with the explanatory power of the linear model that would use all firmwide and industrywide characterizations relevant to the true model if it were in fact linear in the parameters. The comparison shows that we still have much to learn.[13] The motivating force for this book is the hope that understanding purposive diversification and the multimarket contact it engenders can eventually help close the gap between the systematic differences in firms and industries and the portion of those differences that we understand. As seen in Part I, multimarket contact appears to have a significant impact on profitability. Because of its effects on research and development investment, purposive diversification may also explain additional variance in profitability. In Part III, we shall explore the implications of purposive diversification for dynamic efficiency.

# 7

# R&D intensity effects

In Chapter 6 we saw that traditional views of the link from structure to performance explain only a very small portion of the *systematic* variance (the variance *explained* by firm and industry effects) in profits across firms and industries. In other words, we saw that firms differ significantly and that industries differ significantly, yet our traditional models do not explain very much of those significant differences across firms and industries. That finding, as presented in Scott and Pascoe (1986), has attracted some attention in the literature and has been replicated with very different data (Amato and Wilder, 1990). Here in Chapter 7 we shall document the importance of firm and industry effects in R&D intensity and see that the often postulated link from seller concentration to research and development (R&D) intensity is present in the Federal Trade Commission Line of Business (FTC LB) data, but that it disappears once firm and industry effects are controlled. Further, the effect of seller concentration is but a small part of the systematic variance in R&D intensity across business units.

Scherer (1965, 1967a) pioneered the result that technological opportunity is far more important for understanding variance in innovative activity than are measures of rivalry. The result was documented in the FTC LB data by Scott (1984) and confirmed by Levin et al. (1985) using a different procedure with those data. Geroski (1990; 1991a, chapter 6) has, among other things, documented the result using data on major innovations in the United Kingdom for the 1970s, the time period from which the United States observations examined in this chapter were taken. Subsequently, in Chapter 10, we shall ask if the central result – that seller con-

Chapter 7 is a revision of a portion of the material in Scott (1984).

centration is relatively unimportant as an explanation of R&D behavior – can be undone by restructuring competitive groups from the standard FTC classifications into those recognizing that rivalry takes place in the context of multimarket groups.

Although he finds that "opportunity" has the biggest effect, Geroski makes use of his observation that seller concentration may have an indirect positive effect on innovation because in more concentrated markets the firms may anticipate greater returns in the postinnovation market for their innovations. On the other hand, given the level of technological opportunity, seller concentration may have a direct negative effect on innovation. As in the work presented here and in Levin et al. (1985), Geroski's fixed-effects controls for technological opportunity reduce the effect of concentration, and for Geroski's sample the effect becomes significantly negative. Interestingly, in Section 10.5 of Chapter 10, I find a negative effect of seller concentration on R&D intensity after controls for opportunity are introduced, including firm effects that are not included in Geroski's work. Geroski's method allows him to sort out both his expected positive indirect effect and the negative direct effect, and the negative effect dominates. The nature of my sample allows me to control for firm effects, and after establishing their importance in this chapter, I shall proceed in Part III to explore their origins. Here in the present chapter, I shall develop the firm effects and additionally begin to explore the idea of an inverted-U relation between R&D intensity and seller concentration.

Greer (1971), Strickland and Weiss (1976), Scott (1978), Martin (1979), Scherer (1967a; 1980, p. 437), and several other authors studying nonprice competition have hypothesized and found an "inverted-U" relation between media advertising or company-financed R&D and seller concentration. There is nonetheless good reason to question the *cause* of the relation in conventional cross-sectional studies where firms operating in many different industries contribute to the variance in nonprice competition. As will be explored in depth in Chapters 10 and 11, the relation could be explained by variance across industries in the value or cost of nonprice competition, the opportunity (the odds for success) for it, the condition of entry, or the ability to coordinate (tacitly or otherwise) nonprice competition while holding constant the ability to coordinate price competition.

This chapter presents evidence about the *cause* of the inverted-U relation between seller concentration and nonprice competition. If observed inverted-U's are not caused by concentrated sellers attempting to shift supraprofitable sales from rivals to themselves, then they do not imply wasteful competition in the sense hypothesized by the structure-conduct-performance models of the inverted-U that emphasize sellers' cannibalization of rivals' profits. The variance in nonprice competition across firms and industries may have nothing to do with the conjectural interdependence and mutual dependence recognized among sellers, but instead may reflect differing prospective rewards to R&D or advertising *in the absence of* conjectural interdependence. Two different stories fit that possibility. First, the coincidence of middling levels of seller concentration and high R&D intensity could be sheer happenstance. The moderately concentrated industries may just happen to be the ones where sellers would find R&D profitable regardless of concentration or sellers' interdependence. Second, high opportunity may, via variants of Gibrat's law, lead through time to seller concentration (Nelson and Winter, 1982; Scherer, 1984, p. 245, p. 254; Scherer and Ross, 1990, pp. 141–146). Given a probability distribution for a firm's rate of growth, over time an industry of firms of equal size can become concentrated simply because of chance. In an environment with high opportunity the tendency of stochastic growth to generate seller concentration is especially pronounced because we anticipate higher variance for the probability distribution of growth rates (Scherer and Ross, 1990, pp. 144–145; Nelson and Winter, 1982). But as Scherer and Ross (1990, p. 146) observe, entry can offset the tendency toward concentration. Opportunities for entry might hold the evolving concentration in such high R&D, high opportunity markets to moderate levels.

The observations studied in this chapter are for the 3388 manufacturing LBs of the 437 firms reporting for 1974 to the FTC LB Program in 259 FTC four-digit industries and, to check the robustness of the results given the presence of one outlier that was dropped from the 1974 sample, for the 3550 manufacturing LBs of the 474 firms reporting for 1975 in 260 FTC four-digit manufacturing categories.[1] The results are that a statistically significant inverted-U relation exists for these observations if one does not attempt to control for differences across firms and industries in the value, costs, and opportunity for nonprice competition apart from that correlated with concentration, but the relation disappears once controls are added in the form of a fixed-effects model with effects for firms and for two-digit industry categories. Despite considerable variation in concentration within two-digit industries, it apparently has no impact on behavior within them.

The traditional inverted-U relation between company-financed R&D intensity and seller concentration is statistically significant in the LB sample. The inverted-U can be seen in the least squares equation for company-financed R&D intensity (R/S) for an LB (the operations of a firm in an FTC four-digit manufacturing industry) as a function of four-firm seller concentration (CR4) in the four-digit FTC industry. The dependent variable R&D intensity is R, company-financed R&D in the line of business, divided by S, the line of business's sales. I scale by LB sales to control for LB and company-specific effects that are correlated with the firm's LB sales. The four-firm seller concentration variable CR4 is Weiss's adjusted ratio in percentage form. The concentration ratios are adjusted to account for the internal heterogeneity and external openness of the industry categories as they are defined. Weiss and Pascoe (1986) describe the adjustments and show the results for the Standard Industrial Classification's four-digit industries. Here the adjustments are applied to the FTC's four-digit industries. With $t$-ratios in parentheses below the coefficients, the least squares equation for the 3388 manufacturing LB sample for 1974 is

$$R/S = 0.00094 + 0.00049 \, (CR4) - 0.0000038 \, (CR4)^2. \qquad (7.1)$$
$$\phantom{R/S = }(.43) \qquad\quad (4.5) \qquad\qquad\quad (-3.1)$$

The intercept is insignificantly different from zero, and both the coefficient for CR4 and for its square are significant at the 0.01 level for a two-tailed test. One extraordinary outlier was excluded from the sample, so the degrees of freedom equal 3384. The $F$-value for significance of the equation as a whole is 25, significant at the 0.0001 level; $R^2$ equals 0.015. Figure 7.1 illustrates the inverted-U relation; R/S reaches its predicted maximum when CR4 equals 64.5.

However, once we control for company effects and two-digit industry effects, the inverted-U relation disappears. With $D_c$ denoting a dummy variable for the $c$th company and $D_i$ a dummy variable for the $i$th industry, if we fit the least squares equation

$$\frac{R}{S} = b + \sum_{c=2}^{437} b_c D_c + \sum_{i=2}^{20} b_i D_i + f(CR4) + g(CR4)^2, \qquad (7.2)$$

we find that the company effects ($F$-value = 3.7) and the industry effects ($F$-value = 7.5) are each significant at better than the 0.01 level, but that neither of the two coefficients for the seller concentration terms are significantly different from zero ($F$-values of 0.02 and 0.06). The $F$-value for the equation as a whole is 3.8, significant at the 0.0001 level and $R^2$ is 0.37. With the one outlier excluded from the sample, the degrees of freedom are 2929. Scott (1984) reports additional technical details, but for our purposes here we can provide an overview of the results by observing first that seller concentration has no significant effect on R&D intensity once company and industry effects are controlled – even though the inverted-U relation exists in the data without such controls. Second, even before its effect is eliminated with the controls, the effect of seller concentration is

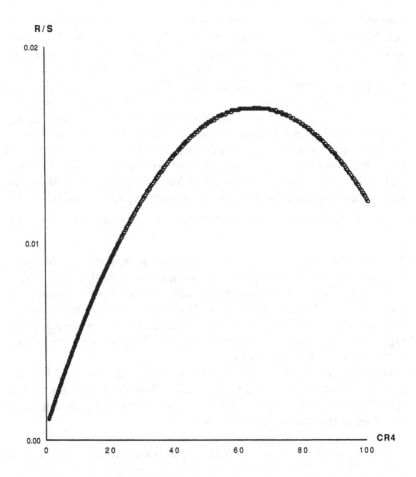

Figure 7.1   The inverted-∪ relation.

quite small relative to the systematic variance that is explained by the company and industry effects. Of course, regarding the first point, the strong two-digit industry effects may capture the influence of seller concentration or some other, interactive variable like barriers to entry. However, as observed below, a considerable amount of variance in seller concentration remains even after the differences across two-digit industries are eliminated. That remaining variance has no effect on R&D intensity.

To summarize the proportion of variance explained by a complete set of company and industry effects, with the industry effects being for the disaggregated four-digit FTC industry categories, consider the following equation for the 3550 manufacturing LBs of the 474 firms reporting for

1975 in 260 FTC four-digit manufacturing categories. The result with the 1974 data is essentially the same, but the 1975 data did not have any extraordinary outliers and provide a useful check for the robustness of the results.

$$\frac{R}{S} = b + \sum_{c=2}^{474} b_c D_c + \sum_{i=2}^{260} b_i D_i. \tag{7.3}$$

The company effects ($F$-value = 3.7), the industry effects ($F$-value = 3.5), and the equation as a whole ($F$-value = 3.6) were significant at the 0.0001 level. The $R^2$ was 0.49 and there were 2817 degrees of freedom. Scott (1984) provides technical details, but as an overview, the explanatory power is divided as follows. One can explain roughly 32 percent of the variance in R/S with either the company effects or the industry effects fitted first and then explain roughly another 16 percent by fitting second whichever set of effects is left. One could then say that about 16 percent of the variance in LB R&D intensity is clearly from company effects, about 16 percent is clearly from industry effects, and about 16 percent is confounded in the two types of effects.[2]

Thus, the inverted-∪ relation does not remain once differences in value, costs, and opportunity for nonprice competition are controlled for with a fixed-effects model. As shown in detail in Chapter 10, firm effects alone eliminate the inverted-∪ relation. Apparently, the inverted-∪ results because firms face different opportunities apart from those inherent in concentration. The value of and opportunity for innovative investment differs across products even without consideration of the extent of sellers' interdependence, and such value and opportunity differences appear to be the most important reason for different behavior. Scherer (1984, p. 254) makes the insightful argument that the Gibrat's law possibility is unlikely since correlations between seller concentration and R&D intensity are greatest in the economy's traditional sectors, rather than the high-technological sectors with the richest opportunities. My point is that the correlations do not exist once firm effects and a more complete set of industry effects are controlled. Thus, whether it is sheer happenstance or Gibrat's law at work, the causal link from seller concentration to R&D intensity is not supported, although this depends somewhat on what one thinks the two-digit industry effects capture.

I believe my interpretation is valid even though the two-digit industry dummies will capture the variance in concentration to the extent that concentration is homogeneous within two-digit industries. In the extreme case of perfect homogeneity, one could not control at the two-digit level for different types of goods, say food in general versus chemicals in general, *and* seller concentration at the four-digit level. In fact, such control is possible. In general, for the 259 four-digit FTC industries, 74 percent of the variance in concentration is within two-digit industries. In the specific 3388 observation sample, 68 percent of the variance in concentration is within two-digit industries.

The evidence from the fixed-effects models suggests caution when interpreting cross-sectional, multi-industry, inverted-U relations between seller concentration and nonprice competition. This is not to say that a correlation supporting the traditional wasteful competition result would not be found with intricate interactive simultaneous equations, or with modeling of various factors other than firm effects, opportunity classes at the broad industry level, and concentration, or simply with more control variables. Rather, since we find a strong inverted-U in the data without control for variance in opportunity across observations, but eliminate that relation once the opportunity controls are added, there is the presumption that all such previously adduced correlations may be artifacts of insufficient control for opportunity.

The results do suggest that company-specific and FTC industry-specific effects can explain a large amount of the variance in nonprice competition. While seller concentration explained at most 1.5 percent of the variance in LB R&D intensity, company and industry effects explained 49 percent of it. And company effects explain anywhere from 16 to 32 percent of the variance. Clearly, the evidence suggests that company policy may have an important influence on the technological progress of the economy. One cannot explain R&D activity simply by observing the industries within which a company operates. There is more to be understood. In Chapter 10, we shall ask if the concept of multimarket groups of rivals can help us to understand these company effects. Companies in a particular industry category often have very different multimarket strategies.

# PART III

Dynamic efficiency and the diversified firm

# 8

## Theories linking diversification and R&D investment

In this chapter, I use a theory of research and development (R&D) rivalry to explain why an industrial firm would diversify its R&D efforts. The theory is then used throughout Parts III and IV to analyze business strategy and public policy.

### 8.1 Introduction

This chapter's explanation for diversified R&D provides the theoretical underpinning of the observations, in Chapters 9 and 10, about purposive diversification. Further, the formal model of homogeneous R&D rivalry describes the intense form of R&D competition which Chapter 11 suggests may be so unattractive from a private standpoint that a firm, when faced with numerous competitors, would deliberately face the risks of thoroughly new and untried approaches to the R&D problem. Additionally, I shall use the model to explain the social economic welfare consequences for R&D investment in the alternative market structures of monopoly or completely cooperative R&D ventures, Nash noncooperative R&D equilibria, and the free-entry Nash noncooperative equilibrium. Understanding the social economic welfare implications of these different market structures will provide the theoretical backdrop for our discussion of industrial policy in Part IV.

The model that I shall use in this chapter (and throughout the discussions of R&D in the remaining chapters) is essentially Lee and Wilde's (1980) reformulation of Loury's (1979) model, which in turn is an extension of the ideas of Scherer (1967b), Barzel (1968), and Kamien and Schwartz (1982). The model has been a popular and well-accepted one; Hartwick (1991) provides an example of its use to study problems in industrial organization. I shall also use key ideas in Nelson's (1961, 1982b) work about parallel paths in R&D. It will be necessary in Chapter 14, when my suggestion for new policy is introduced, to expand the Lee and Wilde *cum* Nelson model by incorporating ideas (about how a firm views the introduction of its new process or product given that its rivals have introduced a competing innovation first) from Kamien and Schwartz (1982). Section 8.2 develops the model, and Section 8.3 uses the model to compare the social economic welfare consequences of R&D investment in various market structures. Section 8.4 uses the model to explain R&D diversification, and Section 8.5 concludes by using the model to make predictions about the links between diversification and industrial R&D and by providing an overview of Chapter 9's findings about those predictions.

### 8.2 A model of R&D rivalry

For the model, the basic unit of R&D effort is the R&D team or trial. The company chooses the R&D expenditure of $x$ per period for a trial. A company can undertake as many such trials as it wants, and in addition to incurring the chosen expenditure of $x$ per period for each trial, there is a fixed up-front investment cost $C(z)$ that is a function of the number of trials $z$. There is uncertainty about when a given trial will introduce its new product or process – technological uncertainty in the sense of Kamien and Schwartz (1982) or Glennan (1967). The probability of success by time $t$ is $F(t)$, the cumulative probability distribution, with $F(\infty) = 1$ and $\int_0^\infty F'(t)\,dt = 1$.

Conditional on not yet having introduced its R&D product, the conditional probability density for the trial's success at time $t$ is $F'(t)/(1-F(t))$. This conditional probability density for a trial's success, or hazard rate $h$, is determined by the amount of R&D expenditure each period. The R&D expenditure $x$ determines the hazard rate $h$, which is assumed to be constant through time. Mansfield (1968, pp. 47–48) used essentially this description of the R&D project for a firm with a collection of such projects. Thus,

$$\frac{F'(t)}{1-F(t)} = h(x). \tag{8.1}$$

Defining $u = 1 - F(t)$ and integrating Equation (8.1) over time, we have $-\int(1/u)\,du = \int h(x)\,dt$. Since $u$ is positive, we have $-\ln(u) = h(x)t$, which implies that $\ln(u) = -h(x)t$. Then $u = e^{-h(x)t} = 1 - F(t)$. Thus,

$$F(t) = 1 - e^{-h(x)t}, \tag{8.2}$$

and

$$F'(t) = he^{-ht}. \tag{8.3}$$

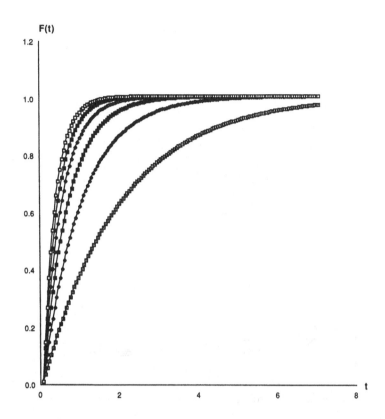

Figure 8.1  The cumulative probability of introduction. $F(t)$ for $h(x) =$ 0.5 (lowest curve) to 3.0 (highest curve) in steps of 0.5.

Figure 8.1 illustrates $F(t)$, and Figure 8.2 illustrates $F'(t)$. The figures show that the larger $h$ is, the faster the probability of success cumulates.

$$F(\infty) = \int_0^\infty F'(t)\,dt = \int_0^\infty (h)e^{-ht}\,dt = (1 - e^{-ht})\Big|_0^\infty = 1.$$

The expected time of introduction is

$$\int_0^\infty (t)F'(t)\,dt = \int_0^\infty (t)(h)e^{-ht}\,dt = \frac{1}{h},$$

as illustrated in Figure 8.3.[1]

To focus on the essence of competitive pressure and, for our subsequent work in Part IV, the idea that competitive duplication can be socially beneficial, I make the simplifying assumption that research trials are identical in the sense that $h(x)$ is the same for all. Further, in the

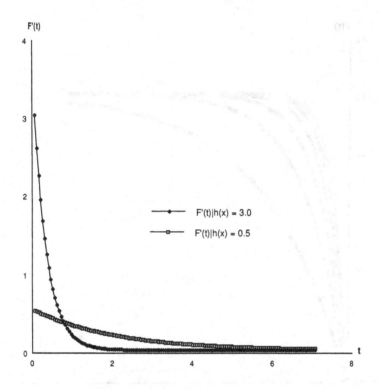

Figure 8.2   The probability density of introduction.

statistical sense their outcomes are independent. Note then that I allow the competing firms to exhibit duplication in research efforts in the sense that the functional relationship between R&D investment and the hazard rate is the same for all firms. However, even when undertaking the same amount of R&D investment, the firms will generate different outcomes because the effect of R&D investment is not certain. As with any R&D investment in the real world, the research efforts generate not certainties but random variables.

Thus, in the model, the firms can all choose "identical paths" in the sense that if we flipped pennies or tossed dice we would be flipping "identical pennies" or "identical dice." Yet the firms would be choosing "different paths" in the sense that if we flipped "identical pennies" or "identical dice" we could come up with different results. Thus the sense in which the model allows the firms to choose different paths is that the results of their R&D trials are not perfectly positively correlated. If they were, then the additional trials provided by rivalry would from society's standpoint just

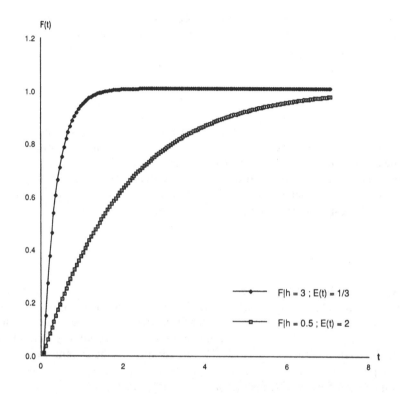

Figure 8.3   The expected time of introduction.

add costs but no benefits – a pure wasteful duplication case. Interestingly, if we made the firms' R&D trials different in the sense of "different pennies" with different values associated with heads or tails, then the parallel paths provided by rivalry are worth less (since we could rank the projects from most to least desirable and adding in the next has less value than it would have if all of the pennies were "identical" to the most desirable one with their outcomes being independently distributed nonetheless; see Nelson, 1961). I believe that my assumption here is a reasonable way to put the idea of "duplication of effort" into a stylized fact, because R&D investment is inherently uncertain even when the form of the investment looks more or less the same.

## 8.3   The social optimality of R&D investment

What would be the socially optimal amount of investment in these circumstances? I shall begin examining this question by asking what are the number of firms, number of R&D units or trials per firm, and amount of R&D expenditure per period per trial that would maximize society's expected profits.

The expected revenues for society would be

$$\int_0^\infty e^{-rt} W_s F_z'(t)\, dt,\tag{8.4}$$

where $r$ is the discount rate applied to future earnings, $W_s$ is the present value to society at the time of introduction of the innovation, and $F_z(t)$ is the probability that at least one trial has been successful by time $t$. Society would care about the probability of success on at least one of the number ($z$) of trials conducted. That probability equals 1.0 minus the probability of failure on all $z$ trials; hence $1 - e^{-zh(x)t} = F_z(t)$.[2]

The expected costs for society would be

$$\int_0^\infty (zx)e^{-rt}(e^{-zh(x)t})\, dt + \sum_{i=1}^{n} C_i(z_i),\tag{8.5}$$

where $n$ is the number of firms that are operating and $z_i$ is the number of trials for each of the firms. Thus, $\sum_i z_i = z$. Equation (8.5) is expected costs because $zx$ in costs per period are incurred as long as none of the trials has succeeded, and as explained in note 2, the probability that none of the trials has succeeded is $e^{-zh(x)t}$. In addition to the expenditure of $x$ per period per trial, there is the fixed cost of $C_i(z_i)$ that depends on the number $z_i$ of parallel trials operated by the $i$th firm.

From Equation (8.4), society's expected revenues are

$$\int_0^\infty (e^{-rt})(W_s)(zh(x))e^{-zh(x)t}\, dt = \frac{W_s zh(x)}{r + zh(x)}.\tag{8.6}$$

From Equation (8.5), society's expected costs are

$$\int_0^\infty (zx)e^{-rt}(e^{-zh(x)t})\, dt + \sum C_i(z_i) = \frac{zx}{r + zh(x)} + \sum C_i(z_i).\tag{8.7}$$

Thus, society's expected profits are

$$\frac{W_s zh(x) - zx}{r + zh(x)} - \sum C_i(z_i).\tag{8.8}$$

Our next step is to ask how a monopolist would look at the problem. The answer is: the same way except that $W_s$ would be replaced by the private value of the innovation $W$ and $\sum C_i(z_i)$ is replaced with $C(z)$, since although the monopolist can choose the number of trials that it wants to operate, the monopolist is one firm by definition. Its up-front investment costs for conducting multiple trials are specified by $C(z)$. If $W = W_s$ and

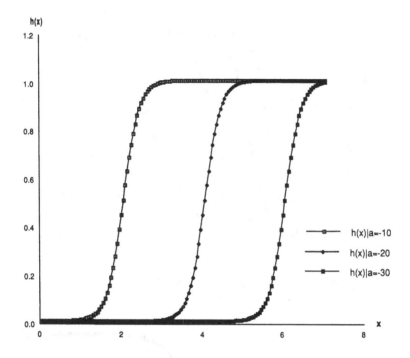

Figure 8.4   $h(x)$ for different values of $a$.

if the maximum value for Equation (8.8) is reached for the number of firms $n = 1$, then the monopolist will choose exactly the socially optimal $z$ and $x$. If, as is often believed to be the case, $W < W_s$, the monopolist will underinvest in R&D.

To provide an illustration, we need to specify $h(x)$ and $C(z)$. Of course a variety of functional forms would do for our present purposes, because we simply need to design a rich enough parameterization to capture the possibilities (for economies and diseconomies of scale and for economies of scope) that define the circumstances for R&D that we have described. First, consider $h(x)$. To be realistic, there should be a range of increasing returns followed by decreasing returns. A general functional form allowing $h(x)$ to behave in that way is

$$h(x) = c/(1 + e^{-a-bx}).  \tag{8.9}$$

Figures 8.4, 8.5, and 8.6 illustrate the function $h(x)$. Figure 8.4 shows that the larger $a$ is, the sooner the expenditure $x$ induces an upward rise in the hazard rate $h(x)$. Figure 8.5 shows that the larger $b$ is, the more

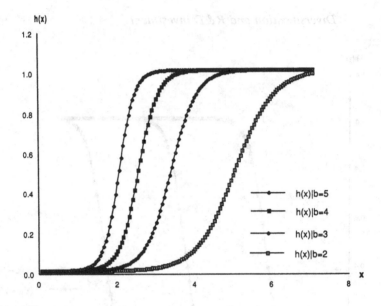

Figure 8.5    $h(x)$ for different values of $b$.

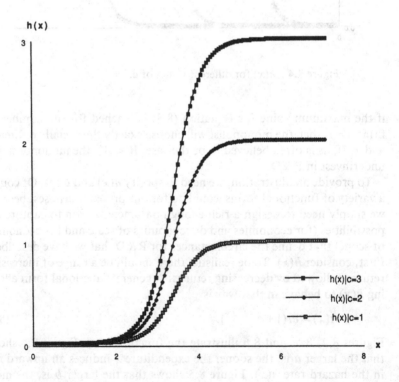

Figure 8.6    $h(x)$ for different values of $c$.

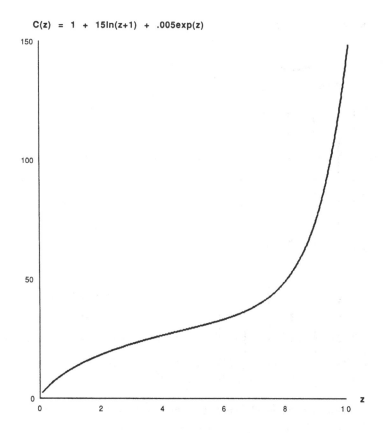

C(z) = 1 + 15ln(z+1) + .005exp(z)

Figure 8.7   A firm's up-front R&D investment costs.

rapid the upward rise will be. Figure 8.6 shows that $c$ provides the upper
asymptotic limit of $h(x)$.

For the function $C(z)$ (the up-front R&D investment costs for a firm
running $z$ trials) costs at first increase at a decreasing rate as the number of trials $z$ increases, but eventually diseconomies of scale set in and
costs increase at an increasing rate. Such diseconomies might be the result of needing a more elaborate corporate information control system.
Mueller (1987, pp. 26–29) reviews the literature and develops the idea that
diseconomies of scale because of control loss are most likely when the
corporation is coping with R&D investment and technological change.
Accordingly, the functional form $C(z) = d + f(\ln(z+1)) + g(e^z)$ captures
increasing returns followed eventually by decreasing returns for combining trials in one firm. Figure 8.7 illustrates $C(z)$ for the parameters that
will be used in the subsequent simulations.

**Expected   Profits**

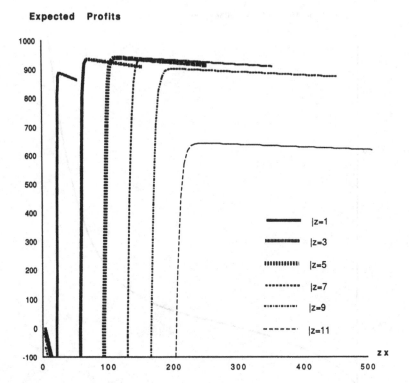

Figure 8.8    Society's expected profits.

Now, in Figures 8.8 and 8.9 we can illustrate the difference between the socially optimal investment configuration and what a monopolist would do given that the social value of the innovation greatly exceeds private value. In the simulation, the social value $W_s = 1000$ while the private value $W = 100$. The parameterization of $h(x)$ is

$$h(x) = 1/(1 + e^{40 - 2x}),$$

and $C(z)$ is parameterized as

$$C(z) = 1 + 15\ln(z + 1) + 0.005e^z.$$

Because this parameterization implies that at the socially optimal number of trials the range of sharply decreasing returns to parallel trials within a firm has not yet been reached, society would prefer just one firm. Note that I have deliberately chosen such a parameterization because we want to explore the issue of exactly why pure competitive pressure can be desir-

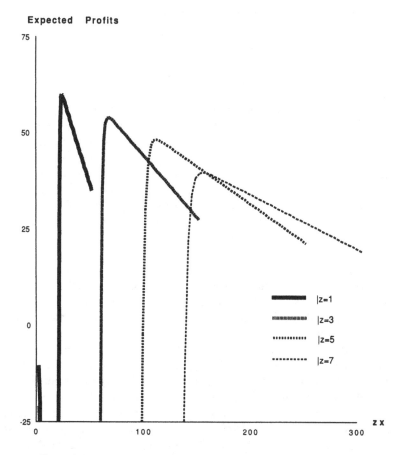

Figure 8.9 A monopoly's expected profits.

able even when a single firm is best for achieving technical efficiency. The value of $r$ is set at $r = 0.1$. In the example chosen, the socially optimal amount of innovative investment would be achieved with $n = 1$, $z = 5$, and $x = 22.20$. In Figure 8.8, each curve shows society's expected profits (given Equation (8.8)) for a particular value of $z$ as $x$ is increased symmetrically for each trial.

Now, given that the private value of the innovation $W = 100$ is far less than the value $W_s = 1000$ of the innovation to society, as Figure 8.9 illustrates, the monopolist in this case would underinvest in R&D. The monopolist chooses $z = 1$ and $x = 22.02$. Each curve traces expected profits for the monopolist given a different value of $z$ and then letting $x$ increase symmetrically across the $z$ trials.

Now the question is whether noncooperative rivalry would bring performance closer to the socially optimal level. To answer that question, we need to specify how the $i$th firm among $n$ firms perceives the R&D rivalry. For the $i$th firm, the essence of rivalry in R&D is the $i$th firm's concern that it will be preempted by one of the other $n-1$ firms. To focus on that essence of competition, I continue to follow Loury (1979) and Lee and Wilde (1980) and examine the case where the winner of the R&D race gets the entire private value of the innovation.[3] The assumption that the winner takes all has no effect on the particular points to be illustrated by the model. First, our use of the assumption that the winner of the R&D race takes all will not affect our predictions, at the conclusion of this chapter, about the desire to use diversification to escape the competitive equilibrium, because our predictions would hold a fortiori without the assumption. If the winner did not "take all," the expected value of winning would be even less and the need for the gains from diversification would be even more. Second, we shall see that society will want the *desirable* effect of pure competitive pressure (which we illustrate with the winner-take-all assumption to get "pure competitive pressure" - pressure without erosion in the total private value in the postinnovation market) to induce socially optimal behavior by the technically efficient, complete (monopoly) joint venture.

In Chapter 14, I shall propose new tax policies that theoretically would allow us to duplicate the desirable effect of the competitive pressure and yet have the desired technical efficiency achieved only by monopoly. For example, we could have the technical efficiency of a complete monopoly for an industry's effort to find the solution to an environmental problem specific to the industry, and yet use either of the new taxes to induce socially optimal R&D investment. The new taxes will mimic the desirable aspect of competitive pressure. That is, the new taxes induce pressure analogous to the pressure (to hurry up or be preempted) that is caused by competition. Competition can also have the effect of creating the expectation of competing substitutes in the postinnovation market. That aspect of competition of course reduces the expected reward for a winner and, considered apart from the desirable pressure, is not desirable in our present context. The model will use the winner-take-all assumption to separate out the desirable aspect of competition. Then we can see exactly what the new tax policies to be proposed in Chapter 14 must replace if we are to induce the technically efficient complete, monopoly venture to behave in a socially optimal way. In Chapter 11, when, in order to understand R&D diversity we do need to relax the assumption that the winner of the R&D race takes all, we shall think more about the erosion in total private profits that competition can induce.

I want to focus on what Katz and Ordover (1990, p. 148) have called "the difficult case for welfare analysis" where, because at the margin the R&D effort of the individual firm reduces the expected profitability of its rivals' R&D, "cooperative decisionmaking lowers the amount of R&D, but we cannot be sure whether the initial level was too high or too low." In the formal model, I shall then focus on the case of what Katz and Ordover call negative "competitive spillovers." The R&D of an individual firm will reduce the probability of success for its rivals. Of course, acting noncooperatively, the individual firm will ignore the fact that at the point where its additional benefits from more R&D have fallen into equality with its additional costs, the collective marginal benefits are below marginal costs. In the context of incomplete appropriation of the returns from R&D, the overinvestment (from the private standpoint) in R&D can be socially optimal. Incomplete appropriation of the returns can of course result because of the "technological spillovers" that I omit in order to focus on the benefits of rivalry that exist even with uncertainty and economies of scale and scope. Other sources of incomplete appropriation of the benefits of innovation are the consumer surplus created by an innovator that cannot price-discriminate perfectly and of course the erosion of postinnovation rents caused by rivalry in the postinnovation market.

I shall focus on the "competitive spillovers" case rather than the very different case of "technological spillovers" because it is the case that must be understood if policy is to avoid the pitfalls of overselling R&D joint ventures as a way to solve the international competitiveness problems of a country's manufacturers. With Katz and Ordover's "technological spillovers," the research effort of the individual firm increases the expected value of its rivals' R&D investments. As a result, in the noncooperative equilibrium, the individual firm, by stopping at the point where its own marginal benefit from further investment equals its marginal cost, will underinvest in R&D from the standpoint of a cooperative venture among the firm and its rivals. The venture would internalize the positive externalities from the individual research programs, and the cooperative group would expand R&D beyond the noncooperative equilibrium because at the point that the individual firms stop investing, the collective marginal benefit exceeds marginal costs. The technological spillovers could be built into the model below either by making the costs of each rival a function of its rivals' R&D investments, or by making the value of each rival's innovation a function of its rivals' R&D investments. The effects of such spillovers are easily stated when I need to discuss them. In the Afterword, I shall return to the technological spillovers theme to explain the relative success of Japan's manufacturers in international trade.

Turning now to the development of the case of competitive spillovers, for the $i$th firm, the expected value of revenues from R&D is

$$\int_0^\infty e^{-rt} W(1 - F_R(t)) F_i'(t)\, dt \tag{8.10}$$

where $F_i(t)$ is the probability of success on at least one of the $i$th firm's $z_i$ trials. Thus $F_i(t)$ is 1.0 minus the probability that it fails on all of its trials, or

$$F_i(t) = 1 - e^{-z_i h(x_i)t}.$$

Then,

$$F_i'(t) = z_i h(x_i) e^{-z_i h(x_i)t}.$$

$F_R(t)$ is the probability that at least one of the $i$th firm's rivals has succeeded by time $t$. Thus

$$F_R(t) = 1 - e^{-\sum_{j \neq i} z_j h(x_j)t}.$$

Note that the probability that the $i$th firm innovates during the small interval of time $dt$ is $(1 - F_R) F_i'\, dt$. The $i$th firm then faces not only technological uncertainty, but also the market uncertainty of Kamien and Schwartz (1982) or what Glennan (1967) termed "external uncertainty." The essence of greater competitive pressure is the intensity of external uncertainty.

From Equation (8.10) then, the expected revenues for the $i$th firm are

$$\frac{W z_i h(x_i)}{r + z_i h(x_i) + \sum_{j \neq i} z_j h(x_j)}. \tag{8.11}$$

The expected costs of the $i$th firm are

$$\int_0^\infty (z_i x_i) e^{-rt} e^{-(z_i h(x_i) + \sum_{j \neq i} z_j h(x_j))t}\, dt + C(z_i), \tag{8.12}$$

because the $i$th firm incurs $(z_i x_i) e^{-rt}$ in expenditures per period as long as no one has introduced the innovation, and the probability that no one has introduced the innovation by time $t$ is $e^{-(z_i h(x_i) + \sum_{j \neq i} z_j h(x_j))t}$. From Equation (8.12) then, the expected costs of the $i$th firm are

$$\frac{z_i x_i}{r + z_i h(x_i) + \sum_{j \neq i} z_j h(x_j)} + C(z_i). \tag{8.13}$$

Thus, from Equations (8.11) and (8.13), the $i$th firm's expected profits are

$$\frac{W z_i h(x_i) - z_i x_i}{r + z_i h(x_i) + \sum_{j \neq i} z_j h(x_j)} - C(z_i), \tag{8.14}$$

which for $z_i = z_j = 1$ is precisely Lee and Wilde's equation (1) (1980, p. 431).

To find the noncooperative Nash equilibrium, we observe that since $z_i$ is integer-valued, maximization of its expected profits given the other firms' choices of $z_j$ and $x_j$ requires that the $i$th firm choose $z_i$ and $x_i$ such that the following two conditions hold simultaneously. First, the partial derivative of expected profits with respect to the periodic expenditure $x$ must equal zero (and correspond to a maximum rather than a minimum):

$$\frac{Wz_i h'(x_i)[r + \sum_{j \neq i} z_j h(x_j)] - z_i [r + \sum_j^n z_j h(x_j) - z_i x_i h'(x_i)]}{[r + z_i h(x_i) + \sum_{j \neq i} z_j h(x_j)]^2} = 0.$$

(8.15)

Second, the expected profits $p_i$ (given by Equation (8.14)) for the $i$th firm must be maximized over $z_i$:

$$\max_{z_i} p_i(z_i \mid x_i).$$

(8.16)

Since the $n$ firms in the noncooperative R & D game are symmetric, for the noncooperative Nash equilibrium Equations (8.15) and (8.16) must hold with $z_i = z_j$ and $x_i = x_j$ for all $i$ and $j$. Thus, in equilibrium Equation (8.15) becomes

$$\frac{Wz_i h'(x_i)[r + (n-1)z_i h(x_i)] - z_i [r + nz_i h(x_i) - z_i x_i h'(x_i)]}{[r + nz_i h(x_i)]^2} = 0.$$

(8.17)

Given $n$, the simultaneous system is readily solved using the method of successive approximations. For example, to find the exact solution to the monopolist's problem above, Equations (8.17) and (8.16) can be used with $n = 1$. If $z_i = 5$ is substituted into Equation (8.17) and the equation is then solved for $x_i$, $x_i = 21.91$ for the zero of $\partial p_i / \partial x_i$ corresponding to the maximum. If $x_i = 21.91$ is then substituted into $p_i(z_i \mid x_i)$ and the maximum over $z_i$ is found, $z_i = 1$. Substituting $z_i = 1$ into Equation (8.17) and solving for the $x_i$ corresponding to the maximum yields $x_i = 22.02$. Finally, substituting $x_i = 22.02$ into $p_i(z_i \mid x_i)$ and maximizing over $z_i$ yields $z_i = 1$. Thus, the optimal R & D investment configuration for the monopolist is one trial with periodic expenditure of 22.02. The same method of successive approximations was used to solve for the symmetric noncooperative Nash equilibrium given $n = 2, 3, \ldots, 7$ for the results reported subsequently. In all cases the method converged quickly to the answer.

If entry is possible, then one more condition completes the system and we have fully endogenous market structure. That condition which would hold simultaneously with Equations (8.15) and (8.16) is that

$$n \text{ is such that } p_i(z_i, x_i \mid n) \geq 0 \text{ and } p_i(z_i, x_i \mid n+1) < 0.$$

(8.18)

Now, it is likely that society will prefer the Nash noncooperative equilibrium for some $n > 1$ to the monopoly solution. That is because the

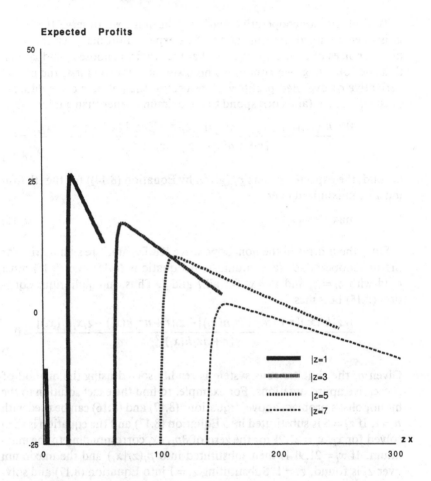

**Expected Profits**

Figure 8.10  Expected profits for the $i$th firm, given $n = 2$.

competitive pressure – which induces concern about preemption caused by $F_R(t)$ – drives the $n$ rivals to collectively do more R&D investment than the monopolist would. Numerous competitors can in effect produce the socially desirable number of trials. Figures 8.10 through 8.15 illustrate respectively the symmetric noncooperative Nash equilibrium for $n = 2, 3, 4, 5, 6$, and $7$ by plotting the $i$th firm's expected profits $p_i(x_i \mid n, z_i)$ against its periodic R&D expenditures $z_i x_i$ for various values of $x_i$ given $n$ and various values of $z_i$ under the assumption that $x_i = x_j$ and $z_i = z_j$. The maximum of the maximums is the symmetric noncooperative Nash equilibrium $\{z_i^*, x_i^* \mid n\}$. As the figures show, the free-entry noncooperative Nash equilibrium is $\{z_i^* = 1, x_i^* = 22.58, n = 6\}$ since the entry of the seventh

**Expected   Profits**

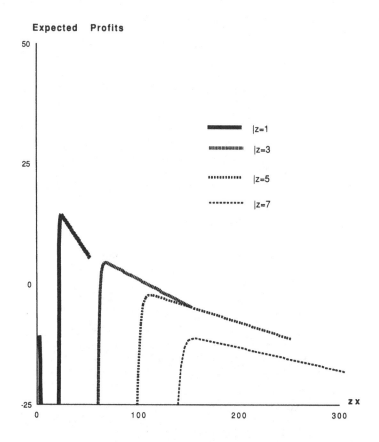

Figure 8.11   Expected profits for the $i$th firm, given $n = 3$.

firm drives expected profits below zero. Table 8.1 summarizes the noncooperative Nash equilibria for the various market structures.

Now, the question remains: Which market structure would society prefer in our case – monopoly or free-entry noncooperative rivalry? Table
8.2 uses Equation (8.8) with the $\{n, z_i, x_i\}$ outcomes for the various market structures, computes the expected profits for society, and shows that
society's expected profits are greater with free-entry noncooperative rivalry, although the expected profits would be greatest if the rivalry were
confined to only three noncooperative firms. In sum, society would prefer one firm conducting five trials with periodic expenditure of 22.2 each
for an expected social profit of 929.511. A monopolist will conduct only
one trial with periodic expenditure of 22.02 for an expected social profit
of 875.89. In the free-entry noncooperative equilibrium, each of six firms

Table 8.1. *Noncooperative Nash equilibria*

| $n$ | $z_i^*$ | $x_i^*$ | $p_i^*$ |
|---|---|---|---|
| 1 | 1 | 22.02 | 59.0152 |
| 2 | 1 | 22.41 | 25.4366 |
| 3 | 1 | 22.50 | 13.5349 |
| 4 | 1 | 22.54 | 7.44483 |
| 5 | 1 | 22.56 | 3.7453 |
| 6 | 1 | 22.58 | 1.25856 |
| 7 | 1 | 22.59 | −0.526752 |

Table 8.2. *Expected social profits*

| Market structure | $z_i$ | $x_i$ | Social profits |
|---|---|---|---|
| Social optimum with $n=1$ | 5 | 22.2 | 929.511 |
| Monopoly with $n=1$ | 1 | 22.02 | 875.89 |
| Noncooperative rivalry with $n=2$ | 1 | 22.41 | 907.687 |
| Noncooperative rivalry with $n=3$ | 1 | 22.5 | 911.383 |
| Noncooperative rivalry with $n=4$ | 1 | 22.54 | 907.695 |
| Noncooperative rivalry with $n=5$ | 1 | 22.56 | 900.976 |
| Noncooperative rivalry with $n=6$ | 1 | 22.58 | 892.714 |
| Noncooperative rivalry with $n=7$ | 1 | 22.59 | 883.566 |

conducts one trial with periodic expenditure of 22.58 for an expected so-cial profit of 892.714.

Table 8.3 shows the expected time of introduction for the various mar-ket structures. Following our earlier explanation, with $n$ symmetric firms with $z$ trials each, the expected time of introduction is $1/(nzh(x))$. In our example, free-entry noncooperative rivalry reduces the expected time of introduction from what it would be with monopoly, but it overshoots the socially optimal time of introduction. This is "excessive" rivalry; none-

Table 8.3. *Expected time elapsed before introduction*

| Market structure | $z_i$ | $x_i$ | Time (in periods) |
|---|---|---|---|
| Social optimum with $n = 1$ | 5 | 22.2 | 0.202 |
| Monopoly with $n = 1$ | 1 | 22.02 | 1.02 |
| Noncooperative rivalry with $n = 2$ | 1 | 22.41 | 0.504 |
| Noncooperative rivalry with $n = 3$ | 1 | 22.5 | 0.336 |
| Noncooperative rivalry with $n = 4$ | 1 | 22.54 | 0.252 |
| Noncooperative rivalry with $n = 5$ | 1 | 22.56 | 0.201 |
| Noncooperative rivalry with $n = 6$ | 1 | 22.58 | 0.168 |
| Noncooperative rivalry with $n = 7$ | 1 | 22.59 | 0.144 |

theless, as Table 8.2 has shown, the expected profits for society with free-entry noncooperative rivalry exceed the expected profits with monopoly. As seen in Table 8.3, the monopolist's R & D program implies an expected time of 1.0 period before the introduction of its innovation occurs. Society would prefer an investment program that has an expected time of introduction at 0.20, or one-fifth of a period from the initial investment date. Five noncooperative firms would carry out R & D implying the socially desirable pace of innovation, while the free-entry noncooperative equilibrium implies that the introduction is expected in just 0.17 of a period.

Although the example that I have worked through in the tables and figures is just one parameterization of the general problem that is specified in the equations, the example is one of countless specific examples that conform to the basic conditions of technological and market uncertainty, economies of scale and scope, and incomplete appropriation of returns. Thus, the problem that I have illustrated is a general problem that could reasonably be expected to plague many cooperative R & D ventures. The basic conditions create situations in which society would prefer only one firm or an industrywide cooperative venture if only the single decision-making entity would choose socially optimal values for the number of

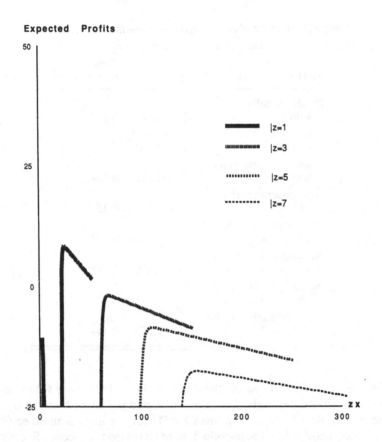

Figure 8.12   Expected profits for the $i$th firm, given $n = 4$.

R&D trials and the periodic expenditure for each. However, the monopolist or industrywide cooperative venture chooses to underinvest in R&D, and, because of that choice, free-entry noncooperative rivalry produces an R&D expenditure pattern that results in better R&D performance from society's standpoint.

### 8.4 Understanding R&D diversification

Now within our model of the firm in its competitive R&D environment, we can understand the role of R&D diversification. Diversification of R&D is a primary tool that firms can use to attempt to escape the low expected profits implicit in the final equilibria depicted in Figure 8.14.

The free-entry Nash noncooperative equilibrium entails low expected profits, and for several reasons a firm could use diversification of R&D

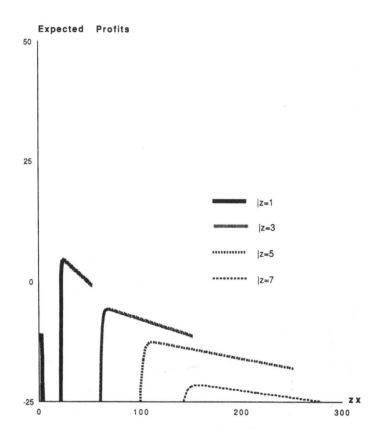

Figure 8.13   Expected profits for the *i*th firm, given $n = 5$.

in the hope of gaining an edge over its rivals and increasing its returns from R&D. First, as Nelson (1959) emphasized, diversification may increase appropriation of returns. The firm with varied activities is better prepared than single-focus firms to perceive applications of a discovery. The improvement in appropriability conditions raises expected profits. I intend appropriability in a general sense, rather than its most narrow definition, which focuses on a firm's ability to prevent imitators from eroding the benefits of the firm's R&D. Second, as Arrow (1962) emphasized, complete insurance against failure of innovative investment is not possible because of the so-called moral hazard – complete insurance would remove the incentive to make the investment succeed. Thus, he hypothesized that diversification may lower risk as the firm provides its own insurance. If financial markets value such diversification, the discount rate

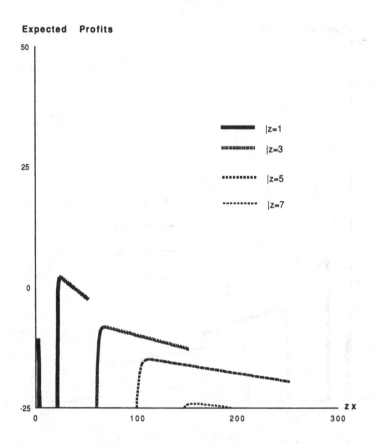

Figure 8.14   Expected profits for the $i$th firm, given $n = 6$.

$r$ falls, raising the present value of the stream of expected profits. Third, diversification may lower costs. As the costs of specialized R & D resources are spread over several areas of R & D investment, expected profits for the collection of investments will rise.

Teece (1980) has emphasized that a diversified enterprise can lower the cost of economic activity when economies of scope (Baumol et al., 1982) require common inputs not readily traded across markets. The two general classes of such common inputs which Teece identifies are know-how and specialized, indivisible physical assets. R & D investment plausibly requires the use of such inputs in a context in which the transactional difficulties for arm's-length trading of technological proprietary information preclude efficient market transactions. "This is because the protection of the ownership of technological knowhow often requires suppressing

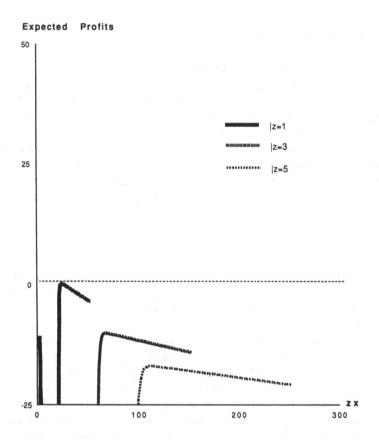

Figure 8.15   Expected profits for the *i*th firm, given *n* = 7.

information in exchange possibilities" (Teece, 1980, p. 227). Helfat (1992) provides empirical support for Teece's ideas by studying the R & D expenditures of petroleum firms.

Fourth, other things being equal, a firm's diversification makes preemption by its rivals less likely, since the diversified firm will recognize potential applications of ideas more quickly. Thus, in the model, diversification improves the firm's own hazard function relative to those of its rivals. In other words, technological uncertainty and market uncertainty are simultaneously reduced. This will raise the firm's expected profits, although in the most general model it need not result in an increase in optimal R & D investment. However, the data studied next in Chapter 9 suggest that diversification typically increases the R & D expenditures of the firm.

### 8.5 Testing the theory

At the risk of getting too far ahead of my story, let me motivate the empirical work to follow and integrate it with the theory of the present chapter by observing that the model's predictions coincide with the descriptive information reported next in Chapter 9. If the theoretical depiction of the role of diversification were true, we would expect to find that (1) diversification of R&D within the firm would not be random, (2) the R&D investments in a given industry category of diversified firms would be systematically different from the investments of undiversified firms in that category, (3) such systematic differences in R&D investments would be systematically related to characteristics of industry categories in ways that imply the pursuit of profits, and (4) spillovers of R&D across industry categories affect productivity. Further, the conjecture that the overall result of diversification is to increase the sum of R&D investments in an area implies that (5) when considering the systematic differences expected in point (2), the cases for which diversified firms do more R&D should dominate. As reported next in Chapter 9, these five expectations are confirmed for the line-of-business data for the mid-1970s.

Regarding point (1), the theory implies that if we look at pairs of firms with diversified R&D, there will be a significant number of instances in which those firms have R&D in the same industry categories. If there are complementarities in R&D investment across industry categories, more than one firm would be expected to recognize those possibilities and attempt to exploit them, causing the set of firms recognizing the opportunities to meet in the group of complementary activities. If a firm diversifies its R&D effort purposely to gain advantage of better appropriability or because of cost advantages of common facilities or complementarities in the process of research across multiple industries, and if similar opportunities are available to other firms, we should find significant grouping of firms. That is, firms purposely combining multicategory R&D activities will meet in the "group" of those activities more than would occur by chance given random diversification.

To find "the groups," in Chapter 9 every possible pair of firms in the sample is examined. Groups of multiple categories within which spillovers of knowledge are a priori likely are defined to be those sets of categories in which "significant" meetings are found. The procedure finds (after elimination of duplicates) 127 groups of related categories, evidently belonging together because the R&D therein was complementary. The null hypothesis that firms are randomly scattering their research across categories is rejected at a high level of significance, since before the elimination of duplicate sets, there were 165 groups significant at the 0.00001 level. Since there were in the sample 352 firms that did R & D, a total of 61,776 pairs were examined. Ignoring the differences in sample space across pairs implies that the ratio of 165 to 61,776 provides a lower bound on the proportion of successes. Thus the number of significant cases exceeded the expected number against the null hypothesis by at least 267 times.

Regarding point (2) above, since our understanding of diversification implies that diversification will change the position of the firm's expected-profits curve, we expect that the intensity of purposively diversified firms' R & D investment in a given industry category would be systematically different from that of undiversified firms in the same category. In fact, Chapter 9's comparison in each industry category of diversified firms' R & D intensity with the undiversified firms' R & D intensity shows statistically significant differences in behavior. The number of comparisons for which the diversified firms have higher R & D intensity at the 10 percent level of significance for a two-tailed test exceeds by 4.55 standard deviations the expected number if there were no difference in behavior. And, at that level of significance, the number of comparisons for which the purposively diversified firms have lower R & D than the undiversified competitors exceeds the expected number by 1.3 standard deviations.

Regarding point (3) above, the differences in behavior seem to be driven by profit-maximizing motives because the cases in which diversified firms have higher R & D intensity occur in industry categories in which appropriability conditions are good, while the cases for which they have lower R & D intensity occur in categories in which appropriation of the returns from R & D is difficult. In Chapter 9, industry categories are ranked from those having the least to the greatest appropriability problems. The average rank of the industry categories in which diversified firms had higher R & D intensity showed those categories to have less than average appropriability problems by 2.4 standard deviations of difference from the mean rank. The cases where the R & D intensity of diversified firms was lower occurred in industry categories with especially poor appropriability conditions. The average rank for these industries was 2.1 standard deviations away from the mean. Thus, purposively diversified firms are either more sensitive to differences in profitability of R & D across industry categories or are better able to exploit such differences.

Regarding point (4) above, if the benefits of R & D spill across industry categories, we would expect to see a higher correlation between R & D intensity and the rate of growth in total factor productivity when the R & D investment and the productivity are observed for the sets of related industry categories determined by the analysis. If the groups of related categories were not economically meaningful groups of industry categories with complementarities in R&D, then the size of the relation and the correlation between productivity and R&D intensity should be the same after grouping as before. In fact, regressions based on the standard productivity–R&D model show that the positive and significant coefficient on R&D intensity increases 2.6-fold and the $R^2$ increases almost 4-fold.

Finally, (5) the cases for which purposively diversified firms have higher R&D intensity than their undiversified counterparts dominate the cases of systematic differences. Considering the cases significant at the 30 percent level or better for a two-tailed test, the number of cases with higher R&D intensity for diversified firms is 3.73 standard deviations above the expected number if the behavior of purposively diversified firms is no different from that of others. But the number of cases with lower R&D intensity for diversified firms falls 1.31 standard deviations below the expected number.

Having used the model to develop hypotheses about diversification and R&D investment, and having outlined briefly the form those tests will take, in Chapter 9 we can turn to the tests themselves.

# 9

## Diversification of R&D and productivity

This chapter explores how purposive diversification of R&D affects R&D behavior and productivity in U.S. manufacturing. The findings support the predictions developed in Chapter 8.

### 9.1 Purposive diversification

The chapter shows that R&D diversification in large U.S. manufacturing firms is purposive, exploiting complementarities of various research activities and forming groups of related industry categories. The purposively diversified firms behave differently from randomly diversified or undiversified firms. One aspect of the behavioral differences between purposively diversified firms and others is that the former allocate relatively more R&D funds to industry categories where the appropriation of the returns from R&D is easier and relatively fewer funds to those categories where returns are more difficult to appropriate. Finally, R&D expenditure and productivity are more closely linked at the group level than at the industry-category level, suggesting that spillovers of knowledge across industry categories are important. The chapter's findings provide a key explanation for the firm effects found in Part II, because firms in the same industry category typically engage in very different forms of purposive R&D diversification and some do not diversify at all.

In Section 9.2, I use my methodology to distinguish nonpurposive or random diversification from any purposive diversification into a set of related, or close, R&D activities. "Nonpurposive" diversification here is discerned as diversification dissimilar to patterns found in significant clusters of firms. It is then not necessarily "random" diversification, although it will be unless it exploits complementarities unavailable to any other

Chapter 9 is a revision of Scott and Pascoe (1987).

Table 9.1. *Diversification of the sampled firms' manufacturing R&D efforts across four-digit FTC industry categories*

| $n$ | Number of firms with $n$ nonsporadic four-digit R&D activities[a] |
|---|---|
| 0 | 24 |
| 1 | 33 |
| 2 | 43 |
| 3 | 48 |
| 4 | 37 |
| 5 | 37 |
| 6 | 30 |
| 7 | 18 |
| 8 | 19 |
| 9 | 16 |
| 10 | 9 |
| 11 | 11 |
| 12 | 6 |
| 13 | 3 |
| 14 | 9 |
| 15 | 10 |
| 16–17[b] | 5 |
| 18 | 4 |
| 19–20[b] | 5 |
| 21–25[b] | 4 |
| 30–42[b] | 5 |
| Total | 376 |

[a] R&D of each category was done in each of the sampled years.
[b] These categories have been combined to comply with procedures to avoid the disclosure of individual company data.

firm in the sample. I use the Federal Trade Commission Line of Business (FTC LB) data for the sample of 376 large publicly traded U.S. manufacturing firms described and studied in Chapter 6. Table 9.1 shows the diversification of manufacturing R&D activities for our sampled firms.

I study here the 352 firms in the sample that reported R&D throughout the sample period for one or more FTC four-digit manufacturing categories. By a manufacturing or industry category, I intend a particular industry, although it is well known that an industry category only imperfectly corresponds to an industry. The procedure in Section 9.2 finds the particular "industries" with activities that are technologically close. This chapter's investigation of the behavioral and performance implications of such groups of related activities complements the studies of Jaffe (1986, 1988), who explores how spillovers of knowledge from R & D performed by technologically close firms can affect another firm's R & D and productivity. Jaffe uses a clustering procedure to form groups of close firms; each firm is assigned to a cluster. In contrast, I apply the method from Chapter 4 to every possible combination of pairs of firms to discern multiple groups of activities within each given firm; thus, firm A may be close to firms B and C, even though the activities of B and C do not overlap. In other words, my procedure allows a given firm to belong to numerous clusters of firms, as will be the case when the firm pursues different sets of related activities. For example, a firm might be part of a group of firms combining research in a food industry and in a chemicals industry, yet also be part of a group of firms combining research in an area of machinery and in a type of transportation equipment.

Given the groups distinguished in Section 9.2, Section 9.3 demonstrates that there is a significant group effect on R & D behavior: Firms tend to diversify into related R & D activities to realize economies of multi-industry operation or better appropriability conditions.[1] Purposive diversification, then, offers a potentially important explanation for Chapter 7's finding that the firm effects on R & D behavior are large and significant. The reason that firms in the same industry category behave differently may be that some are purposively diversified while others are not. Or, more generally, firms in a category may have different patterns of purposive multi-industry diversification. Firms in the same industry category, but differing in the extent or type of multicategory R & D, may behave differently in the category they have in common. For example, a firm combining research in chemicals and in food may behave differently in chemicals research from a firm having research activity in chemicals alone, or from a firm not combining chemicals research purposively with its other research activities, or from a firm combining research in chemicals and in petroleum refining. Section 9.3 demonstrates that some firm effects do result from such group effects. In the same industry category, purposively diversified firms are seen to behave differently from randomly diversified or undiversified firms. In the same industry category, firms purposively diversified in different ways have relatively similar behavior. Further, there is clear evidence that the behavioral differences between purposively diversified firms and others result because the former allocate relatively more R & D funds to industry categories where appropriability conditions are good and relatively fewer funds to those categories where appropriation of the returns from R & D is difficult.

Section 9.4 provides a different view of the interindustry spillover effects pursued by Terleckyj (1977, 1980), Scherer (1982), Griliches and Lichtenberg (1984), Jaffe (1986), Bernstein (1988), Bernstein and Nadiri (1988a), and Geroski (1991c). The total factor productivity data of Griliches are juxtaposed with my restructuring of the FTC LB R&D data into groups of technologically close activities. I demonstrate that R&D expenditure and productivity are more closely linked at the group level than at the industry-category level, suggesting that knowledge spills across industry categories increase productivity.

## 9.2 Distinguishing purposive diversification of R&D effort

I designate as an LB a firm's operations in an industry category – i.e., in what I intend to be a particular industry. For an LB of a large U.S. manufacturing firm, evidence suggests that once we have controlled for the industrial environment, apart from random error the ratio of LB R&D expenditures to LB sales is constant through all observed levels of sales for those LBs with R&D activity.[2] This constant proportion of sales devoted to R&D expenditures is expected to vary across lines of business, even within the same industry category, because as we have seen in Chapter 7, firm effects are quite significant. The issue here is whether changes in the degree and character of purposive diversification would change that R&D intensity.

If a firm diversifies its R&D effort purposively to take advantage of better appropriability or because of cost advantages of common facilities or complementarities of research across multiple industries, and if similar opportunities are available to other firms, we should find significant groupings of firms. That is, firms purposively combining multicategory R&D activities will meet in the "group" of those activities more than would occur by chance given random diversification.

To find "the groups," every possible pair of firms in the sample was examined. Groups of multiple categories within which spillovers of knowledge are likely a priori are defined to be those sets of categories where "significant" meetings are found.

Let $n$ (equal to 253 here) be the number of four-digit FTC manufacturing categories in which our 352 firms have R&D expenditures. For each pair of firms, let $s$ be the number of four-digit categories in which one firm has R&D. Let $t$ $(t \leq s)$ be the number of four-digit categories in which the other firm does R&D. Let $g$ denote the number of categories in which the two firms meet. Let $C_{x,y}$ denote the combination of $x$ things taken $y$ at a time. Then for each pair of firms for which both firms have R&D activity, I compute the probability that the firms would meet as much or more than they do if diversification were random.

Table 9.2. *Some of the 127 groups*

| Industry categories in the group |
| --- |
| {2803, industrial inorganic chemicals, except industrial gases and inorganic pigments; 2804, plastics materials and resins; 2813, industrial organic chemicals, except gum and wood chemicals; 3006, misc. plastics products} |
| {2402, sawmills and planing mills; 2403, millwork, plywood and structural members; 2405, misc. wood products, including wood containers; 2602, paper mills, except building paper; 2610, paperboard containers and boxes} |
| {3420, valves and pipe fittings, except plumbers' brass goods; 3501, turbines and turbine generator sets; 3504, lawn and garden equipment; 3522, pumps and pumping equipment; 3524, air and gas compressors; 3602, switchgear and switchboard apparatus; 3603, motors and generators} |
| {2405, misc. wood products, including wood containers; 2611, building paper and board mills; 2902, paving and roofing materials; 3006, misc. plastics products; 3213, gypsum products; 3216, asbestos products; 3217, mineral wool; 3410, metal doors, sash, frames, molding, and trim} |

$$AP = 1 - \sum_{f=0}^{g-1} p(f) = 1 - \sum_{f=0}^{g-1} \frac{C_{t,f} \cdot C_{n-t,s-f}}{C_{n,s}}. \tag{9.1}$$

Both to reduce the computational burden and to be virtually certain I am studying significant phenomena, I consider only the most significant groupings here. Namely, when AP is less than or equal to 0.00001, the null hypothesis of random diversification is rejected and the alternative, purposive diversification, is accepted. In Chapter 10, where the number of groupings using more aggregate industry categories is less numerous and more manageable, I shall present results using the more conventional 0.01 significance level.

The procedure finds (after elimination of duplicates) 127 groups of related categories, and an illustrative set of examples is given in Table 9.2.[3] I interpret a group to be a set of technologically close industries with complementary R&D activities. Note that a given firm can be a member of more than one group (with some of its LBs in one group and others of its LBs in other groups – but note that the same LB can be a member of more than one group), only one group (with some or all of the firm's LBs in that group), or none.[4]

Note that to form these groups, I have used the 3 years, 1974 through 1976, for which data were available. I use the total R&D expenditures in each line of business for a firm because the decision to combine R&D in various industry categories is expected to take account of the fact that government-financed R&D, and R&D performed under contract more generally, provide knowledge spillovers to the firm.[5] To lessen the importance of outliers that could result from startups or catastrophies destroying sales, in the subsequent analyses I use RS, the sales-weighted average of R&D expenditures to sales during the 3 years for each LB.

### 9.3  Purposive diversification and behavior

I shall focus on the difference within a given industry category between (1) the average behavior for the LBs of firms that are diversified into a particular group of related industry categories and (2) the average behavior for the LBs of firms not in any group. I shall be asking if purposively diversified firms behave differently in a particular industry category than the firms in that category that are not purposively diversified. The simple model used examines, industry category by industry category, the $t$-statistic on the difference in means of RS behavior of purposively diversified firms and those not purposively diversified. The sign and significance of this difference indicates the direction and significance of the differences between the behavior of purposively diversified firms and other firms in an industry category.

Table 9.3 reports the distribution of these $t$-statistics by significance ranges. The table indicates that purposively diversified firms differ from firms that have not purposively diversified. To see this point, imagine a random distribution of $m$ items across $n$ "boxes" of equal size. Let $x_i$ be the random variable, which is 1 if the $i$th item appears in a particular box and 0 otherwise. Then a measure of the number of items appearing in a particular box is the random variable

$$X = \sum_{i=1}^{m} x_i.$$

Its expected value is

$$E(X) = \sum_{i=1}^{m} (1 \cdot 1/n + 0 \cdot (1 - 1/n)) = m/n.$$

Its variance is

$$\mathrm{var}(X) = \sum_{i=1}^{m} \mathrm{var}(x_i)$$
$$= m \, \mathrm{var}(x_i) = m\{[1 - 1/n]^2(1/n) + [0 - 1/n]^2(1 - 1/n)\}.$$

If we consider each of the two top "boxes" of Table 9.3, $n = 20$. This is true because a two-tailed test at the 10 percent level implies that there should be 5 percent of the cases in each tail; there thus are $100\%/5\% = 20$

Table 9.3. *Percentage distribution of t-statistics on 653 differences of means of R&D intensity* (RS) *for firms within a group and a matched set of firms*

| Significance level of *t*-statistics, *p* (two tails) | Percentage of cases | |
|---|---|---|
| | Positive deviations | Negative deviations |
| $p \leq .10$ | 8.88% | 6.13% |
| $.10 < p \leq .15$ | 2.60 | 1.84 |
| $.15 < p \leq .20$ | 2.30 | 1.68 |
| $.20 < p \leq .25$ | 2.76 | 1.84 |
| $.25 < p \leq .30$ | 3.68 | 1.68 |
| "Insignificant" | 34.92 | 31.70 |

*Note:* Based on 127 groups with comparisons at the four-digit industry level. The "nongroup" firms were randomly selected (i.e., each firm had an equal chance of being chosen) from those having R&D expenditures within the four-digit category but not within any group. There were 653 cases for which the matched sample comparisons could be made. See the text for the definition of a group.

such equally likely categories or "boxes" into which cases can fall under the null hypothesis. Here $m = 653$, and for each 5 percent box $E(X) = 32.65$. The $\sqrt{\operatorname{var}(X)} = 5.57$. Now, since there are 58 items in the top left box, the number of items in the box exceeds the expected value by 4.55 standard deviations. And the number of items, 40, in the top right box exceeds the expected value by 1.32 standard deviations.

Thus, purposively diversified firms appear to behave differently from their competitors who have not undertaken such diversification. There is also a tendency for purposively diversified firms not only to behave differently, but specifically to do more R&D than their undiversified competitors. Considering the top five boxes on the left as a single box, or the top five boxes on the right as a single box, $n = 1/0.15 = 6\frac{2}{3}$. Then $E(X) = m/n = 653/(6\frac{2}{3}) = 97.95$, and $\sqrt{\operatorname{var}(X)} = 9.12$. Now, in the top five boxes on the left, there are 132 items, or 3.73 standard deviations above the expected number if the behavior of purposively diversified firms is no different from that of others. But in the top five boxes on the right, there are 86 items, or 1.31 standard deviations below the expected number.

Purposively diversified firms are relatively homogeneous in their behavior, since if I reproduce Table 9.3, but compare the purposively diversified firms of each of the 127 groups to all other firms (purposively diversified or not) in each particular industry category, the pattern of the behavioral differences remains, but its significance is greatly attenuated. I find that of 712 cases, 49 fall in the top left box. Given the null hypothesis, 35.6 are expected, and the standard deviation is 5.82. The number of cases exceeds the expected number by 2.3 standard deviations. But the top right box has 5.1 percent of the sample – not much more than what is expected, and the tendency for positive differences remains but is greatly lessened.

One interesting possible explanation for the different behavior of purposively diversified firms is that such firms are more sensitive to the differences in profitability of R&D across industry categories or are better able to exploit such differences. If so, the positive-difference cases should occur in industry categories where appropriability conditions are good. The negative-difference cases should occur in categories where appropriation of the returns from R&D is difficult.

To test this proposition I examined the 58 positive cases and 40 negative cases for $p \leq 0.10$ in Table 9.3. These cases covered 39 different FTC four-digit categories. Of those, 35 categories always had the same sign – 19 positive and 16 negative. Those 35 cases are reported in Table 9.4.

The Levin et al. (1984) survey asked industries to report imitation time lags and costs for major and minor, process and product, and patented and unpatented innovations. As reported by Levin et al. (1985), these measures are typically highly correlated. For my study, Levin provided IMLAG, the average time needed to duplicate a patented, major product innovation; this is the same variable used in Levin et al. (1985).

I have IMLAG for 156 of the 253 FTC four-digit categories covered by my sample of firms. Because of the nature of the survey, IMLAG really gives ordinal rather than cardinal data. I therefore ranked the 156 industry categories for which the R&D activities of my firms overlap with the four-digit categories sampled in the Levin et al. (1984) survey; the longest lag category was ranked number one, the next longest lag was ranked number two, etc. Our 156 categories of the 253 are distributed over 54 distinct time lag values (i.e., many categories have the same value for IMLAG) ranked from the highest value of IMLAG to the lowest value.

Of the 19 positive-difference cases, I have IMLAG for 13. Of the 16 negative-difference cases, I have IMLAG for 14. If the 13 positive-difference cases were a random sample from all differences, the expected value of the average rank, $r$, would be

$$E(r) = E(1/13) \sum_{j=1}^{13} r_j = (1/13) \sum_{j=1}^{13} \mu = \mu, \qquad (9.2)$$

Table 9.4. *Industry categories with significant differences in means between group and nongroup firms' R & D intensity[a]*

*Positive differences*
2212: Misc. textile goods, except tire cord and fabric
2602: Paper mills, except building paper
2603: Paperboard mills
2607: Sanitary paper products
2803: Industrial inorganic chemicals, except industrial gases and inorganic pigments
2804: Plastics materials and resins
2807: Drugs, ethical
2811: Paints and allied products
2814: Fertilizers
2815: Pesticides and agricultural chemicals, not classified elsewhere
2817: Misc. chemical products, except explosives
2901: Petroleum refining
3419: Ordnance and accessories, except vehicles and guided missiles
3522: Pumps and pumping equipment
3528: Mechanical power transmission equipment, not classified elsewhere
3537: Misc. machinery, except electrical
3601: Transformers
3624: Electronic capacitors, resistors, coils and transformers, connectors and components, not classified elsewhere
3705: Motor vehicle parts

*Negative differences*
2004: Dairy products except fluid milk
2009: Cereal breakfast foods
2029: Misc. foods and kindred products, except roasted coffee
2402: Sawmills and planing mills
2403: Millwork, plywood and structural members
2606: Bags, except textile bags
2610: Paperboard containers and boxes
2809: Perfumes, cosmetics, and other toilet preparations
3311: Nonferrous wire drawing and insulating
3312: Nonferrous foundries
3515: Metalworking, machinery, not classified elsewhere, including metal forming machine tools, special dies and tools, die sets, jigs and fixtures, industrial molds and rolling mill machinery and equipment
3604: Industrial controls
3620: Radio and TV communication equipment
3621: Electron tubes, receiving and transmitting types
3802: Measuring and controlling devices
3904: Dolls, games, toys, and children's vehicles

[a] Significance measured at the 0.10 level for a two-tailed test.

where $\mu = \sum_{i=1}^{54} ip(i)$, $p(i) = n_i / 156$, and $n_i$ is the number of cases in rank $i$. The variance of $r$ is

$$\sigma^2(r) = (1/13) \sum_{i=1}^{54} (i - \mu)^2 p(i). \tag{9.3}$$

If I assume random selection of the 13 positive differences, $E(r)$ is 32.1026, and the standard deviation $\sigma(r)$ is 4.41009. For the 14 negative differences, $E(r)$ is of course again 32.1026, while the standard deviation $\sigma(r)$ is 4.24967. For the 13 positive differences, $r$ is 21.7, which is 2.4 standard deviations below the mean, assuming no relation between appropriability conditions and the R&D behavior of purposively diversified firms vis-à-vis firms that have not pursued such diversification of their R&D activities. For the 14 negative differences, $r$ is 41.0, which is 2.1 standard deviations above the mean.

Thus, the evidence implies that as compared with firms that have not purposively diversified, purposively diversified firms allocate more R&D resources to industry categories where appropriability conditions are good (i.e., where imitation lags are long) and fewer R&D resources to industry categories where appropriability is difficult (i.e., where imitation time lags are short).

### 9.4 Observing the performance effect of purposive R&D diversification

Does R&D in an industry category affect productivity for that industry only, or does the R&D in a set of "technologically close" industry categories affect the productivity for the whole set? For example, we might find only a little R&D in category $i$ but high productivity, and a lot of R&D in category $j$ but low productivity. But if categories $i$ and $j$ are "close," the proper level of aggregation might indicate intermediate R&D and intermediate productivity.

Do such R&D spillover effects exist? They appear to be important. Griliches provided his productivity data for three-digit Standard Industrial Classification (SIC) industries. Except for random error, the aggregate growth rate in total factor productivity in each SIC three-digit industry is assumed to be the same for our sample of 352 large manufacturing firms as it was for the entire population. The questions are (1) whether the variance in their R&D intensity across three-digit industries explains the cross-sectional variance in the rate of growth in their total factor productivity, and (2) whether any additional explanatory power comes from considering the spillovers of knowledge from R&D done in technologically close industries. To answer these questions, I first reestimated the

Table 9.5. *Impact of R&D intensity*[a] *(RS) on the average annual rate of growth in total factor productivity*[b] *(TḞP/TFP) in U.S. manufacturing*

---

*Observations on 133 industry categories*

$$\text{TḞP/TFP} = -0.0089 + 0.14\,\text{RS},$$
$$(t = -4.7)^* \quad (t = 3.8)^*$$

$F$-value $= 15^{**}$, $R^2 = 0.10$, degrees of freedom $= 131$

*Observations on the 93 sets of industry categories*

$$\text{TḞP/TFP} = -0.027 + 0.37\,\text{RS},$$
$$(t = -12)^* \quad (t = 7.6)^*$$

$F$-value $= 58^*$, $R^2 = 0.39$, degrees of freedom $= 91$

---

*Note:* Significance levels (one-tailed test): $^* = 0.0001$, $^{**} = 0.0002$. Significance levels for the $F$-value and $t$-value for the slope coefficient in the first equation differ because a one-tailed test is appropriate here.

[a] Measured as R&D expenditures divided by sales, using the FTC LB data.

[b] Measured as proportions, using Griliches's average annual rates of total factor productivity growth for the 1969–73 to 1974–8 period for three-digit SIC manufacturing industries. A dot denotes a time derivative, and the unit of time is one year. Griliches and Lichtenberg (1984, p. 327) explain the appropriateness of juxtaposing these mid-70s productivity data with the LB R&D data.

group probability model at the three-digit level and found 93 groups of significantly close three-digit industry categories.

If I use conventional industry categories and correlate Griliches's productivity growth measures with R&D intensity, I find the regression relation reported in the first equation of Table 9.5. The regression is derived from a model in which $\text{TḞP/TFP} = \lambda + (\partial Q/\partial R)(\dot{R}/Q) + \epsilon$, where $\lambda$ is an exogenous rate of growth in TFP, $R$ is R&D stock, $Q$ is output, $\partial Q/\partial R$ is the marginal product of R&D, and $\epsilon$ is random error.[6] Thus, the regression suggests that for every 1 percent increase in R&D/sales, the rate of growth in total factor productivity increased 0.14 of a percent. Or, interpreting the coefficient on R&D intensity as the marginal product of R&D, at the margin an increase in R&D stock by one dollar increases the value of annual output 14 cents. For expositions of this interpretation, see Terleckyj (1974) and Scherer (1982, p. 628).

Suppose we then hypothesize that R&D is a public good in the sense that when an industry category is a member of more than one group, the productivity effect of its R&D is felt in all groups. To test this proposition, I combined the productivity growth measures for each industry category within a group[7] to get appropriate productivity growth for the 93 sets of industry categories. If industry categories were combined randomly into a smaller number of groups, or if the population of such combinations were taken, the explanatory power and the coefficients of the productivity relation would be expected to be the same as obtained in the nongrouped data. The least squares line passes through the means of the variables TFP/TFP and $\dot{R}/Q$, and the expected means do not change whether grouped or ungrouped data are used. Both the sum of squared deviations of the observations from the mean and from the least squares line change in the same proportion. Thus both the coefficients and the explanatory power are expected to be the same before and after grouping.[8]

In fact, as seen in the second equation of Table 9.5, both $R^2$ and slope coefficient increase markedly. The slope coefficient for the second equation exceeds that of the first equation by 4.7 standard errors. This result is consistent with the hypothesis that firms purposively exploit knowledge spillovers, since the relationship would be expected to be stronger when the grouped data are used.

Terleckyj (1977, 1980), Scherer (1982), and Griliches and Lichtenberg (1984) have pursued the possible effects of spillovers of knowledge from R&D done in technologically close industries by exploring the possibility that knowledge is embodied in inputs. Our procedure incorporates that possibility but allows for the possibility that knowledge spreads through other channels. As Griliches (1979, p. 104) observes, pure knowledge flows need not be linked to the pattern of purchases of inputs. In pioneering work, Bernstein (1988) and Bernstein and Nadiri (1988a, 1988b) estimate the effects of interindustry and intraindustry spillovers of R&D investments on costs and the relative use of various inputs. My work suggests that the interindustry effects that they estimate would probably be larger if the firms analyzed were first grouped by their particular pattern of purposive diversification. Spillovers across industry categories within multimarket groups of firms purposively diversified in the same way would probably be stronger than spillovers among the firms observed in a given set of standard industry classifications. Further, the intraindustry spillover effects that Bernstein (1988) and Bernstein and Nadiri (1988b) estimate could reflect interindustry spillovers since firms are assigned to particular two-digit industries even though they are diversified. In any case, my results, although they do suggest that more attention should be paid to the fact that firms are diversified across two-digit boundaries and that firms based in the same industries exhibit very different types of purposive diversification, are quite consistent with Bernstein's and Nadiri's findings as well as the findings of Levin (1988), Levin and Reiss (1988), and Jaffee (1986), in the sense that all suggest that spillovers affect productivity.

Geroski (1991c) uses United Kingdom data on major innovations and total factor productivity growth to develop ideas in the foregoing studies and provide estimates of the impact of R&D spillovers on productivity growth within and across two-digit families of United Kingdom industries. His findings suggest that while there are substantial productivity effects in user industries because of the innovations made in producer industries, there are only small spillovers of knowledge among the producers and users of different innovations in technologically close industries. As Geroski (1991c, p. 1448) observes, perhaps the purposive diversification results in this chapter suggest that these spillovers would appear larger if the technological neighbors examined were not restricted to groups of firms within the same two-digit sector but were restricted to groups of firms with similar patterns of purposive diversification. However, Geroski also observes (personal correspondence) that knowledge embodied in an innovation is likely to be too user specific to spill over, while R&D knowledge is typically not yet specific enough to make spillover difficult.

Perhaps paradoxically, my results are also consistent with Lichtenberg's (1990) discovery that the de-diversification movement of the 1980s improved industrial productivity. Lichtenberg finds that productivity is greater if a firm is less diversified. The back-to-basics de-diversification movement of the 1980s dismantled much of the nonpurposive, random diversification of earlier eras – especially the 1960s and 1970s (Ravenscraft and Scherer, 1987; Porter, 1987). I find that *purposive* diversification increases productivity growth; de-diversification increases purposive diversification even as it decreases diversification per se, because what it leaves is diversification that makes sense, i.e., is purposive, exploiting complementarities in R&D across industries.

## 9.5 Discussion

The findings of Mueller and Culbertson (1986) provide an example of one aspect of what must lie behind my finding of a higher correlation between productivity growth rates and R&D intensity when the observations are multimarket groups instead of SIC industries. They provide examples supporting my conjecture that firms purposively diversifying their R&D are trying to exploit complementarities in research, development, and application of innovations across industry categories. They use food-processing innovations to test Rosenberg's (1979) theory of interdependence of technology among industries. Rosenberg's theory predicts that important productivity effects are embodied in purchased inputs, and Mueller and Culbertson believe that the theory can explain why, for food-processing industries, low R&D often coincides with large advances in labor productivity. Mueller and Culbertson tabulated the industry of origin for a sample of the Putman Awards, which recognize innovations that increase efficiency in food-processing industries. They found (Mueller and Culbertson, 1986, table 3, p. 166) that the dominant manufacturing categories that received Putman Awards were SIC groups 20 (food processing), 35 (machinery), 38 (instruments and controls), 26 (packaging and paper), and 28 (chemicals and paint). In the next chapter, I shall apply the methodology used in the present chapter and establish such groups of related or technologically close two-digit industries into which firms have purposively diversified. Among the multimarket groups of two-digit industries identified in Chapter 10 are {20, 26, 28}, {20, 26, ..., 35, ..., 38}, and {20, 28, 35, 38}. The Putman Award data studied by Mueller and Culbertson were for 1971, 1973, 1975, and 1977, while my data were for 1974, 1975, and 1976, so the time period of their study is essentially the same as the time period studied in Chapter 10. Thus, the Mueller and Culbertson (1986) findings for food processing are consistent with the evidence in Chapters 9 and 10 for U.S. manufacturing in general.

The evidence in this chapter about the R&D behavior of purposively diversified firms and about the link from purposively diversified R&D to factor productivity growth supports the view that the firms I have called "purposively diversified" are in fact deliberately exploiting complementarities in R&D. But my findings raise a new question. What is the explanation for nonpurposive activity? Note that even a firm that is purposively diversified into a set or sets of categories that "belong together" may have some R&D activities that "don't belong." This may reflect growth via diversification for reasons other than the R&D complementarity of the acquired fields. And what are the "nonpurposive" firms up to? Are they not as smart about the spillovers of knowledge? Do they find it harder to finance diversified R&D? Since all firms in the sample are among the largest 1000 U.S. manufacturers, none is absolutely small; yet, 69 percent of the R&D performing firms in my sample do not "purposively diversify" their R&D. If I compare the "purposively diversified" firms with the others by industry category, I find that the purposively diversified firms are absolutely more diversified.[9] Why so many firms do not purposively diversify poses a mystery for future research. I shall venture an answer in Chapter 11, but first I shall explore purposive R&D diversification at the two-digit level.

# 10

# Multimarket rivalry and R&D intensity

This chapter explores an important possibility suggested by the findings of Chapter 7 and Chapter 9 taken together. Chapter 7 showed that the correlation between seller concentration in standard industry categories and research and development (R&D) intensity may not reflect the Schumpeterian hypotheses that market power begets R&D activity as commonly supposed. Chapter 9 showed that purposive diversification of R&D occurs and shapes R&D behavior and productivity performance. Might it not be, then, that within the universe of the very largest firms the state of competition should be evaluated not for standard industry categories but instead for the multimarket groups of related categories and the firms within them whose operations span the set of categories in the group?

## 10.1 Introduction

Many economists have been intrigued by Schumpeter's (1942) vision of technological progress driven by firms fighting to survive competition from new products, new processes, or new organizational forms. But his proposition that the firms at the heart of that potentially socially beneficial struggle are necessarily large and monopolistic – that firm size and monopolistic power promote technological advance – has not found strong empirical support.[1] Focusing on the big facts about how technological change has benefited society, Schumpeter argued that any static allocative and technical inefficiencies caused by monopolies would be overwhelmed by the good effects of the desirable technological change that the monopolies induce. Schumpeter's hypothesis is of course distinct from the empirical tests used to explore it. The tests usually explore a "Schumpeterian" hypothesis that firm size and market power promote R&D efforts

Chapter 10 is a revision of Scott (1990).

and ultimately technological change. This chapter explores the possibility that previous empirical tests, such as those discussed in Chapter 7, have been incapable of revealing proof of the Schumpeterian hypothesis because the phenomenon of purposive diversification has been ignored. As explained in Chapters 8 and 9, purposive diversification of R&D is a firm's systematic attempt to improve the net value of innovative investment by diversifying its R&D across a group of industry categories for which research efforts are complementary. Complementary research efforts may share facilities and personnel, and knowledge gained from the R&D in one activity may spill to another activity.

Section 10.2 reviews the recent evidence that suggests that firm size, among the largest 1000 U.S. manufacturers, and monopolistic power, as measured by seller concentration in manufacturing industries, do not affect R&D intensity. The rest of the chapter will use the concept of purposive diversification of R&D to reframe the tests. Section 10.3 explains the methodology (as with Chapter 9 an adaptation of the methodology introduced in Chapter 4) for discerning it and illustrates it by developing new evidence at the level of broad manufacturing industries.

Section 10.4 shows that differences in purposive diversification of R&D provide firm-specific characteristics associated with differences in firms' R&D behavior even within the same industry category. Size per se may not matter, but differences among firms in purposive diversification do matter.

Section 10.5 pursues the idea that the pertinent competition in R&D is taking place within each group of technologically close, related industries. Each group is occupied by firms that have purposively diversified in similar ways. The firms in each such group are likely to be competing in R&D with strategies aimed at introducing similar innovations. Arguably concentration of *R&D* resources among the firms in a given *group* of related activities and the effect of that concentration on behavior should then be the focus of any exploration, via the relationship between seller concentration and R&D intensity, of the "Schumpeterian" hypothesis about monopolistic power. Previous work has examined seller concentration in *sales* within the industry categories determined by the old, existing products – just as we did in Chapter 7. True, Schumpeter argued (1942, pp. 87–106) that monopolistic power in old product markets gives firms the extra revenue needed to support R&D and provide "insurance," while expected monopolistic profits in new product markets provides the incentive. But, our review in Section 10.2 of the behavioral reasons for a link between seller concentration and R&D intensity suggests that the concentration of *R&D* resources would be a key determinant of R&D

behavior. Key are expectations about the ability to coordinate price competition in the postinnovation market and the ability to coordinate nonprice competition in the preinnovation market. Both should depend on the number and size distribution of sellers competing in R&D in the preinnovation market. Thus, Section 10.5 explores the impact of concentration of *R&D* resources in the *groups,* holding constant all relevant firmwide and industry category–wide variables (including their nonlinear effects), assuming only that the true model is linear in the parameters (but not linear in the variables).

After assessing the chapter's findings, Section 10.6 points up how the concept of purposive diversification provides new directions for research about industrial R&D.

### 10.2 Previous evidence about the Schumpeterian hypotheses

Studies of firm size and innovation have often explored the relationship between size and R&D intensity, usually measured as the ratio of R&D expenditures to sales. In my exploration of the differences in R&D intensity across the over 3000 lines of business (LBs)[2] of the over 400 firms reporting to the Federal Trade Commission Line of Business (FTC LB) Program in the 261 four-digit FTC manufacturing industry categories, I found that after controlling for all four-digit FTC industry effects, LB (i.e., business unit) size had no effect on R&D intensity.[3] Cohen et al. (1987) uses direct measures of appropriability and opportunity differences across industries to provide controls and corroborates my finding regarding business unit size as well as the finding of previous literature that firm size does not, among the largest U.S. manufacturing firms, affect R&D intensity once one controls for industry differences.[4] Freeman (1982, chapter 6, pp. 131-147) and Acs and Audretsch (1988) consider a wider range of firm sizes; I shall focus here on the evidence that among the largest – top 1000 – U.S. manufacturers, size does not appear to be important for innovative activity.

The diversification of a firm's R&D effort, however, is another prominent characteristic of a firm, arguably more important for R&D performance than size. Nelson (1959) advanced the hypothesis that a firm's size in terms of its diversification – production in several industry categories – would increase its ability to perform and to benefit from R&D, especially basic research. Studying basic research, Link (1981, 1982, 1983a) and Link and Long (1981) provide support for the hypothesis. Scherer (1984, p. 236) examines *applied* R&D and in a variety of experiments finds only a small but statistically significant effect of diversification on patenting, other things being equal.[5]

Chapter 9 provides support for the idea that *purposive* diversification of *applied* R & D across FTC four-digit industry categories is an important determinant of differences in applied R & D intensity across firms. Section 10.4 will add to that evidence by observing the purposive diversification of R & D (and its effects on behavior) at the level of the broad two-digit manufacturing industries. We then explore the idea that this characteristic of a firm – the presence or absence of purposive diversification – is the key to understanding why the industry-level tests of the relationship between concentration and R & D intensity have been so inconclusive. The firms in a given industry are typically pursuing very different R & D strategies. They are not all competing in one industry group, but rather fall into different groups according to their different strategies. Each firm competes in R & D with those firms with similar strategies and expecting similar products in the future. Thus, the type of purposive diversification pursued by a firm should be used to determine the extent of competition that it faces in its R & D, although the number or character of the groups in which a firm competes may be affected by industry concentration.

The relationship between R & D intensity and seller concentration has been the focus of studies of the Schumpeterian hypothesis that monopolistic power promotes innovation. Chapter 7 showed that the effect of seller concentration was only a small percentage of the systematic variance in R & D intensity across the over 3000 business units. Further, control for firm effects and two-digit industry effects eliminated the significance of seller concentration. Without the controls, seller concentration was significant and exhibited the familiar inverted-∪ relationship with R & D intensity,[6] in which R & D intensity rises with seller concentration initially but eventually decreases as concentration increases. Assuming that seller concentration does measure the ability to coordinate behavior, a behavioral reason for the inverted-∪ would be a difference between the ability to coordinate price competition in the postinnovation market and the ability to coordinate nonprice competition in the preinnovation market. At very high levels of seller concentration, coordination of both price and nonprice competitive devices is possible. At intermediate levels of seller concentration, each firm may reckon that its price cuts are readily matched effectively, yet it may also believe that others will not so readily match its R & D program effectively. If so, then R & D performers may anticipate more cooperation on price in the postinnovation market than they are able to coordinate for R & D in the preinnovation market. With low levels of seller concentration, the competition among substitutes (patented or not) in the postinnovation market may severely reduce appropriation of returns and hence R & D in the preinnovation market.

The distinction between cooperation before and after an innovation is often forced in the theoretical models by assuming Cournot behavior in R&D while maintaining that the R&D competitors are competing for a fixed total amount of quasi-rents to accrue to the winner of the R&D race or to be shared among several winners. Hence, although there is monopoly in the postinnovation market or implicitly a joint profit–maximizing coordination of price by multiple sellers in that market, coordination does not occur in the preinnovation market. Instead, there is a Cournot outbreak of "wasteful" nonprice competition in the form of rivalrous innovative investments. Of course, if the monopoly solution would have resulted in too little R&D investment because of the monopolist's inability to appropriate all of the social returns, the rivalry in R&D, although reducing private profits, may increase R&D toward the socially optimal level. Thus, the inverted-U results when, in a middle range of seller concentration, overbidding (from a private but not necessarily a social perspective) for innovative rewards dominates any appropriability problems in the postinnovation market.

Support for the inverted-U has been found in numerous data sets and in numerous papers. But based on the findings in Chapter 7, there is no strong evidence supporting the Schumpeterian notion that seller concentration is an important determinant of R&D intensity, since in all studies finding such a relationship the result was arguably an artifact of insufficient control for differences in the value, cost, and opportunity for R&D across firms and industries apart from the differences caused because seller concentration differed. The effect of concentration disappeared despite its considerable variance within the sets of observations isolated to allow control of opportunity and appropriability differences other than those generated by concentration itself. At the FTC four-digit industry level, Levin et al. (1985) replicates the elimination of the inverted-U effect by directly controlling for the variance in appropriability and opportunity conditions across industries.[7] As explained in Chapter 7, Geroski's (1990; 1991a, chapter 6) results with U.K. data are also consistent with the basic findings of Chapter 7, although he successfully explores additional issues and although he cannot control for firm effects in the way I do with the FTC LB sample.

One potential problem with the foregoing tests has been the failure to take account of purposive diversification. Chapter 8 has explained why such diversification occurs, and Chapter 9 has provided evidence supporting the hypotheses developed in Chapter 8. In the present chapter, we can explore the impact of the concentration of R&D resources across the multi-industry groups of firms resulting from purposive diversification.

## 10.3 **Distinguishing purposive diversification of R&D effort**

If a firm diversifies its R&D effort purposely for the reasons discussed in Chapters 8 and 9, and if similar opportunities are available to other firms, we should find significant grouping of firms. Firms purposely combining a particular set of multicategory R&D activities will meet in the "group" of those activities more than would occur by chance from random diversification.

To find "the groups," I examined every possible pair of firms in the subset (376 large U.S. manufacturing firms) of the FTC LB sample (U.S. FTC, 1981a, 1981b, 1982) that was used and described in Chapter 6. Adapting the methodology introduced in Chapter 4, I define groups of multiple categories within which spillovers of knowledge are likely as those sets of categories where "significant" (0.01 level) meetings are found.

Chapter 9 uses this same sample and methodology to find and report significant groups of FTC four-digit industries. Here I work with the broad two-digit SIC (and FTC) manufacturing industry categories, both to provide new evidence about purposive diversification and because subsequently I focus on the effect of competition within these broad groups. In his seminal article hypothesizing the importance of diversification, Nelson (1959, pp. 302–303) emphasized the breadth of the large technological leaders in manufacturing:

A broad technological base insures that, whatever direction the path of research may take, the results are likely to be of value to the sponsoring firm. It is for this reason that firms which support research toward the basic-science end of the spectrum are firms that have their fingers in many pies. The big chemical companies producing a range of products as wide as the field of chemistry itself, the Bell Telephone Company, General Electric, and Eastman Kodak immediately come to mind. It is not just the size of the companies. . . . Rather it is their broad underlying technological base, the wide range of products they produce or will be willing to produce if their research efforts open possibilities.

Here I work with the *applied* R&D of large U.S. manufacturing firms rather than their *basic* research, yet Nelson's 1959 reasoning and the ideas of others (used in Chapter 8 to understand the motives for diversifying R&D) suggest that technological leaders in manufacturing will use their applied R&D to compete for positions in the markets of the future within groups of the broad industry categories.

Let $n$ denote the number (20 here) of two-digit SIC manufacturing categories in which the firms have R&D expenditures. For each pair of firms, $s$ is the number of two-digit categories in which one firm has R&D, while $t$ ($t \leq s$) is the number of two-digit categories in which the other firm does R&D. Let $g$ denote the number of categories in which the two firms meet, while $C_{x,y}$ denotes the combination of $x$ things taken $y$ at a time. Then for each pair of firms for which both firms have R&D activity, we can compute a probability

$$AP = 1 - \sum_{f=0}^{g-1} p(f) = 1 - \sum_{f=0}^{g-1} \frac{C_{t,f} \cdot C_{n-t,s-f}}{C_{n,s}},$$

which is the probability that the firms would meet as much or more than they do if diversification were random. Note that $C_{t,f}$ is the number of different combinations of $f$ activities in which the two firms could meet. Conditional on the two firms meeting in particular $f$ activities, $C_{n-t,s-f}$ is the number of possibilities for $s$ minus $f$ categories that do not coincide with the $t$ activities of the other firm. $C_{n,s}$ is the total number of ways the firm with $s$ activities can be configured. So $p(f)$ gives the proportion of $C_{n,s}$ taken by all the cases where the two firms meet in $f$ categories. When AP is less than or equal to 0.01, the null hypothesis of random diversification is rejected and the alternative, purposive diversification, is accepted. Chapter 4 provides numerical illustrations.

The procedure finds (after elimination of duplicates) 165 groups of related categories, and an illustrative set of examples is given in Table 10.1. Table 10.1 shows, for example, that 32 of the sample's firms performed R&D in both the two-digit SIC categories 20 (food) and 28 (chemicals). Note that a given firm can be a competitor in more than one group (with some of its LBs in one group and others of its LBs in other groups – but note that the same LB can be a member of more than one group), one (with some or all of its LBs in that group), or none.

### 10.4 Purposive diversification and R&D intensity

To study the effect of purposive diversification on LB R&D intensity, I used the 3 years, 1974 through 1976, for which data were available. Total (applied) R&D expenditure in each LB for a firm was used. I chose total R&D because the decision to combine R&D in various industry categories is expected to take account of the fact that both government-financed R&D and R&D performed under contract more generally provide knowledge spillovers to the firm.[8] To lessen the importance of equilibrium-obscuring outliers that could result because of startups or catastrophies destroying sales, I used RS, the sales-weighted average of R&D expenditures to sales during the 3 years for each LB, for the 355 firms in the sample that maintained R&D expenditures throughout the 3 years in one or more two-digit manufacturing industry categories. Thus, there were 21 firms in the sample of 376 that had no nonsporadic two-digit R&D activities.

Purposive diversification of a particular type has a significant effect on the behavior of the firms with that particular type of diversification

Table 10.1. *Some of the 165 groups: Examples from those combining research in chemicals with research in other areas*

| Industry categories in the group | Number of firms in the sample and in the group |
|---|---|
| {20, food and kindred products; 28, chemicals and allied products} | 32 |
| {22, textile mill products; 23, apparel and other fabric products; 28, chemicals and allied products; 30, rubber and miscellaneous plastics products} | 4 |
| {28, chemicals and allied products; 29, petroleum refining and related industries; 30, rubber and miscellaneous plastics products} | 11 |
| {28, chemicals and allied products; 33, primary metal industries; 34, fabricated metal products, except machinery and transportation equipment} | 23 |
| {28, chemicals and allied products; 35, machinery except electrical; 36, electrical and electronic machinery, equipment, and supplies; 38, measuring, analyzing, and controlling instruments; photographic, medical, and optical goods; watches and clocks} | 10 |

strategy. The firms in a purposive diversification group behave differently from the other firms in any particular industry category in common, even when the other firms include some which also have purposively diversified in their own way. To make that point, rather than comparing within each industry category the firms of each type of purposive diversification with firms that have not purposively diversified at all, Table 10.2 examines the difference, industry category by industry category, of the mean of R&D intensity, RS, for firms within each type of purposive diversification group and a matched set of firms outside the group. Recall that RS is, for each *two-digit* LB (an LB – i.e., the operations of a firm in a *two-digit* industry category), the sum of the 3 years of total applied R&D – company-financed R&D plus R&D billed to the federal government plus R&D billed to other outsiders – divided by the sum of the 3 years of LB sales. Table 10.2 shows that the firms purposely diversified in a particular way do not necessarily have greater R&D intensity in a particular industry category than the average R&D intensity in that category of the firms not so diversified. The R&D intensity of the particular purposively diversified firms is clearly significantly different, but the difference may be positive or negative.

Table 10.2. *Significance of R&D differences
between group and nongroup firms*[a]

| Significance level, $p$ (two tails) | Sign of the difference | |
|---|---|---|
| | + | − |
| $p \leq .10$ | 8.9 | 5 |
| $.10 < p \leq .30$ | 16.1 | 13 |
| "Insignificant" | 28.5 | 28.5 |

[a] Using each of the 165 groups, and each two-digit industry category within each group, the percentage of cases at each level of significance for the difference in mean R&D intensity, RS, between firms within the group and an equal number of firms randomly selected (each firm had an equal chance of being chosen) from those having R&D expenditures within the two-digit category but not within the group. The results are for the 740 cases for which the matched sample could be formed.

To assess the statistical significance of the results in Table 10.2, imagine a random distribution of $m$ items across $n$ boxes of equal size. Let $x_i$ be the random variable, which is 1 if the $i$th item appears in a particular box and 0 otherwise. Then, just as in Chapter 9, a measure of the number of items appearing in a particular box is the random variable

$$X = \sum_{i=1}^{m} x_i.$$

Its expected value is

$$E(X) = \sum_{i=1}^{m} (1 \cdot 1/n + 0 \cdot (1 - 1/n)) = m/n.$$

Its variance is

$$\text{var}(X) = \sum_{i=1}^{m} \text{var}(x_i)$$

$$= m \, \text{var}(x_i) = m\{[1 - 1/n]^2 (1/n) + [0 - 1/n]^2 (1 - 1/n)\}.$$

Considering the top two categories on the left as a single "box," or the top two categories on the right as a single "box," $n = 1/0.15 = 6\frac{2}{3}$. This is true because a two-tailed test at the 30 percent level implies that there should be 15 percent of the cases in each tail. There are then $100\%/15\% = 6\frac{2}{3}$ such equally likely categories or "boxes" into which cases can fall under the null hypothesis. Then, since 740 cases are examined in Table 10.2,

$E(X) = m/n = 740/(6\frac{2}{3}) = 111$, and $\sqrt{\text{var}(X)} = 9.71$. Now, in the top two "boxes" on the left, there are 25 percent of the 740 items, or 7.62 standard deviations above the expected number if the behavior of purposively diversified firms is no different from that of others. In the top two "boxes" on the right, there are 18 percent of the items, or 2.29 standard deviations above the expected number.

As Chapter 9 shows by also comparing purposively diversified firms with matched sets of firms not purposively diversified, firms purposively diversified in different ways are more alike in their R&D intensity than are purposively diversified firms and firms that have not so diversified. And although purposively diversified firms may have higher or lower R&D intensities in particular industry categories than the firms that have not purposively diversified, there is a significant tendency for the R&D intensity of the purposively diversified firms to be higher.

## 10.5 **R&D concentration within multi-industry groups and R&D intensity**

Despite the elimination in Chapter 7 of the effect of seller concentration on R&D intensity, a simple descriptive relation consonant with a simplified view that competition promotes technological progress is still possible. Arguably, seller concentration should be measured by the concentration of R&D resources, and, arguably, concentration within industry categories should be replaced by concentration within complementary R&D activities. In this section, we explore both possibilities. If we find that, using R&D concentration within complementary sets of R&D activities, the relationship between concentration and R&D intensity survives the controls for other differences across firms and industries, then the simple descriptive relation is resurrected. However, if the relation again disappears, we are clearly left with the need to explore more intricate models.

First, the experiments of Chapter 7 at most caution that previously estimated inverted-U relations between seller concentration and R&D intensity may not reflect the theory of competition in R&D. Further, the observations on seller concentration may be incorrect if effective competition in R&D occurs within industry boundaries that differ from those conventionally defined. For example, with R&D, the cutomary distinction between "the food industry" and "the chemical industry" may – unfortunate as it may seem – be blurred. Finally, seller concentration in R&D activity may well be the relevant factor. Traditional sales concentration measures have previously been used, yet the anticipation of the degree of competition in the postinnovation market as well as conjectural variations in the preinnovation market may well depend on the concentration of R&D activity.

With CR denoting four-firm concentration ratios and H denoting Herfindahl indices, and with I denoting conventional industry categorization and G denoting our group categorization, and $D_i$ and $T_j$ denoting firm and industry dummy variables, respectively, Tables 10.3 and 10.4 undertake the new experiments suggested by these thoughts. These tests are rough, because I must capture the variance in the number and size distribution of R&D performers with their distribution in my sample.

Equation (1) in Table 10.3 shows that, using conventional industry categories and no controls for other effects, there is the conventional inverted-∪ relation between R&D intensity and concentration. R&D intensity peaks for a four-firm R&D concentration ratio of 0.50 (i.e., when 50 percent of an industry's R&D is controlled by the four firms with the largest R&D expenditures). Equation (1) of Table 10.4 shows that when the R&D concentration of our multimarket groups is used, the peak of R&D intensity occurs when four-firm R&D concentration is 0.55 (or 55 percent).

However, the tests show that although firm effects ($\beta$'s), or firm and industry effects ($\gamma$'s) where both can be estimated,[9] eliminate the inverted-∪ in the data, a statistically significant negative effect of sellers' concentration (of R&D activity) on LB R&D intensity remains. As comparison of the two tables shows, however, the result is not markedly different when concentration within the group rather than concentration within the industry category is used to condition the R&D behavior of an LB. A simplified view that competition stimulates R&D is weakly supported by the negative sign of the coefficient on seller concentration. In a manner analogous to Geroski's (1990; 1991a, chapter 6) results as discussed in Chapter 7, the negative sign persists even when industry and firm effects are controlled. However, the concentration variables explain only a minuscule proportion of the variance in R&D at the two-digit LB level. Thus, our attempt to resurrect a simple empirical relationship between concentration and R&D intensity has failed. However, we have at least explored systematically one possibility for resurrecting the relation, and we have presented at the two-digit industry level the evidence for the inverted-∪, for the negative effect of concentration, and for firm and industry effects.[10]

### 10.6 Summary

The results are promising for further exploration of the effects of "size" along the dimension of purposive diversification across several

Table 10.3. *Industry R&D concentration and LB R&D intensity,*
*with the concentration associated with an LB observation being the*
*concentration for the conventional industry to which the LB belongs*\*

(1) $RS = -0.018 + 0.17\,ICR - 0.17\,(ICR)^2$
$\quad\quad\quad (t=-0.90) \quad (t=2.3)^b \quad\quad (t=-2.4)^b$
$\quad F\text{-value}=3.1,^c \ R^2=0.0049, \text{ degrees of freedom}=1256$

(2) $RS = 0.018 + 0.12\,IH - 0.53\,(IH)^2$
$\quad\quad\quad (t=2.8)^b \ (t=1.3)^d \quad\quad (t=-2.0)^c$
$\quad F\text{-value}=3.5,^c \ R^2=0.0055, \text{ degrees of freedom}=1256$

(3) $RS = 0.027 - 0.0073\,ICR$
$\quad\quad\quad (t=3.6)^b \quad (t=-0.52)$
$\quad F\text{-value}=0.27, \ R^2=0.00021, \text{ degrees of freedom}=1257$

(4) $RS = 0.029 - 0.050\,IH$
$\quad\quad\quad (t=7.9)^a \quad (t=-1.7)^{c,k}$
$\quad F\text{-value}=3.0,^{d,k} \ R^2=0.0024, \text{ degrees of freedom}=1257$

(5) $RS = z + \sum_{i=2}^{355}\beta_i D_i - 0.010\,ICR - 0.017\,(ICR)^2$
$\quad\quad\quad (F=1.5)^{a,e} \quad\quad (t=-0.11) \quad\quad (t=-0.20)$
$\quad F\text{-value}=1.5,^a \ R^2=0.37, \text{ degrees of freedom}=902$

(6) $RS = z + \sum_{i=2}^{355}\beta_i D_i - 0.14\,IH + 0.22\,(IH)^2$
$\quad\quad\quad (F=1.5)^{a,f} \quad (t=-1.4)^d \quad (t=0.74)$
$\quad F\text{-value}=1.5,^a \ R^2=0.38, \text{ degrees of freedom}=902$

(7) $RS = z + \sum_{i=2}^{355}\beta_i D_i - 0.028\,ICR$
$\quad\quad\quad (F=1.5)^{a,g} \quad (t=-1.8)^c$
$\quad F\text{-value}=1.5,^a \ R^2=0.37, \text{ degrees of freedom}=903$

(8) $RS = z + \sum_{i=2}^{355}\beta_i D_i - 0.068\,IH$
$\quad\quad\quad (F=1.5)^{a,h} \quad (t=-2.2)^c$
$\quad F\text{-value}=1.5,^a \ R^2=0.38, \text{ degrees of freedom}=903$

\*Significance levels (one-tail): $^a=0.0001,\ ^b=0.01,\ ^c=0.05,\ ^d=0.10.$
$^e$ To reduce the size of the $\mathbf{X'X}$ matrix, the firm effects were absorbed. Nonetheless, the $F$ test is for the effects when fitted last. That is, $F$ for the company effects is the ratio of the reduction in residual sum of squares, as we go from Equation (1) to Equation (5), divided by 354, to the residual sum of squares for Equation (5) divided by 902.
$^f$ This is the $F$ test for the effects when fitted last. The $F$-value was derived using Equations (2) and (6) in the manner described in note $e$ for Equations (1) and (5).
$^g$ Fitted last, using Equations (3) and (7).
$^h$ Fitted last, using Equations (4) and (8).
$^k$ Note that the discrepancy between the significance of the slope coefficient and the significance of the equation as a whole results because we are using a one-tailed test to determine the significance of the $t$-value. With a two-tailed test, the probability of $|t|$ being larger is of course the same as the probability of $F$ being larger, which in this case is 0.085.

Table 10.4. *Group R&D concentration and LB R&D intensity, with the concentration associated with an LB observation being that for the group (or the average for the groups) to which that LB belongs, or for the conventional industry to which the LB belongs if the LB is not part of a group*

(1) $RS = -0.0067 + 0.12\,GCR - 0.11\,(GCR)^2$
$\quad\quad\quad (t=-0.29)\quad\quad (t=1.7)^c\quad\quad\quad (t=-2.1)^c$
$\quad F\text{-value}=5.5,^b\ R^2=0.0087,\ \text{degrees of freedom}=1256$

(2) $RS = 0.025 - 0.0038\,GH - 0.018\,(GH)^2$
$\quad\quad\quad (t=5.5)^a\quad (t=-0.13)\quad\quad (t=-0.46)$
$\quad F\text{-value}=1.4,\ R^2=0.0022,\ \text{degrees of freedom}=1256$

(3) $RS = 0.040 - 0.024\,GCR$
$\quad\quad\quad (t=6.0)^a\quad (t=-2.6)^b$
$\quad F\text{-value}=6.6,^b\ R^2=0.0052,\ \text{degrees of freedom}=1257$

(4) $RS = 0.027 - 0.017\,GH$
$\quad\quad\quad (t=9.2)^a\quad (t=-1.6)^{d,g}$
$\quad F\text{-value}=2.6,^g\ R^2=0.0021,\ \text{degrees of freedom}=1257$

(5) $RS = z + \sum_{i=2}^{355}\beta_i D_i + \sum_{j=2}^{20}\gamma_j T_j - 0.050\,GCR + 0.014\,(GCR)^2$
$\quad\quad\quad\quad (F=1.4)^{e,b}\quad\quad (F=3.5)^a\quad\quad (t=-0.40)\quad\quad\quad (t=0.16)$
$\quad F\text{-value}=1.7,^a\ R^2=0.42,\ \text{degrees of freedom}=883$

(6) $RS = z + \sum_{i=2}^{355}\beta_i D_i + \sum_{j=2}^{20}\gamma_j T_j - 0.063\,GH + 0.050\,(GH)^2$
$\quad\quad\quad\quad (F=1.4)^{f,b}\quad\quad (F=3.7)^a\quad\quad (t=-1.0)\quad\quad\quad (t=0.74)$
$\quad F\text{-value}=1.7,^a\ R^2=0.42,\ \text{degrees of freedom}=883$

(7) $RS = z + \sum_{i=2}^{355}\beta_i D_i + \sum_{j=2}^{20}\gamma_j T_j - 0.031\,GCR$
$\quad\quad\quad\quad (F=1.4)^{f,b}\quad\quad (F=3.5)^a\quad\quad (t=-1.4)^d$
$\quad F\text{-value}=1.7,^a\ R^2=0.42,\ \text{degrees of freedom}=884$

(8) $RS = z + \sum_{i=2}^{355}\beta_i D_i + \sum_{j=2}^{20}\gamma_j T_j - 0.020\,GH$
$\quad\quad\quad\quad (F=1.4)^{f,b}\quad\quad (F=3.7)^a\quad\quad (t=-0.85)$
$\quad F\text{-value}=1.7,^a\ R^2=0.42,\ \text{degrees of freedom}=884$

*Significance levels (one-tail): [a]=0.0001, [b]=0.01, [c]=0.05, [d]=0.10.

[e] Although the firm effects were absorbed to reduce the size of the $\mathbf{X'X}$ matrix, this $F$-value is for the 354 firm effects when fitted last. It is the ratio of the reduction in the sum of squared residuals, as we move from the specification with industry effects, GCR, and $(GCR)^2$ to that including additionally the firm effects, divided by 354, to the sum of squared residuals in Equation (5) divided by 883. Thus, when fitted last, $F$ for the company effects is 1.4 with 354 and 883 degrees of freedom. This is obviously highly significant, but unlike the 1.5 case in Table 10.3, I have not worked out the integral which is tedious when the number of degrees of freedom in the numerator and the denominator are so large. Although the result is actually more significant, I have conservatively labeled it as "b."

[f] This $F$-value is for the firm effects when fitted last, in the same manner as explained in note e. Again, "b" is very conservative; the result is actually more significant.

[g] Note that the discrepancy between the significance of the slope coefficient and the significance of the equation as a whole results because we are using a one-tailed test to determine the significance of the $t$-value. With a two-tailed test, the probability of $|t|$ being larger is of course the same as the probability of $F$ being larger, which in this case is 0.11.

industry categories. As the theory of Chapter 8 predicts, purposively diversified firms clearly behave differently from those that are not purposively diversified. There is also a tendency for purposively diversified firms to have higher R&D intensity, other things being equal.

The results were not promising for concentration in any simple form, although it may well be that in interactions with other industry variables it has a lot to do with the variance in behavior explained by industry effects. In any case, the implication from the work here in conjunction with that in Chapter 7 is that seller concentration does not appear to be an important determinant of LB R&D intensity, whether measured in terms of current sales or R&D expenditures, and whether measured for conventional industry categories or for the multicategory groups of related categories combined by purposively diversifying firms.

More generally, the idea of purposive diversification has a lot to add, even if it cannot save the simple view of concentration and Schumpeterian competition. I think progress in the empirical research about market structure and technological change will require measures of behavior other than R&D intensity and measures of performance other than patenting.[11]

Since productivity growth is in part determined by R&D, such growth provides one possible alternative variable which can be used to frame and test hypotheses about Schumpeterian competition. For example, Scherer (1983b) has explored the association between concentration, R&D intensity, and productivity growth.[12] Purposive diversification could usefully be considered in such tests, because, as the theory of Chapter 8 would predict, Chapter 9's analysis of productivity data affords evidence of spillovers of knowledge among the industry categories in each group of categories combined by purposive diversification.

Chapter 11 will model "component gestalt" – the integrated product structure or components' performance-attribute pattern necessary for a complex innovation – and provide a framework for further analysis of "Schumpeterian" hypotheses and purposive diversification. Many industrial R&D projects require the integration of several components. Purposive diversification undoubtedly results in part because the development of multiple component projects requires integration of research in several industry categories.

Chapter 9 finds that firms in the same four-digit industry category have different patterns of purposive diversification and in many cases do not purposively diversify at all. That same phenomenon occurs at the two-digit industry level observed in this chapter. In Chapter 11, I shall describe the sample space for industrial R&D and suggest that the reason that firms differ so dramatically in their extent and type of purposive diversification is that they find it profitable to research different niches in that sample space. Chapter 11 will argue that such diversity reflects a link from rivalry to R&D behavior even though, as seen in Chapter 7, the simplest concentration–R&D intensity tests offer little support for theories about R&D rivalry, and even though the lack of support remains when, as in the present chapter, the tests are defined over the multi-industry groups determined by purposive diversification.

# 11

## Research diversity induced by rivalry

This chapter will depart from the standard theoretical formulation in which all of the firms in the research and development (R&D) race anticipate the same single prize. Chapter 8 developed the standard formulation to explain that when, from society's perspective, firms underinvest in R&D because they do not appropriate all of the social value of their innovations, more competition can increase R&D investment toward the socially optimal amount. This chapter treats research possibilities as diverse among firms, because the point of the chapter is that another potential gain from competition is more diversity in research.

To develop the idea theoretically, I shall use the Chamberlin/Osborne type of model discussed in Chapter 2. As explained there, we could also develop the idea using the theory of multiperiod games; however, my point can be made most simply by using what Chapter 2 called the Chamberlinian shortcut. To explore diversity empirically, I shall use the variance within and across industries in the systems orientation of patent portfolios. Industry effects will be used to control for the differences across industries in the applicability of systems research, while firm effects will capture the idea that industry traits do not determine completely the systems orientation of firms. Firms can employ different strategies even when in the same industry category. The intra-industry diversity associated with the firm effects that I estimate could of course be associated with things other than the rivalry mechanism that I shall posit. My point is that diversity that has typically been thought of in those other ways could instead have been caused by the extent of rivalry through the mechanism described in this chapter. Further, a firm's particular form of purposive diversification is likely to be the structural manifestation of the diversity

Chapter 11 is a revision of Scott (1991a).

reflected in the firm (i.e., company) effects that demonstrate something unique about the firm as a whole regardless of the one of its industries in which we observe it.

## 11.1 Overview

Scholars have often asked whether competition or instead Schumpeterian monopoly is more likely to promote technological progress. But from Chapter 7, we have seen that the conventional story about the importance of seller concentration does not have any evidential power. Even in Chapter 10, which applied Chapter 9's idea that firms compete within multimarket groups of industry categories, we have seen that the simple traditional story does not work. Arguably, Schumpeter's vision, though, is that in an evolutionary context competition and monopoly are part of the same process. Greater competition implies a greater incentive to use divergent research strategies to lessen the anticipated erosion of quasirents caused by competition among rival innovations in the postinnovation market. In this chapter, we shall explore the idea that the important link from structure to performance is that greater competition increases socially desirable diversity in research.

Thus, we shall consider the possibility that the rivalry of numerous competitors causes them to establish unique research strategies. The competitors will pursue different variations of the one general type of innovation being sought by them all, and the competitors will use different methods of search. Greater structural competition, then, is associated with a larger number of sellers, each of which is monopoly-like in the sense that each has a unique R&D strategy. My evidence in this chapter shows a correlation between structural competition and the significance of such monopoly-like distinctions among sellers. I shall explain that such diversity may well be socially optimal.

Section 11.2 describes industrial R&D in a way that allows research diversity to be understood. Section 11.3 explains why rivalry may increase such diversity by employing a very simple model that differs from our model in Chapter 8, which focused on the case in which competitors were pursuing the same R&D result. The model of Chapter 8 was designed to explain the motives for a firm to diversify its R&D efforts – that is, the firm's motives for spreading its R&D effort over several industries – and to provide the analytical framework for our policy suggestions in Chapter 14. To explain the motives for R&D diversification, Chapter 8's model focused on the equilibrium in R&D among firms seeking the same result and observed that product-line diversification can be a way that the individual firm tries to increase its expected profits. We focused on the case in which all of the firms pursued the same R&D result because some of the motives for diversification that are deduced result from the competition that the case models. Motives present in the absence of such competition, such as cost reduction, are present as well in the case examined in Chapter 8. Our use of the assumption that the winner of the R&D race takes all did not affect our predictions about the desire to use diversification to escape the competitive equilibrium. Our predictions would hold a fortiori without the assumption. Further, Chapter 8's model focused on the case where the R&D rivals pursue the same result with a winner-takes-all assumption, because study of that case lets us understand the value of pure competitive pressure. Then in Chapter 14 we can suggest policies that mimic the desirable aspects of such pressure. But in the present chapter, in Section 11.3, we shall focus, with a very simple uncluttered model, on how relaxing the assumption that the winner takes all provides an explanation for another type of behavior. In particular, relaxing the assumption provides an explanation for research diversity – that is, for R&D competitors using different approaches to the R&D effort and R&D outcome.

Section 11.4 offers evidence of firm effects in R&D strategies and a correlation between structural competition and the significance of monopoly-like distinctions among sellers. Section 11.5 argues that the diversity in R&D strategies that is created by R&D competitors can be socially beneficial, just as the product differentiation created by Chamberlin's (1933) monopolistically competitive firms can create social benefits.

## 11.2 Research as a way to find a component gestalt

Innovations are new bundles of components that work together; the components have consistent attributes. The integration of an innovation's components achieves *component gestalt* – the necessary integration of components. Basic research and the creative inventive act conceive the components in their essential working configuration. Development refines their integration. With the development process, enough is known so that trial and error by the firm, although typically costly, focuses on the possibilities for performance attributes of the R&D project's components.[1]

A component here could be a part of what might itself be viewed as a component. For example, the development of a hypersonic transatmospheric aircraft would entail development work on the aircraft's exterior. That work could be construed as a project in itself requiring development of "components" including the material, the fabrication process, and the design.

A complete R&D product requires research on all components of the project (not *necessarily* in-house, but perhaps most efficiently so – within a diversified firm – Chapter 8 and Teece, 1980), and success requires an outcome for which the components' performance attributes are consistent.

Table 11.1. *The extent of component gestalt:*
$C = 5; Z = 840$

| $x^a$ | General patterns[b] | Occurrences[c] $= y$ |
|---|---|---|
| 1 | 5 | 840 |
| 2 | 4, 1 | 3,523,800 |
|   | 3, 2 | 7,047,600 |
| 3 | 3, 1, 1 | $5.9058888 \times 10^9$ |
|   | 2, 2, 1 | $8.8588332 \times 10^9$ |
| 4 | 2, 1, 1, 1 | $4.9432289 \times 10^{12}$ |
| 5 | 1, 1, 1, 1, 1 | $4.1325394 \times 10^{14}$ |
| | $\sum y = 4.1821194 \times 10^{14} = Z^C = (840)^5$ | |

[a] $x$ denotes the number of components that are distinct in the sense that they do not mesh.
[b] The general patterns for sets of distinct components consistent with $x$ are shown as integers ordered from largest to smallest, with each integer being the number of consistent components with a particular set of performance attributes.
[c] The number of ways that each particular general pattern could occur is shown in this column.

For example, the research on fabrication must discover a technique compatible with the material developed. A technique requires a material of particular weight and strength. Further, the configuration of the aircraft must be consistent with certain types of materials and fabrication techniques, because the design requires materials and a fabrication process with particular attributes.

The extent of component gestalt achieved can be high or low. Thus, we need the same probability distribution that we used in Chapter 3; the differences are only in interpretation. Table 11.1 illustrates a project that has five components. The component gestalt is greatest when all five components mesh; it is lowest when none of the components function together. Letting $x$ denote the number of distinct project components – distinct in the sense that they do not mesh, $x$ ranges from 1 through 5 as the project's component gestalt varies from high to low. When $x$ is one, all five components work together. If $x$ were two, either four components function together and one does not mesh, or one group of three compatible components and another group of two constitute the outcome. Thus, when $x = 2$, the general patterns for sets of distinct components are 4 and 1 or

3 and 2. When $x = 5$, the only general pattern is 1, 1, 1, 1, and 1. Each of the five components is distinct – does not mesh. To mesh, their performance attributes must be compatible. If the project is the development of a pollution-free engine, and the fuel developed burns hot, but the combustion chamber cannot take the heat given the design and the materials, then the fuel and the combustion chamber do not mesh.

Let $C$ denote the number of project components, where the project could be the grand project (such as the plane) or a proper subset (such as the fuselage). Let $Z$ be the number of ways each component could turn out for the set of characteristics that must mesh across all components. That meshing or consistency is necessary for a successful innovation. Yet for the typical R&D project given $C$ and $Z$ only a small proportion of the $Z^C$ possible outcomes will exhibit the necessary consistency. As in Chapter 3, let $y$ be the number of ways that each particular general pattern for sets of distinct components could occur. Then, the expression for $y$ given in Section 3.2 of Chapter 3 is precisely the expression needed here. The variables $q_{ij}$ and so forth take their appropriate meanings (see Scott, 1991a) for the new context.

For a nontrivial R&D problem $Z$ is large relative to $C$, and consequently, most of the possible development outcomes have low degrees of component gestalt.[2] The absolute number of development outcomes with a high degree of component gestalt is typically large and increases with complexity (measured directly by $Z$). As a proportion of the total number of outcomes, however, the high component gestalt cases are rare – increasingly rare as project complexity increases. The small proportion of the sample space associated with high component gestalt shrinks as the complexity of the development task increases. Table 11.2 illustrates how complexity increases the large proportion of the sample space for which none of the components mesh.

The foregoing abstraction, which is used throughout this chapter, is consistent with the following observations about innovation:

(a) Genius, or at least the flash of insight, is necessary to conceive the $C$ components of an innovation; accumulated knowledge and trial and error are necessary to develop the consistency of the components' performance attributes.

(b) Unless basic science and applied experience are strong, the development process for complex innovations entails costly trial and error to uncover consistent outcomes, because the proportion of the sample space for which components are consistent is small.

(c) There are an immense absolute number of potential solutions to an R&D problem; hence, there is room for diversity of solutions.

Table 11.2. *For an R&D project with five (C = 5) project components, the proportion of the sample space for which there is no component gestalt - i.e., all project-component vectors are distinct - as the project becomes more complex (as Z increases)*[a]

| Z | $y/Z^C$ |
|---|---|
| 100 | 0.90345 |
| 1,000 | 0.990035 |
| 10,000 | 0.999 |
| 100,000 | 0.9999 |
| 1,000,000 | 0.99999 |

[a] For comparison, in this (1, 1, 1, 1, 1) case where $x = 5$ and $Z = 840$ in the numerical example provided in Table 11.1, $y = 4.1325394 \times 10^{14}$, and $y/Z^5 = 0.988145$.

## 11.3  Rivalry and diversity

A research strategy includes a choice of the number of components $C$ and of complexity $Z$. My hypothesis is that competing firms, with identical capabilities and opportunities, choose different R&D strategies to increase the expected value of their innovative investment. Given that patents, trade secrets, or first-mover advantages protect innovations from imitation, and given that innovating firms would not anticipate a sole winner of a patent on the innovation sought (but rather patented, competing substitutes), the firms would want research strategies that make more likely a single winner, rather than multiple winners, for each R&D rivalry. Assuming that the rich technological opportunities suggested by Section 11.2 are sufficiently valuable, greater competition implies greater incentive to use such divergent research strategies, because in their absence the erosion of quasi-rents, caused by competition among rival innovations in the postinnovation market, would be more severe. Of course, with somewhat diverse anticipated outcomes and no sole winner, even a free-entry Nash equilibrium in research will leave some lumps of rent. Those rents, however, will be less the greater the number of postinnovation rivals.

To develop the idea that rivalry may drive firms to use more diverse research strategies, I shall use a simple model of independent R&D trials to explain why R&D rivals would have an incentive to create, for any particular innovation, a competition that only one firm will win. Research entails an outlay of resources in anticipation of an uncertain return. Suppose that a unit of R & D input allows one trial with the probability of success equal to $n_1/(n_1 + n_2)$, where a trial has $n_1$ chances for success and $n_2$ chances for failure. Since not all consistent outcomes have value, $n_1 < Z$, the number of consistent outcomes.

Let $V$ denote a monopolist's total private value of successful innovation, regardless of the number of successful, consistent component configurations introduced. Thus, whether one, two, or more of the $n_1$ potential successful innovations were introduced, multiple innovations would share the market and total private value would be $V$.

What then is the monopolist's expected net benefit, $B$, from innovative investment? It is

$$B_m = \left\{ \sum_{i=1}^{f} (V)\Omega_{f,i} \left[ \frac{n_1^i n_2^{f-i}}{(n_1 + n_2)^f} \right] \right\} - \text{Cost}(f),$$

where $f$ is the number of research trials and $\Omega_{f,i}$ denotes the number of combinations of $f$ things taken $i$ at a time. The formulation follows because $n_1^i n_2^{f-i}/(n_1 + n_2)^f$ is the probability of each set of $i$ successful trials and $\Omega_{f,i}$ gives the number of such sets. The monopolist conducts trials up to the point where one more trial would add less to the expected benefit than to cost. Since, as trials increase, the marginal benefit of a trial diminishes, there is an optimal number of trials (Nelson, 1961; Nelson, 1982b; Evenson and Kislev, 1976).

We can now depict a noncooperative equilibrium that is identical to the monopoly solution. If each firm conducts only one trial, then with $V(i)$ denoting the value of innovative investment to an individual firm when $i$ firms succeed in discovering one of the $n_1$ substitutes, expected profit for the individual firm given $f$ firms in the market is

$$B_c = \left\{ \sum_{i=1}^{f} V(i)\Omega_{f-1,i-1} \left[ \frac{n_1^i n_2^{f-i}}{(n_1 + n_2)^f} \right] \right\} - \text{Cost}(1).$$

As before, the expression containing $n_1$ and $n_2$ denotes the probability of each set of $i$ successful trials and $\Omega_{f-1,i-1}$ is the number of ways the individual firm can be among $i$ winners.

Now, we have the following result: With each firm maximizing its expected profit under the assumptions that it will do $(1/j)$th of the total innovative investment (where $j$ is the number of firms undertaking innovative investment) and that its postinnovation market share will be $1/i$ (where $i$ is the number of firms innovating in a given state of nature), the total amount of innovative investment in the industry will be *in equilibrium* at an amount equal to the amount undertaken by a monopoly if the number of firms equals the number of units of innovative investment that would be undertaken by the monopoly.

For the proof of our result: First, $B_m(f) = f[B_c(f)]$, since each term within the summation sign for $B_c$ is $(1/f)$ times the corresponding term for $B_m$. From Chamberlin (1929) and Osborne (1976), we know (given our assumptions) that $V(i) = V/i$. Then, for $B_c$ the terms are

$$V(i)\Omega_{f-1,i-1}\left[\frac{n_1^i n_2^{f-i}}{(n_1+n_2)^f}\right]$$

$$= \frac{V}{i}\frac{(f-1)(f-2)\cdots((f-1)-(i-1)+1)}{(i-1)(i-2)\cdots(1)}\left[\frac{n_1^i n_2^{f-i}}{(n_1+n_2)^f}\right]$$

$$= \frac{1}{f}V\Omega_{f,i}\left[\frac{n_1^i n_2^{f-i}}{(n_1+n_2)^f}\right].$$

Since by assumption $\text{Cost}(f) = f(\text{Cost}(1))$, we have $(1/f)B_m(f) = B_c(f)$. But if the number of firms is equal to the $f$ that maximizes $B_m$, those $f$ firms will find that they have no incentive to change their innovative investment. To undertake more investment *symmetrically* clearly lowers total profits $B_m(f) = fB_c(f)$ and, in fact, individual firm profits, since $2fB_c(f+f) < fB_c(f)$ implies $2B_c(f+f) < B_c(f)$. To undertake less investment would mean abandoning a profitable project. Thus, this noncollusive outcome, identical to the monopoly outcome, is an equilibrium and the proof of the result is complete. It is a specialized, stochastic version of the equilibrium adduced in Chapter 2 for multimarket oligopolists.

The exposition of the result clarifies why rivalry in research will usually not result in an equilibrium identical to the monopoly solution. The conditions needed to get the monopoly solution included (1) symmetric innovative investments for each of the firms, with the number of firms exactly equal to the ratio of the monopolist's number of trials to the number of trials undertaken by each competitor, (2) no scale economies for multiple trials, and (3) Chamberlin's (1929) or Osborne's (1976) noncooperative joint profit–maximizing equilibrium in the postinnovation market. Typically we would expect these conditions to be violated in the real world, and we would expect that rivalry in R&D would cause firms to expect rivalry among competing substitutes in the postinnovation market. Would R&D then be higher or lower? Would it be qualitatively different?

With the expectation of competing substitutes, for competition the total expected profit for all of the firms together would typically be less than what the monopolist expects. Of course, many theorists have shown that, in spite of the low profits, the competitors in such a game might well spend more on R&D than would the monopolist (Baldwin and Scott, 1987). But the low profits and high R&D expenditures make this an unattractive game from a private standpoint, and consequently, R&D competitors have an incentive to incur costs that a monopolist would not want to incur, solely to change the R&D game for a particular innovation into one that only a single firm could win. For then, given that the rivals do all pursue a unique form of the innovation and do not simply allow each other to pursue particular innovations alone, each firm's innovative investment costs would yield the expected benefit $(1/j)$th of the monopolist's benefit given $j$ trials, an expectation greater than the expected benefits with competition:

$$\left\{ \sum_{i=1}^{j} V(i)\Omega_{j-1,\,i-1}\left[\frac{n_1^i n_2^{j-i}}{(n_1+n_2)^j}\right]\right\},$$

given that $V(i) < V/i$.

To create a research game that only one firm could win, the rivals would pursue diverse strategies aimed at producing a unique product unlikely to be considered a mere substitute for competing innovations, but instead likely to have a decisive advantage that would drive other innovations from the postinnovation market. Even if one R&D strategy seems more promising than the next best alternative, once the preferred strategy has been preemptively taken by a rival, a firm can prefer an alternative that has some chance of finding a dominant innovation. However, our discussion of the sample space suggests that the immense number of possible solutions may yield numerous strategies that are, a priori, equally likely to succeed. A monopolist would not have an incentive to incur the costs of ensuring diverse outcomes for trials in order to increase the likelihood of just one dominant product, since regardless of the number of trials producing successful, substitutable innovations, the monopolist gains the same expected benefit. Substitutable products commercialized as a result of the monopolist's R&D trials will not create rent-eroding price competition in the postinnovation market.

## 11.4 Evidence of competition-induced diversity

The evidence below suggests that at least in a special statistical sense rivalry and diversity are synonymous; differences among an industry's firms are more significant when seller concentration is lower. However, the effect of rivalry on diversity is not captured by traditional correlations of R&D behavior and market structure. Instead of the traditional observations, I observe, given competitors in an area of R&D, distinct R&D strategies, including differences in systems orientation, R&D intensity, and purposive diversification of R&D.

If rivalry does induce diversity, I should observe differences in R&D strategies of firms in the same area of R&D. My test assumes that, in the absence of random error, a complete model would exhibit a definite relationship among $n$ nonstochastic variables, $(y_1, y_2, \ldots, y_i, \ldots, y_n)$, describing industries, firms, and lines of business (LBs), where an LB is the operation of a firm in a particular industry category. That relationship would be $\Gamma(y_1, y_2, \ldots, y_i, \ldots, y_n) = 0$, where, for example, one of the variables is the LB variable $y_i$, which is the proportion of the LB's patent portfolio devoted to systems or subsystems – i.e., developments that integrate components (in the ordinary sense). Then, we observe $y_i$ where $y_i = \Psi(y_1, y_2, \ldots, y_{i-1}, y_{i+1}, \ldots, y_n) + \epsilon$, where $\epsilon$ is homoskedastic random error, with mean zero, uncorrelated with $y_j$, $j \neq i$, and where the function $\Psi$ is approximated well by a function linear in its parameters but not in its variables. Then estimations ask whether LB, firm-specific, and industry variables explain a substantial portion of the variance in $y_i$ in ways predicted by theory.

As we have seen in Chapters 7 and 10, Schumpeterian hypotheses about LB size, firm size, diversification, and industry concentration have not explained much of the variance in R&D intensity.[3] The discussion here, however, suggests new tests using $y_i$. First, it predicts strong firm effects since firms in the same industries will choose different strategies (including different $C$'s and $Z$'s) and thus have different proportions of their patent portfolios devoted to developing systems – i.e., collections of innovations that work together in an integrated whole to accomplish a typically complex task. The various strategies of the firms should vary markedly in outlays for R&D; the strategies span different sets of industry categories.

*Systems orientation of patent portfolios:* Conceivably, the often examined characteristics of firms could affect their choice of the portions of their R&D portfolios to devote to the development of systems. Very large firms and diversified firms might be more likely to undertake the more costly development projects that attempt to integrate greater numbers of components. Smaller and less diversified firms might tend to focus on the less costly, less integrated projects as well as on less costly, more basic research. That would be consistent with, but not the same as, the observations of Jewkes et al. (1958), Scherer (1980, pp. 416–417), and Mansfield et al. (1977a) that smaller firms may tend to *invent* but larger firms tend to *develop* industrial products and processes.

Whether the choice of $C$ and $Z$ (the number of components and the complexity of their integration) in *development* projects differs significantly across firms of different size is the issue in this chapter. Since the proportion of the sample space for which component gestalt is high is typically quite small for complex systems developments, greater R&D outlays will be necessary to find solutions not among the relatively plentiful low gestalt solutions. My theory also predicts strong industry effects.

Industries differ in the value and cost of achieving various degrees of component gestalt, and that will cause differences in systems orientation, apart from any effects of differences in competition. Other dimensions of the diversity of firms' patent portfolios could of course be explored. Most important, the concept of systematic gestalt will be inapplicable to some research-intensive industries. The estimated industry effects should capture such differences across industries, and the question is whether or not intraindustry variance in systems orientation remains.

While we can extend earlier studies by asking if the Schumpeterian characteristics of size, diversification, and concentration are correlated with systems orientation, the new approach is to ask if more rivalry – i.e., more firms doing R&D – does lead to diversity in the form of a filling of more sample space niches. Such diversity will be indicated if we discover firm effects in R&D activity. Rivalry can lead not only to more socially desirable levels of R&D, but to more socially desirable composition of R&D – indeed to less duplication in the sense that less of the R&D effort is focused on a given strategy or portion of the sample space. Perhaps seller concentration is correlated with rivalry and is therefore important for understanding differences in systems R&D across industries. But my theory predicts intra-industry differences among firms rather than a conventional partial correlation between firm behavior and seller concentration.

F. M. Scherer provided me with the patent characteristics data for the mid-1970s patents of the 1819 Federal Trade Commission (FTC) LBs described and studied in Scherer (1983a). His data are used here to explore the extent to which LB, firm, and industry characteristics are correlated with systems developments among large U.S. manufacturing firms. The LB-level variables include a measure of $y_i$, the dependent variable, denoted SYST; it is the fraction of an LB's patents pertaining to systems or subsystems. SYST is measured as a proportion with mean equal to 0.39. All other variables are described in detail in the Appendix. They include two additional LB variables. One is the ratio of contract R&D outlays to total R&D outlays; the other is the sales in an LB. Company-level variables are a measure of diversification and a measure of firm size. Additionally, $D_i$ denotes a dummy variable for the $i$th firm. A measure of seller concentration is an industry-level variable, and $T_j$ denotes a dummy variable for the $j$th industry.

Scherer (1983a, pp. 124–125) uses the 1819 observation sample and regresses SYST on a measure of LB sales and technological class dummies. After duplicating those results, I extended the analysis as follows.[4]

Equation (11.1) shows that industry effects alone explain 49 percent of the variance in SYST, and Equation (11.2) shows that firm effects alone can explain 46 percent of SYST's variance.

$$\text{SYST} = z + \sum_{j=2}^{238} \gamma_j T_j$$
$$(F = 6.5)^a$$

(11.1)

$F$-value $= 6.5,^a$ $R^2 = 0.49$, degrees of freedom $= 1581$.

$$\text{SYST} = z + \sum_{i=2}^{397} \beta_i D_i$$
$$(F = 3.1)^a$$

(11.2)

$F$-value $= 3.1,^a$ $R^2 = 0.46$, degrees of freedom $= 1422$.

In equation (11.3), we see that firm and industry effects together explain 64 percent of the variance in SYST.[5]

$$\text{SYST} = z + \sum_{i=2}^{397} \beta_i D_i + \sum_{j=2}^{235} \gamma_j T_j$$
$$(F = 1.3)^{a^*} \quad (F = 2.6)^a$$

(11.3)

$F$-value $= 3.4,^a$ $R^2 = 0.64$, degrees of freedom $= 1188$.

When interpreting the results, remember that when firm (industry) dummies are included, firm (industry) level variables cannot be. The effects of the latter are nested within the effects controlled by the dummies.[6] Further, remember that I am describing correlations and their strengths, not identifying the direction of causal links. Formally, the direction of causality is not specified, but I assume that the error in an equation is uncorrelated with the included variables.

Unlike models of symmetric Nash equilibria, my description of industrial R&D implies that firm effects as well as industry effects will be important. Further, the hypotheses about Schumpeterian variables imply that both firm and industry effects will be present and important in SYST. They clearly are. Beyond that observation, we cannot proceed with confidence to unambiguous effects of particular firm-specific or industry variables, other things being equal, because as shown in the Appendix, the traditional variables explored here explain only a small portion of the variance explained by the dummy variables, and hence, by all relevant firm and industry variables. The results, as shown in the equations provided in the Appendix, are as follows.

Although left-out industry variables no doubt affect the coefficient, even after control for firm effects, seller concentration is associated with relatively extensive systems developments. Possibly the correlation reflects fewer niches to be filled in industry categories where systems development is important, but the left-out variable problem renders any story inconclusive. Here, as with the variables studied subsequently, if we had found that the particular industry (firm) level variable or variables explored explained a large portion of the variance explained by the industry (firm) dummies, we could have had some confidence in the correlations as reflections of effects, other things being equal. However, seller concentration alone explains at most only 1.6 percent of the variance in systems orientation.

More diversified firms did more systems work, but that is because they tend to be in industries where more systems work is done. Further, diversification explains less than 1 percent of the variance in SYST. An increase in overall firm size is associated with a lower proportion of an LB's patents devoted to systems, but the effect is small, is barely significant, and explains far less than 1 percent of the variance. As we would expect, contract work tends to support development of systems (since federal government contracts often support such work), but firm and industry effects explain the presence of contracted R&D, which when entered alone explains about 3 percent of the variance in SYST. LB sales is not significant in complete specifications, adding virtually nothing to explanatory power.[7]

*R&D intensity:* Evidence of firm effects in R&D intensity also supports the idea that firms in the same industry categories pursue different R&D strategies. The importance of firm versus industry effects in R&D has been documented in Chapter 7. Table 11.3 shows new evidence. Instead of controlling for FTC four-digit industry effects as we did in Chapter 7, the effects of the differences among 20 Standard Industrial Classification (SIC) two-digit manufacturing industries and the 127 groups are controlled, each group being a related set of FTC four-digit industries found in Chapter 9. Each group consists of a set of industry categories for which R&D activities were found to be complementary, with shared R&D facilities or spillovers (among the categories) of knowledge generated by R&D. The dependent variable is an observation of R&D intensity for 1974–76 for each LB (i.e., the activities of a firm in an FTC four-digit manufacturing category) in Chapter 6's sample for which there was R&D activity throughout the sample period. R&D intensity is measured as the ratio of LB total (applied) R&D to LB sales.

Table 11.3 is consistent with the prediction that firms differ in their R&D intensity, even after industry or group effects have been accounted for in the statistical procedure. The discussion in Section 11.3 implies that firms will differ simply because they choose to differ, thereby increasing the likelihood that for any given project only one competitor will win the R&D contest. In Table 11.3, the firm as well as the industry and group effects are significant.[8] Yet previous studies of R&D intensity have shown

Table 11.3. *Observations for 352 sample firms reporting R&D throughout the sample period for one or more FTC four-digit manufacturing categories*[a]

|  | (1) | (2) | (3) | (4)[b] |
|---|---|---|---|---|
| 351 Firm effects | $F=1.7$ |  |  | Fitted last $F=1.5$ |
| 19 2-Digit industry effects |  | $F=14$ |  | Fitted last $F=4.7$ |
| 127 Group effects |  |  | $F=2.3$ | Fitted last $F=1.7$ |
| Intercept | $z$ | $z$ | $z$ | $z$ |
| $F$-ratio | 1.7 | 14 | 2.3 | 2.0 |
| $R$-square | 0.23 | 0.10 | 0.12 | 0.36 |
| Degrees of freedom | 1963 | 2295 | 2187 | 1817 |

[a] The dependent variable is RS (LB total R&D)/(LB sales) for the 2315 observations on LBs existing for all three years and in which some R&D was performed. All $F$-ratios are highly significant, far beyond the conventional 0.01 level. To reduce the size of the $X'X$ matrix for computational purposes, in some specifications firm effects were absorbed, and then the $R^2$ and $F$-tests were constructed using the information from several regressions.
[b] To get column (4), with variables in deviation form, I regressed RS on the industry dummies, RS on the group dummies, RS on the industry dummies and the group dummies. And then, with the variables not as deviations, I regressed RS on the industry dummies and the group dummies. In other words, I fit everything except the group effects, everything except the industry effects, everything, and then everything except the firm effects. I then used the sums of squares thereby obtained with the appropriate degrees of freedom to construct column (4). For a complete description, in a simpler context, of how these regressions are used to get the $F$'s for effects fitted last, see Scott (1984, p. 244).

that the traditional variables identified as factors in Schumpeterian competition explain very little of that systematic variance in R&D intensity.[9]

My hypothesis suggests as a conjecture that, in the FTC LB sample of very large firms, the firm effects in R&D intensity will be more pronounced in markets with more competitive structures (in the sense of more firms), because there is more need for a firm to strive for a different outcome to avoid erosion of quasi-rents in the postinnovation market. Thus, somewhat paradoxically, more competitive structure would imply more monopoly in the sense of more significant monopoly-like differences among sellers. Although undoubtedly a very indirect test, we would find, then, a positive correlation between insignificance of firm effects and the magnitude of seller concentration. To test this conjecture, let INSIG measure directly the insignificance of the firm effects in R&D intensity within each of the 20 two-digit SIC industries. INSIG is the probability of a larger $F$-value for the $F$ test against the null hypothesis of no firm effects within each two-digit SIC industry. INSIG is taken from Scott (1984, table 10.4, pp. 238–240). Further, let ACR be the adjusted concentration ratio in percentage terms for each of the 20 SIC two-digit industries. ACR is a sales-weighted average of the underlying four-digit FTC adjusted concentration ratios described in Chapter 6.

Then, the conjecture is that INSIG and ACR are positively correlated, and I do find that correlation. For the 20 two-digit industry observations, ACR explains 20 percent of the variance in INSIG, with a significant positive correlation coefficient of 0.45. Inspection of the plot of INSIG on ACR suggests that INSIG increases at an increasing rate as ACR increases. Fitting a quadratic relation gives an insignificant coefficient on the unsquared term; the more parsimonious functional form with only the squared term yields:

$$INSIG = 0.0629 + 0.000126\,ACR^2$$
$$(t = 0.520) \qquad (t = 2.33)$$

with $R^2 = 0.232$. ACR, then, as it ranges from 15.66 to 73.84 in the sample, has a large predicted inverse impact on the significance of differences in R&D intensity. Moving from the least concentrated to the most concentrated two-digit industry increases from 0.0938 to 0.750 the predicted probability of a greater $F$-value for firm effects. Thus, greater competitive structure is associated, in a sense, with more monopoly.

*Purposive diversification:* Chapters 9 and 10 provide another test of the idea that firms in the same industry will pursue different R&D strategies. Our evidence in those chapters shows that firms in a given industry category typically have quite different patterns of purposive R&D diversification and that, even in the same industry category, R&D intensity differs for firms with different diversification patterns. That a firm's idiosyncratic research strategy encompasses multiple industries is consistent with firm effects in the statistical sense: A firm effect is associated with the firm regardless of the industry category where the firm is observed.

## 11.5 Conclusion

Models of R&D rivalry have typically described symmetric innovative investment outcomes for the firms in an industry and have not addressed the presence of firm effects. The paradoxical fact is that different firms in the same industries pursue different R&D strategies. There are two possible explanations: (1) firms are fundamentally different in their capabilities; (2) the R&D environment would lead to asymmetric strategies even if all firms were identical. The second explanation for firm effects was developed in Section 11.3; both explanations are consistent with evidence of firm effects in Section 11.4. The absence of any identifiable variables that explain the variance in the systems orientation of LB patent portfolios, however, supports the second explanation, because without such variables it appears that different strategies are chosen by firms otherwise identical, not differing in any LB, firm, or industry variables other than those like SYST that reflect the deliberate choice of a different strategy in order to avoid rent-destroying competition. Further, the previous studies of R&D intensity have shown that the traditional Schumpeterian variables explain very little of the systematic variance in R&D intensity. Yet, as we have seen, unidentified firm and industry effects do explain a large part of that variance; hence, our examination of R&D intensity also supports the second explanation, which could usefully be pursued with case studies. Indeed, that second explanation – *firms with identical capabilities and opportunities employ different strategies* – could also explain the failure, documented in Chapter 6, of traditional industrial organization models to capture much of the systematic variance in LB profitability.

Rivalry among firms, then, causes them to pursue different R&D strategies in order to turn each innovation project into a game that only one firm can win. Such research diversity induced by rivalry could improve social economic welfare if a monopolist of R&D would underinvest in diversity. Arguably a monopolist would underinvest in research diversity because much of its social value would not be appropriated by the monopolist.[10] As with innovative investment more generally, rivalry can induce behavior that is socially optimal even though it reduces the total industry profits appropriated privately (Barzel, 1968; Scherer, 1980, p. 431, note 79; Scott, 1988). Paradoxically, such socially optimal behavior induced by Schumpeterian rivalry occurs in markets that are both competitive in the sense that there are several firms vying for the innovation, and monopolistic in the sense that the firms use distinctive R&D strategies and anticipate only one dominant innovation.

### Appendix

In addition to SYST, which is discussed in the text, the line of business-level variables include FED, the ratio of contract R&D outlays to total R&D outlays, measured as a percentage. The mean of FED is 6.57. SALES, the sales in an LB, is the final LB variable, measured in millions of 1974 dollars, and its mean is 266.38. There are two company-level variables. The first is a measure of diversification,

$$\text{DIVERS} = 1 \bigg/ \sum_{i=1}^{n} s_i^2,$$

where $s_i$ is the share of the company's sales in the $i$th of its $n$ LBs, and the second is a measure of firm size, FIRMSIZE, which is total sales for the entire company. For a firm having equal sales in each category, DIVERS therefore would show the number of different industry categories in which the firm operated. For the 1819-observation sample, the mean of DIVERS is 6.035. FIRMSIZE was measured in thousands of 1974 dollars. Additionally, $D_i$ denotes a dummy variable for the $i$th firm. CR4 is an industry-level variable which is a weighted average index of 1972 four-firm seller concentration in meaningfully defined components of the FTC LB categories. The variable is developed, discussed, and used in Scherer (1983a, p. 118). It is measured as a percentage, and its mean in the 1819-observation sample is 43.37. Finally, $T_j$ denotes a dummy variable for the $j$th industry.

The additional equations estimated are given here in the order in which they are discussed in the text. Although to estimate the firm effects in the following specifications the effects were absorbed to reduce the size of the $X'X$ matrix, the $F$-values for firm effects (as well as the industry effects) are for the effects when fitted last and are derived using additional estimations in the same manner as in Scott (1984, p. 244). Significance levels for a one-tailed test are noted as $a = 0.0001$ or better, $b = 0.05$ or better, $c = 0.10$ or better, and $a^*$ is recorded for the $F$-value that I computed as in Scott (1984, p. 244) and for which I did not have a computer-generated probability value. Computing the relevant integral is burdensome given the large numbers of degrees of freedom, but the result is obviously highly significant.

$$SYST = z + \sum_{i=2}^{397} \beta_i D_i + 0.00074\,CR4$$
$$(F = 3.0)^a \qquad (t = 1.5)^c \tag{11.4}$$

$F$-value $= 3.1,^a\ R^2 = 0.47$, degrees of freedom $= 1421$.

$$SYST = 0.27 + 0.0027\,CR4$$
$$(t = 12)^a \qquad (t = 5.4)^a \tag{11.5}$$

$F$-value $= 29,^a\ R^2 = 0.016$, degrees of freedom $= 1817$.

As noted above, FIRMSIZE was measured in thousands of 1974 dollars. When I began this project I was no longer a consultant at the FTC's LB Program and had to write the research design before the program lost its last research assistant, submit it for the research assistant to carry out, and then, because of strict confidentiality requirements, had to wait to see the results until after they had been cleared through the FTC and after the last research assistant had left the program. Therefore, I did not realize until receiving the cleared printouts that with the scaling of FIRM-SIZE and the number of spaces allocated on the printout for a coefficient, the statistically significant (barely – at the 0.10 level for a one-tailed test) negative coefficient for FIRMSIZE was reported to me as a negative sign followed by a zero, a decimal point, and then a string of seven zeros. I had asked for FIRMSIZE as $\Sigma$ SALES, which would have scaled it in millions, but the proper variable was taken directly from the reporting form in thousands. I report the coefficient below in Equations (11.6) and (11.7) as $d$. The computer did report the ratio of the coefficient to its standard error. Thus, all I can report for this variable is that its effect is negative, barely significant, and not large. Its absolute value must be less than 0.0000001. Thus, an increase in overall firm size is associated with a lower proportion of an LB's patents devoted to systems, but an increase in firm size of 1 billion 1974 dollars lowers that proportion by less than 0.1. How much less, however, I cannot say.

$$\text{SYST} = z + \sum_{j=2}^{238} \gamma_j T_j - 0.00023\,\text{DIVERS} - d\,\text{FIRMSIZE}$$
$$(F = 6.4)^a \qquad (t = -0.12) \qquad (t = -1.4)^c \qquad (11.6)$$

$F$-value $= 6.4$,$^a$ $R^2 = 0.49$, degrees of freedom $= 1579$.

$$\text{SYST} = 0.34 + 0.0082\,\text{DIVERS} - d\,\text{FIRMSIZE}$$
$$(t = 20)^a \qquad (t = 3.8)^a \qquad (t = -0.33) \qquad (11.7)$$

$F$-value $= 7.1$,$^b$ $R^2 = 0.0077$, degrees of freedom $= 1816$.

$$\text{SYST} = z + \sum_{i=2}^{397} \beta_i D_i + \sum_{j=2}^{235} \gamma_j T_j + 0.00043\,\text{FED} - 0.0000011\,\text{SALES}$$
$$(F = 1.3)^{a^*} \quad (F = 2.54)^a \qquad (t = 0.73) \qquad\qquad (t = -0.09) \qquad (11.8)$$

$F$-value $= 3.4$,$^a$ $R^2 = 0.64$, degrees of freedom $= 1186$.

$$\text{SYST} = 0.37 + 0.0036\,\text{FED} - 0.0000081\,\text{SALES}$$
$$(t = 37)^a \quad (t = 7.7)^a \qquad (t = -0.82) \qquad (11.9)$$

$F$-value $= 30$,$^a$ $R^2 = 0.032$, degrees of freedom $= 1816$.

$$\text{SYST}$$
$$= z + \sum_{i=2}^{397} \beta_i D_i + 0.00069\,\text{CR4} + 0.00094\,\text{FED} - 0.0000045\,\text{SALES}$$
$$(F = 2.9)^a \qquad (t = 1.4)^c \qquad (t = 1.9)^b \qquad (t = -0.48) \qquad (11.10)$$

$F$-value $= 3.1$,$^a$ $R^2 = 0.47$, degrees of freedom $= 1419$.

$$\text{SYST} = 0.27 + 0.0023 \text{ CR4} + 0.0033 \text{ FED} - 0.000013 \text{ SALES}$$
$$(t = 12)^a \qquad (t = 4.5)^a \qquad\qquad (t = 7.0)^a \qquad\qquad (t = -1.4)^c \qquad (11.11)$$

$$F\text{-value} = 27,^a \ R^2 = 0.043, \ \text{degrees of freedom} = 1815.$$

Finally, the small negative effect associated with firm size does appear to be independent of the size of the LB. Controlling for the 237 industry effects, DIVERS, FED, and SALES, the coefficient on FIRMSIZE is again negative with a $t$-ratio of $-1.26$. Against the null hypothesis of a zero coefficient, the probability of a $t$-ratio that low or lower is 0.10435.

# PART IV

## Industrial policy

# 12

## Diversification versus cooperation in R&D

In this chapter, I shall use the ideas and findings from the preceding chapters to compare the diversification of R&D in the mid-1970s with the mid-1980s cooperative R&D that is protected by the National Cooperative Research Act of 1984 (NCRA, U.S. 98th Congress, October 1984). The evidence suggests that the effect of the law may well be to reduce innovative investment and cause investment to be further away from the socially optimal amount. Yet the NCRA model has been touted by business executives, economists, and policymakers as a way to improve U.S. industrial performance, and has become the basis for new law encouraging production joint ventures, as we shall see in Chapter 13.

I shall ask whether the initial response to the NCRA suggests that the act stimulated the types of activity envisioned by those supporting the new law. With the exception of a few examples, I use the first year and a half of data about the coooperative ventures registering under the new law because that seemed a large enough amount of information about initial reaction to gain some insight into whether the behavior reflected the concerns of the law's architects. I explore the issue in its historical context. For example, did the NCRA stimulate R&D in industries where the productivity slump hit hard, as the arguments made in support of the legislation suggested that it would? Of course, the desire to stimulate R&D in industries subject to a productivity slump may have been misguided. I shall compare the initial NCRA activity with the expectations for the law and then speculate about the social economic welfare implications of the law. What happened subsequently reflects a different historical context, although the results would perhaps be quite similar. Further, since I make my comparisons using the data of the now defunct U.S. FTC LB Program, I cannot carry the sample too far.

Chapter 12 is a revision of Scott (1988).

### 12.1 Introduction and outline

I shall use both theory and evidence to compare firms' diversified R&D with the cooperative R&D protected by the NCRA. R&D diversification and cooperative R&D are related theoretically because both can be understood by studying the behavior of a firm in a competitive environment for which the private and the public value of innovative investment diverge, and because diversification and cooperation provide alternative ways of improving appropriation of the returns to R&D. Empirically R&D diversification and cooperative R&D are related because the NCRA-protected cooperative activity occurs in areas similar to those pursued with the R&D of diversified firms.

As shown in Chapter 8, our model of a firm's choice of R&D describes plausible reasons for the diversification of R&D in manufacturing. The model is based on the theoretical literature about market structure and technological change, and it implies that striving for market value via diversified R&D investment will carry firms toward an equilibrium for which the rate of return to innovative investment is normal. The model accords with Chapter 8 where the diversification of R&D effort is hypothesized to be an important driving force behind firms' attempts to appropriate returns from R&D. That hypothesis is supported by the evidence in Chapters 9 and 10 about R&D diversification in U.S. manufacturing.

As Chapter 8 has also explained, cooperative R&D can provide an alternative way of increasing the appropriation of the returns from innovative investment. In Section 12.3, comparison of the diversification of R&D in the mid-1970s with the mid-1980s cooperative R&D that is protected by the NCRA shows that cooperation combines multi-industry research areas that have been combined previously by diversified firms. However, because of the confidentiality of the FTC LB data, I have had to opt for the indirect procedure of juxtaposing the facts about industries combined by diversified firms in the FTC LB sample with the facts about the specific partners listed by the U.S. *Federal Register* for the specific R&D projects protected by the NCRA. Cooperative R&D among partners who plan to use the research output in different product markets is analogous to the increase of R&D productivity through the diversification of the firm. On the other hand, the cooperative R&D may eliminate direct R&D competition of diversified firms if the agreements are between partners who do compete directly in their multimarket R&D. However, my empirical evidence cannot concentrate directly on the extent to which direct R&D rivalry is a property of the participants in the ventures that I study.

In short, although both diversification by individual firms and cooperation among them can increase appropriability, cooperative R&D sacrifices the competition that is present with diversification alone. I shall argue that the evidence about R&D diversification, juxtaposed with evidence about the types of industry categories in which NCRA cooperative ventures are being formed, suggests that diversification in the absence of the NCRA carried innovative investment toward the social optimum while the law discourages investment and takes it away from the social optimum.

Thus, I have fashioned in Chapter 8 a theory of the role of diversification and then in Chapters 9 and 10 observed that the theory seems to be well supported by existing evidence. In this chapter, I go beyond that and hypothesize that diversification by individual firms can probably do more for social economic welfare than the new cooperative R&D protected by the NCRA. My analysis will suggest that the law may not be working well. Given existing data, I cannot test, but instead must settle for developing, a hypothesis that is contrary to conventional wisdom.[1] I shall use the data to suggest that the hypothesis is at least plausible, but I do not confirm it. I think it is important to develop and suggest the plausibility of the possibility that the NCRA is not working well, because an extraordinarily important aspect of economic public policy – namely, public policy promoting industrial organization conducive to technological progress – is at issue. Further, as will be explained further in Chapter 13, the law is being extended to cover cooperative ventures in production, increasing the chances that cooperation will lessen desirable rivalry.

## 12.2 Diversification, cooperation, and the social optimum

Chapter 8 described the equilibrium for rivalrous R&D. The number of competitors is determined endogenously. A major presumption of the NCRA is that firms cannot appropriate a significant amount of the social returns to their innovative investment. That need not be true, especially if cannibalization of existing rents is prevalent. But the presumption is true for those cases in which we want public policy to stimulate R&D. What Chapter 8 has shown is that even when there are appropriability problems, the free-entry Nash noncooperative equilibrium can provide a better solution from society's standpoint than the cooperative result. With diversification to improve expected profits for the individual competing firms, a socially desirable outcome for their R&D investment seems even more likely. Of course, appropriability problems could be so great that without cooperation there would not be enough R&D investment. In this chapter we shall want to ask empirical questions that help to shape our understanding of whether rivalry or cooperation will give superior results.

As shown in Chapter 8, the social value of any particular total amount of R&D depends on market structure. The calculations there of the R&D investment with joint venture activity are for a "short run" which precludes further entry. Such a focus on the short run is perhaps reasonable since the pace of technological change may preclude new long-run adjustments to a zero net present value equilibrium, and since examination of the NCRA filings in the *Federal Register* show that the NCRA ventures typically leave open the invitation for new members. Indeed, the continued filings by NCRA ventures as they add new members suggest that the invitations are important, even though the antitrust enforcement agencies might reasonably prefer that ventures not leave membership open and thereby perhaps leave more competition in the market. In cases where membership is not open or new members are not forthcoming, potential entrants may be disadvantaged to an extent that precludes profitable entry despite the profits of incumbent firms. But it is certainly possible that the effects of NCRA cooperation could be undone by the entry of new firms or new combinations of firms creating equilibria with wasteful duplication. As Nelson and Winter (1982, p. 333) observe, even if we can pin down the relation between market structure and performance, structure is not an obviously manipulatable policy variable.

Our theory in Chapter 8 has shown that it is reasonable to assume that a certain amount of "duplication" of R&D effort, in the sense in Nelson's (1961) parallel paths (and also in the models of Evenson and Kislev, 1976, and Tandon, 1983), is desirable.[2] The innovative efforts of firms have value outcomes which are random variables, but these variables are not perfectly correlated. Each firm provides an experiment, or trial, and for the particular example worked out carefully in Chapter 8, from the standpoint of the socially optimal amount of innovative investment, competition (which we could equate with the outcome under the existing antitrust laws before the NCRA) results in better performance than cooperation.

To understand why this could occur, we need to think about why firms undertake cooperative R&D. They may do so to realize economies of joint operations, including the elimination of wasteful duplication, and to avoid competition that lessens appropriation of returns to innovative investment. If firms cooperating in innovative investment appropriated all of the social returns to their investment and all costs were internal, then the venture would undertake the socially optimal amount of investment in R&D, since social and private marginal benefits and marginal costs would coincide. Since complete appropriation is unlikely, however, the cooperating firms may do too little R&D. Competing firms, on the other hand, anticipate lower returns and hence may also do too little

R&D. However, competitors also overbid for the innovative rewards as they try to preempt one another and as they look only to their own profitable opportunities without regard to the erosion of the total expected profits in the particular area of R&D. It is possible that the stimulus to do R&D because of overbidding will offset the tendency of poorer appropriability conditions and result in a competitive R&D environment getting closer to the socially optimal amount of innovative investment. That is just what happened in our example in Chapter 8.

Our example, it should be pointed up, was constructed to include many features of the industrial R&D environment that are conventionally thought to imply the need for cooperation. Consider now the circumstances believed to favor cooperation. I shall describe five circumstances that are conventionally believed to imply that noncooperative R&D rivalry is undesirable and cooperation among an industry's firms would be socially desirable. Then I point up an important class of joint ventures that would seem to conform to the five conditions and, as it turns out, would be a likely setting for the application of the novel approach to taxation that I shall propose in Chapter 14.

*Five stylized conditions:* First, uncertainty is usually cited as a reason that firms will underinvest in R&D unless they receive tax breaks or cooperate with rivals. In our model of Chapter 8, there is both technical and market uncertainty. Technical uncertainty means that the output of an R&D unit is not certain. Market uncertainty results when for a known R&D output a firm may face profit-reducing competition in the market.

Second, duplication of R&D efforts by uncooperative rivals is cited as a reason for cooperation. In our model of Chapter 8, the R&D efforts of the rivals in an industry are identical to each other in the sense that the relationship between R&D effort and R&D output is the same for every firm. Key, though, *is* technical uncertainty. Thus, although "identical," the relationship between R&D and output *can* yield different results for the competing firms.

Cooperation is usually believed to be desirable when there are, eventually, sharply diminishing returns to R&D units, but at the same time there is a substantial range of increasing returns to combining those units. Thus, third, in our model of Chapter 8, after an initial range of increasing returns, there are sharply diminishing returns to R&D in individual units or trials. But, fourth, there is a substantial range of increasing returns to combining R&D units or trials in a single firm or venture before decreasing returns take hold.

Fifth, cooperation is usually considered necessary when an industry's firms can appropriate only a small portion of the total social returns to an innovation. In our model of Chapter 8, the private value of innovation is just a small fraction of the social value.

*An important class of R&D joint ventures:* Now, these five conditions are not only precisely those that lead firms to argue that cooperative ventures (and tax breaks examined in Chapter 14) are necessary for innovation, they are often considered by policymakers and academics to necessitate such policies. For example, an approximation to the five conditions is perhaps reasonably associated with one type of research joint venture that has been prevalent under the National Cooperative Research Act of 1984 (NCRA) – namely, consortia to carry out research manifestly displaying a social conscience. By this I mean R&D projects for which very little of the social value can be captured privately – even by a monopolist. In extreme form, as Katz and Ordover (1990) observe, such projects might increase fixed costs and simply reduce profits at the optimum price. Or they might provide a benefit which is not perceived directly by consumers or which more generally changes inframarginal consumers' surplus but does not affect the optimal price. However, since the innovations produced by the projects are valued, indeed required in many cases, by government regulators, they will have some private value for the innovator.

Jorde and Teece (1988, p. 100) report that about 30 percent of the NCRA filings (other than membership changes) from January 1985 through June 1988 addressed environmental and health concerns. The continued importance of such filings is apparent from inspection of the NCRA filings during 1991. The filings fitting the category have included for example the Electrically Heated Catalyst Testing Program. Several major petroleum companies and the California Air Resources Board are members of the cooperative program which researches automobile exhaust emissions and potential improvements in air quality that could be obtained by using electrically heated catalysts. The venture's membership remains open but in any case certainly seems to have the major players in the relevant market where the California Clean Air Act has required attention to air pollution.[3]

Such cooperative ventures are clearly aimed at developing new products or processes that will improve the social value of the industry's production. As Katz and Ordover (1990, pp. 172–173) observe, ". . . review of the stated objectives of the registered ventures reveals that many of them are engaged in industry-specific environmental research, safety-related research, or research undertaken in response to governmental directives. These lines of research could potentially be characterized by spillovers (poor appropriability) worse than in the average R&D project in a given industry." The poor appropriability characterizing these projects and the likelihood that they will not impose competitive injury on rivals and hence would not affect firms' best-reply functions and competitive interactions lead Katz and Ordover to conclude (p. 173) that the ". . . pattern suggests that cooperation in these areas has not served as a means of retarding the rate of R&D investment to minimize competitive spillovers."

Katz and Ordover do note (p. 173) that there remains the possibility that the industry's members will use the cooperative venture as a way of coordinating a game against government regulators. However, even if there were no hint of such a game, our models (drawn together in Chapter 8) of noncooperative R&D rivalry suggest that these ventures which so clearly demonstrate an awareness of society's goals – i.e., the ventures with a social conscience – may well be especially likely to lower the social value of the R&D because they eliminate competitive pressure. Chapter 8 shows that this can be true despite the presence of technological and market uncertainty, economies of scale for individual projects and for combining several projects, and most remarkably not only despite but indeed because of the presence of poor appropriability and the duplication of R&D efforts in the absence of the cooperative R&D venture.

The ventures in question certainly look innocuous – indeed, they appear at first blush to be clearly in the public interest. So no one has thought to ask seriously if society is really better served by cooperation or instead by noncooperative rivalry among firms trying to be the first to achieve a technology that would then be diffused rapidly to all in return for a reward far short of its social value. However, it is debatable whether cooperation is a good thing in such cases. Chapter 8 has used theory to demonstrate why. The theory shows that society might well prefer a Nash noncooperative free-entry equilibrium, while the industry's members would prefer to conduct the research jointly with their joint venture controlling the research and then licensing the patented technology to the industry's members.

Thus, if firms had complete appropriability of the social benefits of their research, the cooperation fostered by the NCRA could reduce the waste of the overbidding via R&D investments that noncooperative, competitive R&D would induce. However, in the more realistic environment of incomplete appropriability, the cooperation promoted by the NCRA could reduce spending below the socially optimal level. If circumstances were as described in Chapter 8, cooperation would increase appropriability (in the sense of avoiding the competing away of profits) and reduce waste thus eliminating what is, from the private perspective, overbidding. R&D investment would be reduced from the noncooperative level to the cooperative level. Although the cooperative level is privately optimal, the noncooperative level is socially preferable since the net social value of innovative investment is larger then. Because cooperation eliminates overbidding as well as increasing appropriability and increasing technical efficiency, it is still possible, as in the case developed in Chapter 8, for the cooperative solution to be socially inferior to the competitive solution.

Katz (1986) develops economic welfare possibilities of cooperative R&D assuming that firms are not cooperative, each choosing at each stage of a four-stage game its own action while assuming that rivals' actions for that stage are given. The firms ultimately compete in the product market using the level of cost achieved with the "cooperative R&D." More generally many detailed stories, including a truly cooperative venture sharing R&D costs and jointly marketing patented R&D products, are possible. The basic point is that independent diversified firms may effect an equilibrium with higher social net present value than cooperation would effect because the increase in appropriability resulting from cooperation is incomplete. Society would gain from the additional imperfectly correlated research efforts of competing firms even though from the standpoint of the cooperating firms the marginal value of such efforts falls short of their marginal cost.

## 12.3 Evidence about NCRA cooperative R&D

Obviously this scenario in which the NCRA will reduce economic welfare is just a possibility. However, it is reasonable because the cooperative R&D protected by the NCRA is quite similar to diversification of individual firms in the past, and because the cooperation tends to occur in industries where productivity growth and seller concentration have been high. Further, there is no evidence that cooperative R&D protected by the NCRA is occurring in industries where appropriability has been a problem. Then, in the industries with NCRA-protected R&D, fragmentation of R&D effort is perhaps not a problem needing a remedy as much as may be the case in other industries. Thus, comparison of the diversification of R&D during the mid-1970s with the cooperative R&D protected by the NCRA suggests that the possibility developed in Chapter 8 in which cooperation results in investment further from the socially optimal amount could be a reasonable qualitative approximation to the actual performance of the new law.

The productivity slump that hit hard in the mid-1970s (Link, 1983b) fostered the NCRA. The framers and supporters of the law hoped (U.S. 98th Congress, September 1984) that the promotion of cooperation would increase net social benefit of R&D investment by improving appropriability, lowering costs, lowering risks, decreasing wasteful overbidding (in the sense of too many trials), and reducing actual duplication (in the sense of perfectly correlated trials). The evidence suggests, though, that the improvement of social economic welfare may not result. Proof that social economic welfare is lessened by the NCRA is not my goal here; rather, given the policy establishment's and business community's naive exuberance about the possibilities for the act, adducing evidence merely making plausible the naysayer's view is important.

If the NCRA is to be beneficial, we would expect the act to promote cooperative R&D in those areas where the productivity slump hit hard. To turn around the productivity performance of the economy, the act would stimulate R&D in those industries that were poor performers during the heart of the slump. In the context of our theoretical understanding, the gains expected from the act would be most likely if the act furthered cooperative R&D in the unconcentrated, fragmented industries, in the lower productivity growth industries, and in industries where the salubrious effects of R&D diversification could not work because the R&D activities in those industries had not been combined with the R&D in other industries. In fact, what we find is quite the opposite: NCRA-protected cooperative R&D is largely in those industries which, during the heart of the productivity slump which lay the groundswell for the NCRA, were already concentrated (including foreign competitors in the market definition), had higher productivity growth, and whose R&D was already purposively combined with the R&D activities of other industries. Further, there appear to be no unusual appropriability problems in the industries where protected cooperative R&D is occurring.

The *Federal Register* (1985, 1986), provided the complete set of cooperative R&D projects that were filed under the NCRA during the first 18 months (January 1985 through June 1986) of filings. During this period filings were made for 61 separate cooperative projects.[4] The 18 months of observations seemed to me to be a sensible cutoff point to provide a sample allowing an initial assessment of the NCRA. The *Federal Register* filings revealed the participants in each cooperative project, the nature of the project, and usually some information about its organizational structure.

To compare the characteristics of industry categories in which there is NCRA cooperative R&D with the characteristics of industry categories without NCRA help, the first task was to assign each cooperative project to a FTC four-digit industry category or to a set of such categories where appropriate. That is not an easy task, so I must explain my approach.

For example, suppose the good being developed is an output, say an industrial inorganic chemical, for one industry $x$ and an input for another $y$. Should I assign category $x$ where it is a product innovation, or category

$y$ where it is a process innovation? Does it matter for what I do if all the cooperating firms are in industry $x$, or all in industry $y$, or if the participants come from both industries? I obviously needed to set out a consistent set of rules and follow them. And I obviously need to report the rules followed.

One might be tempted to use the following categorization technique. Assign the cooperative R&D to $x$ alone if the participants are all from $x$, and call this a product innovative investment. And assign the R&D to $y$ alone if the participants are all from $y$, and call this a process innovative investment. Finally, the R&D would be assigned to $x$ and $y$ if the participants are from both industries. But this approach is too mechanical. The product of the $x$ industry often has many more applications than those in industry $y$. For example, suppose that $x$ denotes the computer industry and $y$ the aerospace industry. Even if all the participants in the venture are firms in the aerospace industry, they are likely to realize spinoffs from their research that will be useful as products of the $x$ industry for sales to industry $z$ or even to other producers in industry $y$. In such a case, I would assign the project to both category $x$ and category $y$, but not $z$, unless there were some indication, such as sales by the participants in category $z$, that the participants were likely to produce in industry $z$ using the new inputs from industry $x$, rather than simply sell the new product to $z$ producers. *My bottom line for assigning projects to industry categories was to assign the cooperative project to those industry categories in which the investors in the cooperative R&D would probably expect to reap the return on their investment.*

So, if the venture's participants are $y$ producers making a product of $x$ for input to $y$ and if they do not have fairly clear prospects for sales of the $x$ product to other industries or to other producers of $y$, then I assign the project to $y$ alone. But if they seem likely to sell $x$, then the project is assigned to $x$ too. And if they do seem likely to be using $x$ to enter with new products or processes in other industry categories, then those too are assigned. If the project participants are $x$ producers making a good that is sold to $y$ as an input, but they do not expect to be setting up production of $y$ but setting a price of their new input, then I assign the project to $x$. If the cooperating firms are from both $x$ and $y$, then I assign their project to both category $x$ and category $y$.

Before actually looking at specific cooperative R&D projects, one can tie oneself in conceptual knots over all of this. Examining the ventures, however, one finds that the assignments are, following the basic guideline above, not so difficult. Further, I expect that for my present purpose of identifying the industry categories with NCRA cooperative R&D, errors in assignment will largely offset one another. That is because omissions of relevant industry categories in the assignments for venture $i$ are very likely to be picked up because they are correctly identified for venture $j$. And, industry categories improperly assigned to venture $s$ are likely to be correctly noted in our sample of NCRA industry categories because they belong to some other venture or ventures. In all, for the 61 cooperative projects filed during the period from January 1985 through June 1986, a total of 81 of the 261 FTC four-digit industry categories were associated with the ventures.[5]

To describe the differences between the 81 industry categories with NCRA activity and the remaining 180 categories, I use the simple regression model

$$y = \alpha + \beta d + \epsilon$$

where $y$ is the industry characteristic of interest, $\alpha$ is an intercept term, $\beta$ is the coefficient on $d$, a dummy variable taking the value of 1 for each of the 81 industries with NCRA cooperative R & D and 0 for the remaining 180 categories, and $\epsilon$ is random (approximately) normal error with zero mean. Thus, for industry characteristic $y$, we have, from the ordinary least squares regression of $y$ on $d$, estimates, denoted with "hats" (^'s), of the parameters. The estimates are used to interpret descriptive differences as follows. For characteristic $y$, the expected value for observations without NCRA R & D is $\hat{\alpha}$, while the expected value for the observations with NCRA R & D is $\hat{\alpha} + \hat{\beta}$. The standard tests for significance provide a test of the statistical significance of the difference $\hat{\beta}$ between the characteristic for the two groups. Here are my questions and the answers using the differences for the industry characteristics I have surveyed.

First, are the cooperative projects predominately in unconcentrated industries where joint ventures would arguably be needed to overcome fragmentation of R & D effort? No, the fact is quite the opposite. With $y$ being the industry four-firm concentration ratio (as a proportion) adjusted to reflect, among other things, import competition,[6] we have, with the $t$-ratio with 259 degrees of freedom in parentheses, $\hat{\alpha} = 0.403$ (28.9) and $\hat{\beta} = 0.0673$ (2.69), with $R^2 = 0.0271$. Katz and Ordover (1990, p. 172) observe that the firms in concentrated industries may perceive that their antitrust risks are higher and are therefore more likely to register their ventures under the NCRA. Paul Geroski (personal correspondence) observes that they may also lobby more effectively and may be more effectively benefiting from federal government largesse.

Second, are the cooperative projects predominately in lower productivity growth industries where joint ventures would arguably be needed to improve productivity? Again, the answer is no. With $y$ being the average annual growth rate (as a percentage) of industry total factor productivity for the 1969–73 to 1974–78 period,[7] we have, with the $t$-ratio with 259 degrees of freedom in parentheses, $\hat{\alpha} = -0.758$ ($-5.15$) and $\hat{\beta} = 0.690$ (2.61), with $R^2 = 0.0257$.

Third, are the cooperative projects occurring predominately in industries where we have not observed purposive diversification and where the appropriability advantages from such diversification would not have been able to offset appropriability problems caused by competition in R&D? No again; joint ventures are more likely to be found in industry categories where we found purposive R&D activity. With $y$ taking the value 1 when the industry category is one found to be purposively combined with others and 0 otherwise, we have, with the $t$-ratio with 259 degrees of freedom in parentheses, $\hat{\alpha} = 0.467$ (12.8) and $\hat{\beta} = 0.237$ (3.63), with $R^2 = 0.0484$.

Fourth, are the cooperative projects occurring predominately in industries where company-financed R&D intensity has been low and where extra stimulus is arguably needed to get innovative investment? Once more, the answer is no. With $y$ being the ratio (as a percentage) of company-financed R&D to sales in the 248 FTC four-digit categories for which the figure was available,[8] we have, with the $t$-ratio with 246 degrees of freedom in parentheses, $\hat{\alpha} = 1.06$ (9.57) and $\hat{\beta} = 1.14$ (5.84), with $R^2 = 0.122$.

Levin's variables measuring appropriability are never significantly different for the categories where cooperative R&D is found as compared with the remaining categories. Thus, there is no evidence that the cooperative R&D is in categories where there have been appropriability problems. This result is surprising since one might expect to find cooperative R&D in a higher proportion of those industry categories where firms perceive appropriability problems than for categories without such problems, for if appropriation of returns were easy, then cooperation would offer no advantage. True, if it were impossible and any entrant could ride free, there would again be no gain. But conditional on appropriability problems, cooperation will be able to address those problems if the cooperation serves as a "club" that precommits a sufficient proportion of the potential free-riders to contribute to the predicted costs. I am surprised by the result, because cooperation can offer an advantage even if "appropriability is easy" in the sense of there being little erosion in the value (before deducting the cost of innovative investment) of the total prize. Even in that case, Levin's firms might be expected to say that "appropriation is difficult" because the expected share of the prize falls as competition intensifies. Katz and Ordover (1990, pp. 172–173) observe that Levin's appropriability measure may not be the one we want here, because it characterizes the entire industry's appropriability conditions on average, whereas the projects for which ventures are formed are likely to be those where appropriability difficulties are especially likely to be severe. Since many of the cooperative ventures have been in the areas of environmental or safety research, Katz and Ordover believe that positive spillovers are especially likely for those projects. In the absence of government directives requiring that production processes and products themselves meet certain environmental or safety standards, it would indeed be difficult to appropriate the social value of process and product innovations that reduce environmental and safety problems. However, the NCRA ventures in these areas appear to be in response to new or impending governmental standards, so innovators would probably expect to be able to market their new product or process successfully. On balance, then, I am not convinced of the importance of the Katz and Ordover argument about the likelihood of positive spillovers for the environmental and safety NCRA projects.

If the joint ventures being formed are designed to exploit multi-industry spillovers and economies of scope, the combining firms will bring together experience in broad industry categories that are "technologically close." I have shown that cooperative R&D is more likely to occur in a category that I have found to be purposively combined with other categories by diversified firms. But additionally, at the level of broad industry categories, are the sets of categories brought together in observed NCRA joint ventures congruent with the sets of categories brought together by purposively diversifying firms? The sets of firms brought together in observed joint ventures imply sets of industry categories being brought together. I shall ask if those sets, at the broad two-digit FTC (and SIC) level, overlap to a significant extent the sets of industry categories combined by purposively diversified firms and therefore considered "close." Let the sets of industry categories brought together by joint ventures number $\Sigma$, and let the number of sets of close industry categories be $\Omega$. Chapter 10's purposive diversification test, with each firm's R&D allocated over the 20 two-digit manufacturing industry categories, yielded (after the elimination of duplicate sets) $\Omega = 165$ sets of close (with significance level of 0.01) industry categories. There were $\Sigma = 19$ distinct groups of two-digit industry categories found among the 61 cooperative projects that filed for NCRA protection through June 30, 1986. Let the total number of possible sets of two or more industry categories be $\phi$. Since there are 20 two-digit manufacturing categories, $\phi = 1,048,555$. Then where $p(f)$ is the probability that $f$ of the $\Sigma$ sets coincide with $f$ of the $\Omega$ sets, we have, given random choice of the $\Sigma$ sets,

Table 12.1. *Probability of f identical sets of "close" industry categories*

| $f$ | $p(f)$ |
|---|---|
| 0 | 0.997014 |
| 1 | $2.98142 \times 10^{-3}$ |
| 2 | $4.19753 \times 10^{-6}$ |
| 3 | $3.69822 \times 10^{-9}$ |
| 4 | $2.28587 \times 10^{-12}$ |
| 5 | $1.05313 \times 10^{-15}$ |
| 6 | $3.75026 \times 10^{-19}$ |
| 7 | $1.0563 \times 10^{-22}$ |
| 8 | $2.3879 \times 10^{-26}$ |
| 9 | $4.37065 \times 10^{-30}$ |
| 10 | $6.50357 \times 10^{-34}$ |
| 11 | $7.86709 \times 10^{-38}$ |
| 12 | $7.70413 \times 10^{-42}$ |
| 13 | $6.05409 \times 10^{-46}$ |
| 14 | $3.7618 \times 10^{-50}$ |
| 15 | $1.80605 \times 10^{-54}$ |
| 16 | $6.4601 \times 10^{-59}$ |
| 17 | $1.62023 \times 10^{-63}$ |
| 18 | $2.5414 \times 10^{-68}$ |
| 19 | $1.87548 \times 10^{-73}$ |

$$p(f) = [(C_{\Omega, f})(C_{\phi - \Omega, \Sigma - f})]/(C_{\phi, \Sigma})$$

where $C_{x,y}$ denotes the combination of $x$ things taken $y$ at a time and where $p(0) + p(1) + p(2) + \cdots + p(\Sigma) = 1$. The correctness of $p(f)$ is readily seen. $C_{\Omega, f}$ is the number of ways to get $f$ of the $\Omega$ sets. $C_{\phi - \Omega, \Sigma - f}$ is the number of ways to get $\Sigma - f$ of the non-$\Omega$ sets. Finally, $C_{\phi, \Sigma}$ is the number of ways to draw $\Sigma$ sets. With this distribution, I can ask if the overlap of the $\Sigma$ and $\Omega$ sets is significant. In fact 10 of the 19 sets observed in the NCRA cooperative projects are identical to sets among the 165 found among the purposively diversified firms. Thus, the multimarket cooperative research was quantitatively extensive for the sample of NCRA research projects; and further, the multimarket cooperative research overlaps significantly the multimarket diversified research in the FTC LB sample. The probability of an equal or greater number of congruent sets is

$$\sum_{f=10}^{19} p(f).$$

As Table 12.1 shows, that probability is quite close to zero.

Thus, to an extraordinary extent the NCRA-protected cooperative projects combine R&D in precisely the same general industry categories as diversified firms combined individually. Multi-industry research coalitions may then be a substitute for multi-industry firms exploiting R&D spillovers. This empirical result aligns nicely with the findings of Lemelin (1982) and MacDonald (1985) about research intensity and diversification, because they find that diversification joining science-based, research-intensive industries is especially likely.

NCRA cooperative R&D appears to be very similar to diversification behavior except that some competition is eliminated. The cooperative R&D protected by the NCRA has occurred in industries that were concentrated during the 1970s, with higher productivity growth, and that had R&D activities purposively combined by diversified firms with R&D in other industries. Further, cooperative R&D has not been more prevalent in those industries for which Levin et al. (1984) found appropriability difficulties; therefore, the act does not appear to be fostering R&D where competing firms dared not invest because of appropriability problems. Moreover, cooperative R&D appears to be more likely in industries where diversified firms were already investing relatively heavily, and to be less likely in those industries where they had low R&D intensity. Finally, broad areas of R&D investment combined by the cooperative R&D projects protected by the NCRA in the mid-1980s parallel closely the areas combined by the diversified firms of the mid-1970s. The NCRA may, therefore, stimulate cooperative projects that change innovative investment in the way modeled in Chapter 8, and thus reduce the net social benefit of R&D investment.

## 12.4 Discussion

Joint ventures in R&D generally – i.e., those not protected by the NCRA – are perhaps another matter; certainly I have not presented any evidence here about them.[9] Further, with regard to the cooperative R&D protected by the NCRA, I emphasize that my evidence only makes my theoretical story an important possibility. At best I have made it plausible, but I think it is important to emphasize such a possibility because the Justice Department's assessments of cooperative R&D have been uncritical. I have offered an alternative scenario for the effects of the NCRA.

To criticize my own inference that the NCRA will lessen desirable competition in R&D, I have two points. First, the Department of Justice has said that it wants to preserve competition and will block ventures that lessen it significantly. For example, stating in a "business review letter" its enforcement intentions regarding one of the cooperative projects, the

Department observes that: "Joint R&D ventures generally are procompetitive, and are condemned by the antitrust laws when they have a net negative effect on competition. Generally, R&D joint ventures rarely will raise competitive concerns – [they will do so] only when the venture's membership is "overinclusive," because an insufficient number of entities are left outside the venture to perform competitive R&D, or when the venture results in a significant restraint on competition that precludes or retards the production or sale of goods or services that do not employ the technology developed by the venture" (U.S. Department of Justice, June 25, 1985). But as I look at the cooperative R&D granted NCRA protection, the projects appear to have quite inclusive memberships, sometimes even when one does not look for a particular niche in the general area of research.

For example, the business review letter quoted above concerned the cooperative R&D of Computer Aided Manufacturing–International, Inc. (CAM-I) in the area of computer-aided design and manufacturing. CAM-I's membership includes the U.S. and foreign leaders in the areas being researched. The problem of inclusiveness, though, runs deeper than cases where leading manufacturers from around the world are combined in R&D projects. There could be problems if only U.S. leaders are combined. For example, in aerospace, foreign competition for our defense establishment's dollars is not terribly important. Further, significant reduction in competition could occur even when many other U.S. firms do "similar" research. For example, suppose the leading aerospace firms combine to do software research. Innumerable U.S. firms do "similar" research. Yet there may be no viable competitors in developing applications in aerospace. And firms outside aerospace that develop software applicable to aerospace and then need to license the technology to aerospace firms would be licensing to the set of firms in the venture who would then have bargaining power that could lessen the value of the license to the innovator,[10] perhaps retarding the pace of innovation.

To illustrate both of these potential problems, consider the Software Productivity Consortium formed to develop complex computer software. Numerous organizations not party to the venture conduct R&D in this area. However, the venture, at the time of its filing, included all of the largest (by sales or R&D) eight firms listed in *Business Week*'s aerospace category. Other important firms in aerospace were also included in the venture, but did not appear in *Business Week*'s aerospace category because of their diversified sales. Our policy establishment is too willing to look at an R&D venture and find that "apparently numerous organizations and firms not currently members . . . , both in the U.S. and in other countries, can and do perform R&D that competes with the R&D

performed under [the venture's] sponsorship" (U.S. Department of Justice, June 25, 1985).

Second, my inference that the NCRA is reducing desirable competition in R&D and reducing investment below socially optimal levels is vulnerable because it is possible that there are further gains to be made in concentrated, higher productivity growth industries where diversified firms have previously invested heavily in R&D. That may be so, but it turns out that the relations observed are not simply the result of cooperative R&D occurring in high-technology industries where R&D intensity is high. We are not simply observing that cooperation is most likely where R&D is most likely when we compare in the same sample old traditional or smokestack industries with high-technology industries. The relation between R&D intensity and cooperation holds throughout the sample, even for the leading quartile of industry categories ranked by R&D intensity. As noted above, I have the R&D intensity of 248 industry categories. Considering only those categories for which R&D intensity exceeds 1.9 percent leaves 62 observations, the top quartile by R&D intensity. Repeating the pertinent experiment described above, I find that for R&D intensity, with $t$-statistics with 60 degrees of freedom in parentheses, $\hat{\alpha} = 3.05$ (9.13) and $\hat{\beta} = 0.717$ (1.61), with $R^2 = 0.0415$. Thus, even among the most R&D–intensive categories, cooperation and high research intensity continue to go together. I think it highly likely that cooperation will reduce R&D investment in these cases. That may be desirable, but, as I have explained earlier, it may not be.

Thus, there is a sound case for not being so comfortable with the belief that cooperative R&D protected by the NCRA will improve social welfare, although there are surely private gains. It is likely that the diversification of firms in the absence of the NCRA promoted socially, as well as privately, optimal innovative investment, while the cooperative projects protected by the NCRA may well lessen R&D performance in manufacturing.

I emphasize that I am not arguing against joint ventures generally, but rather suggesting that the NCRA is probably less of an improvement than is currently thought. The evidence makes plausible the theoretical scenario in which cooperative R&D actually reduces social welfare because from society's standpoint the gains from increases in appropriability may be outweighed by the losses from decreases in competitive races (overbidding from a private standpoint) for the innovative rewards. The evidence supports that scenario because the joint ventures appear to be taking place where R&D activity and productivity growth have been relatively robust. Private gains remain to be captured by cooperative R&D, but it is not clear that society at large will gain. While increases in private net present value are likely, social net present value may well fall.

As Nelson (1959) observed, diversification and cooperation are ways to increase appropriability broadly defined. But diversification increases appropriability while maintaining more competitive pressure than is the case with cooperative R&D. In an uncertain world with incomplete appropriability, competition adds desirable duplication and diversity. Diversification of R&D may well allow appropriability to be compatible with competition.

# 13

## From cooperative research to cooperative production

In June 1990, the U.S. House of Representatives passed a bill (U.S. House, 1990) designed to extend to joint ventures in production the protection offered cooperative research and development (R&D) efforts by the National Cooperative Research Act of 1984 (NCRA).[1] By the following summer, both the U.S. House and the U.S. Senate hammered out and passed similar bills. The historical context of the NCRA is important; the act was passed during a dramatic redirection of U.S. government policy toward business combinations. Uncritical pronouncements about the efficacy of such combinations abounded. Recounting in this chapter the history of those pronouncements, from which the proposed laws on production joint ventures have evolved, and questioning their economic validity, suggests first that the laws promoting cooperation are not likely to be a panacea for lagging U.S. competitiveness and second that they may actually do great harm.

### 13.1 Introduction

The Reagan administration expected much good from business combinations. The declining international competitiveness of U.S. industrial products added importance to the expectations. The claims of advocates of change in antitrust laws led to new laws and proposals for still more new laws championing combinations among U.S. industrial competitors as ways to promote efficiency and meet the challenges of international competition.

That historical context of the NCRA, reviewed in Section 13.2, implies that the act would have passed even if it were not sound economic policy. Section 13.3 reviews economic theory explaining why the NCRA may not

Chapter 13 revises Scott (1989b).

promote desirable R&D behavior. In Section 13.4, the administration of
the NCRA is juxtaposed with the economics and the unique historical
context to suggest that the policy is not based on serious evaluation –
probably because policymakers were blinded by their uncritical assessments of the efficiencies of business combinations or, particularly for Congress, perhaps by their desire to establish an image of doing something
for U.S. competitiveness. Despite the fact that the policy analysis has
been superficial, the ventures encouraged by the NCRA may nonetheless
promote desirable behavior. The evidence reviewed in Section 13.5, however, does not hold much promise for that sanguine conclusion, yet it
has become the model for further relaxation of antitrust laws. Section
13.6 suggests that new policies should be used to replace the competitive
pressure lost because of cooperation, and we shall turn to that task in
Chapter 14.

### 13.2 The historical context
The NCRA encourages research combinations among competi-
tors. To establish the context of uncritical advocacy of business combinations, this section provides an overview of the Reagan administration's
antitrust initiatives, describes its policy toward horizontal and conglomerate mergers, and explains the similarities in the approach to them and
the NCRA's approach to R&D ventures.

"Government regulation" commonly denotes policies as diverse as the
regulation of a public utility and the enforcement of our antitrust laws.
Perhaps as a result, policies proscribing certain combinations among competitors are often considered unwarranted interferences with markets. The
regulation of a public utility is direct regulation in which a regulatory
authority prescribes prices and services. In contrast, our antitrust laws
establish indirect regulation under which firms are free to compete according to the rules of the game legislated by the antitrust laws. The Department of Justice (DOJ) and the Federal Trade Commission (FTC)
enforce those laws, and the courts interpret them. Such laws most promi-
nently proscribe competing firms from colluding to set prices or merging
if competition decreases.

The Reagan administration was tough on price fixers, but it was more
relaxed than past administrations about other business combinations. Often that was good; some combinations promote efficiency. Undoubtedly
in the past, antitrust enforcement at times went too far in *blocking* mergers.[2] But the enforcement policies of the Reagan administration may have
gone too far in *promoting* combinations. If so, the desire to promote
U.S. international competitiveness and to reduce government "regulation"
stimulated the excesses. Understanding the uncritical reorientation of

antitrust policy toward business combinations is crucial for interpreting the NCRA and its enforcement.

*New directions for antitrust policy:* William Baxter, antitrust chief at DOJ in the early years of the Reagan administration, initiated many important antitrust policies. As an Assistant Attorney General heading DOJ's Antitrust Division, he played a key role in antitrust policy. Baxter considered many Supreme Court rulings "rubbish," "wacko," or "ludicrous" (Taylor, 1982); he set out to instruct courts on proper application of the law. By simply not bringing cases which would traditionally have been brought to court, he could to a large extent make the administration's view the law. Policy was redirected for mergers – horizontal, vertical, and conglomerate – and for vertical restraints such as resale price maintenance. Published guidelines codified these new enforcement policies.[3]

President Reagan's first FTC chairman, James Miller, changed the focus of the commission's work dramatically from its traditional orientation and the orientation of the commission under the previous chair, Michael Pertschuk, who had been appointed by President Carter. Many observers believe that under Pertschuk there was too much consumer activism. Apart from that possibility, the FTC was transformed from an agency that looked for inefficient markets where performance could be improved by government action, to one that sought cases where government intervention in the marketplace had decreased economic performance.[4]

The Reagan administration introduced new laws promoting business combinations as well as new enforcement policies. The Commerce Department championed and won passage of new law – The Export Trading Company Act of 1982 – promoting formation of export cartels by U.S. firms. Commerce and Justice promoted and won passage of the NCRA, which encourages research joint ventures among firms. In 1986, the Reagan administration's antitrust establishment proposed the enactment of five new laws which, among other things, would have codified its view of appropriate merger policy and reduced the damages that plaintiffs in certain types of antitrust suits could win from firms found in violation of the law (U.S. Department of Justice, February 19, 1986).

These initiatives share a common philosophical foundation – namely, the belief that the performance of the economy will be improved if government interference with business behavior is lessened. Antitrust laws aim to set out rules of the competitive game, which, if followed, can allow a system of markets to work well. The question is how stringent those rules should be. In the area of mergers, should we begin to worry about a lack of competition, and therefore single out mergers for further scrutiny when the number of sellers in the industry would be decreased to, say, seven or eight, or four or five, or two or three? At what point should we begin to worry about the concentration of an industry's resources in the control of a few sellers? What other factors must we examine to estimate the potential for less competition?

An important theme, subsumed in the Reagan administration's general philosophy that government interference with the market should be lessened, is that policy should be less concerned with business combinations, whether via merger or joint venture. One can argue that the new policies regarding horizontal mergers, conglomerate mergers, and joint ventures in research and development show too little concern about business combinations. More importantly, as documented below, the Reagan administration – surely at least in part because of its concern with declining competitiveness of U.S. firms in global markets and in part because of its desire to "deregulate" markets – justified these policies by extraordinarily selective reference to theories and facts.

*Horizontal mergers:* The new policy for a horizontal merger (one between firms competing in the same product and geographic market) explicitly weighs evidence of potential efficiencies from a merger against the likelihood of increased market power. But the U.S. Supreme Court's rulings under the current version of Section 7 of the Clayton Act state that if a merger is likely to increase market power (the ability of the new firm, or the industry's firms together, to control price) the fact that it also increases productive efficiency (lowering costs) cannot make it legal. Potential operating efficiencies provide no defense for a merger that is otherwise illegal because of its probable effect on competition. "Possible economies cannot be used as a defense to illegality. Congress was aware that some mergers which lessen competition may also result in economies but it struck the balance in favor of protecting competition" *FTC v. Procter & Gamble,* 386 U.S. 568 (1967).[5]

Yet administrative procedure has now diverged from the precedent embodied in the Court's opinions. Baldwin's (1987) review traces the evolution of merger policy. Since the Merger Notification Act of 1976, firms involved in a prospective merger above a certain size must notify both DOJ and the FTC. Notification is followed by a waiting period before the merger can be consummated. If either enforcement agency questions the proposed merger, a negotiated settlement is typically reached during the waiting period. Thus, most challenged mergers are no longer fought in the courts after the fact. As Baldwin (1987, pp. 383–385) emphasizes, the decisions about whether mergers are allowed are not being made so much by the courts in a legal setting as by the departments and agencies, most notably DOJ and the FTC, of the administration holding power.[6]

The Reagan administration accepted greater levels of postmerger concentration than would have been accepted by earlier administrations, and it explicitly incorporated an efficiency defense for otherwise illegal mergers.

Undoubtedly, if we *could* confidently identify the efficiencies of a merger, the absence of an efficiency defense for an otherwise illegal merger *would* in some cases lessen economic welfare, because gains from cost savings can outweigh losses from increased market power. Such efficiencies are difficult to establish yet very easy to allege.[7]

Further, most potential economies could be achieved by internal expansion, which is often pro-competitive and evidently far more likely to achieve efficiency than a merger (Mueller, 1987; Ravenscraft and Scherer, 1987). Nothing in antitrust law prevents the internal growth of firms that provide better products or produce at lower costs, although Section 2 of the Sherman Act (1890) has been interpreted as proscribing internal growth to dominance of a market when the growth was not achieved by chance or better products or lower costs. Case law under Section 2 of the Sherman Act has made clear that internal growth resulting from innovation is accepted under the "rules of the game." In the 1945 *Alcoa* case and the 1962 *Brown Shoe* case, the courts interpreted the antitrust laws as embodying the desires of Congress not only to promote economic efficiency narrowly construed, but also to ensure the dispersion of social and political power – to fulfill the Jeffersonian ideal of decentralized power. The courts have therefore been willing to give up the uncertain efficiencies a merger might bring, in return for the lower seller concentration maintained by blocking the merger. Yet the Reagan administration repeatedly said that the antitrust laws were intended to promote economic efficiency only. According to antitrust chief Baxter, "The sole goal of antitrust is economic efficiency" (Taylor, 1982).[8]

In introducing DOJ's 1984 *Merger Guidelines,* Attorney General William French Smith referred to what he called "the latest legal and economic learning – recognizing that most merger activity does not threaten competition, but actually improves our economy's efficiency and thus benefits all consumers" (U.S. Department of Justice, June 14, 1984). In these guidelines, the Reagan administration, although it claimed otherwise, made efficiency a defense to challenges by the enforcement agencies, whatever the courts may hold. In the statement accompanying the release of the revised merger guidelines, the Department claimed ". . . that efficiencies do not constitute a defense to an otherwise anticompetitive merger but are one of many factors that will be considered by the Department in determining whether to challenge a merger" (U.S. DOJ, June 14, 1984, p. 15). In the guidelines themselves, the Department states: "Some mergers that the Department otherwise might challenge may be reasonably necessary to achieve significant net efficiencies. If the parties to the merger establish by clear and convincing evidence that a merger will achieve such efficiencies, the Department will consider those efficiencies in deciding whether to challenge the merger. . . . The parties must establish a greater level of expected net efficiencies the more significant are the competitive risks . . ." (U.S. DOJ, June 14, 1984, pp. 35–36). The same approach is retained in the *1992 Horizontal Merger Guidelines* (U.S. DOJ and U.S. FTC, 1992, pp. 55–56).

Clearly, with these guidelines, DOJ allowed efficiency gains (from lower costs) to be weighed against any loss in efficiency (from higher prices) resulting from a merger. Further, one of the proposed laws sent to Congress in 1986, the Merger Modernization Act of 1986, would have amended Section 7 of the Clayton Act to require weighing efficiencies against any possible increase in market power. The new language implied that a ruling of illegality would require demonstration of a probability of increased market power greater than required under the current law.

The reorientation of policy has been based on unsubstantiated claims, and this reorientation and similar faith in combinations underlies the NCRA and the bill (U.S. House of Representatives, 1990) on production joint ventures. The Conference Report on the NCRA (U.S. 98th Congress, September 21, 1984) describes the rule of reason that is to be applied to antitrust evaluation of R&D joint ventures. The same weighing of losses from market power versus efficiency gains is required. Again, especially with R&D ventures, this is sensible in principle. Yet, given the enforcement agencies' uncritical advocacy of business combinations, joint ventures may pass muster even when unwise from a social standpoint.

On what evidence did the Reagan administration change the course of merger law? To quote Reagan's Secretary of Commerce Malcolm Baldrige, "Economists now believe that the positive relationship between industry profitability and concentration is due to the comparatively greater efficiency of larger firms in the industry rather than collusion. Recent studies show that firm profitability in a given line is related to its market share regardless of whether or not the industry is 'concentrated.' . . . This is powerful evidence that the larger firm has achieved profitability through economies of scale rather than collusion."[9] There *is* evidence (Demsetz, 1973; Gale and Branch, 1982; Ravenscraft, 1983), especially from the mid-70s, that can be misconstrued as supporting Baldrige's position. But what is of importance for objectively analyzing the reorientation of antitrust policy, including the new policy embodied in the NCRA, is the way that the Reagan administration supported its position while ignoring contrary evidence.

Many observers have interpreted the evidence Baldrige cited as suggesting that better products or lower costs have resulted in expansion and profitability of certain firms and thus relatively large shares of an industry. To these observers, therefore, the profits associated with concentrated industries have resulted from the efficiency associated with market share, not from the price-raising inefficiency allowed by mutual dependence recognized (tacit collusion) among concentrated sellers. The evidence they see says that large-share firms have high profits whether concentration is high or low, while low-share firms have low profits regardless of the level of industry concentration. Concentration appears to have no profit-increasing effect.[10]

There are problems with the popular interpretation of the evidence. One could argue that the existing literature about market share and profits is irrelevant for merger policy. Even if the relationship exists, we do not know what the causality is. The Demsetz (1973) story could be that efficiency causes market share and profits. The leading firms we observe could have been more efficient in the sense that they had better products and grew big *internally*. To understand the effects of external growth, mergers must be studied separately. Thus, the evidence does not support Baldrige since it has not been developed for firms that grew to dominate their markets because of mergers.

Even assuming that the correlations between market share and profits reflect efficiencies for merger-intensive firms, there are other problems with the evidence. The evidence about the profitability of high-share firms could be interpreted quite differently. The conventional dominant-firm model associates market power with high profits for the large-share firm (or a group of leading firms), while a competitive fringe without such power does less well. Shepherd (1972) interprets the relation between share and profit in that way. Salop and Scheffman (1983) explain that large-share firms may increase their profits by carrying out socially wasteful policies that raise smaller rivals' costs, decreasing the output from the smaller firms and ultimately increasing the market share and profits of the leading firm or firms. Caves and Porter (1977) hypothesize segmented industries, with a market power problem for some segments of the industry but not others, with barriers to the mobility of resources preventing entry into the segments of the industry where excess profits are earned. In none of these hypotheses is market power necessarily required for efficiency to be attained.

Yet another problem is that, as we have seen in Chapter 6, the very data the Reagan administration marshaled in its favor suggest an opposing view. The mid-70s were turbulent times for our economy, and oligopolistic consensus is difficult to maintain during periods when demands and costs are unstable. Such consensus should be especially likely to break down if sellers have high fixed costs, tempting them to undercut their rivals' prices in an attempt to spread fixed costs over more sales, but ultimately causing a collapse of the industry price. Using measures of seller concentration that include the impact of foreign firms, Chapter 6 suggested that the evidence on which the Reagan administration relied, the evidence showing no positive effect of concentration on profits and hence suggesting that the concentration problem is no problem, is the result of averaging the low profits of high fixed-cost concentrated industries, where oligopolistic coordination had evidently broken down, with the high profits of the remaining concentrated industries.

More significantly, none of the structural variables which are so prominent in the policy debate appear to be very important in terms of explaining variance in line of business profitability. Yet, unidentified firm and industry variables are quite important, explaining a large part of that variance. Thus, the results cited by the Reagan administration are quite likely driven by the unidentified variables which have been left out of traditional specifications that have informed the policy debate. The data, then, do not support a revolution in policy regarding the traditional concern of antitrust with the oligopoly problem caused by the concentration of sellers in an industry.

*Conglomerate mergers:* New policy toward conglomerate mergers also illustrates a willingness to ignore the potential problems of business combinations. The policy is relevant here both as another example of unsubstantiated claims about the effects of business combinations and because, as seen in Chapter 12, joint ventures often combine the resources of firms doing R & D in different manufacturing industries. Assistant Attorney General Baxter believed that "During the 1960s, in its general hostility to conglomerate mergers, the Supreme Court cooked up a variety of esoteric and totally baseless theories about the harm caused by conglomerate mergers" (Taylor, 1982).

I do not believe those theories were baseless. But in any case, Baxter's view became the official view of the enforcement agencies. Assistant Attorney General for Antitrust Douglas Ginsburg stated that "In the case of a purely conglomerate merger, on the other hand [as contrasted with horizontal mergers in concentrated markets], no serious anticompetitive problems arise because the firms involved in the deal, by definition, do not actually compete with one another in any relevant market. One exception to this occurs in cases where one firm is properly characterized as a potential competitor of the other . . ." (U.S. DOJ, March 5, 1986). This belief was embodied in the Justice Department's 1984 merger guidelines and is cited as the current policy in the joint DOJ and FTC statement (U.S. DOJ and U.S. FTC, 1992, p. 3) accompanying the release of the *1992 Horizontal Merger Guidelines.*

The foregoing received wisdom about conglomerate mergers is mistaken because, as we have seen in Part I, theory and evidence suggest that such mergers can, in some circumstances, significantly enhance the likelihood of noncompetitive behavior and performance in industry, even when there is no issue of potential competition. As explained in those chapters from Part I, if a conglomerate merger increases multimarket contact, it can make the market-power-inducing understandings that follow from recognition of mutual dependence more likely, yet the merger would not be challenged given the new policy.

We do have evidence that conglomerate mergers that increase multimarket contact matter. Most of the evidence about the multimarket contact of sellers shows no effect of multimarket contact on prices or profits. But the evidence in Chapter 4 suggests that findings of no effect of multimarket contact on prices or profits result because the effect of multimarket contact works in opposite ways in concentrated and unconcentrated markets. When seller concentration is high, high multimarket contact can enhance the ability to coordinate behavior legally and result in high prices and excess profits. But when seller concentration is low, diversification across many industries is expected to increase sellers' awareness of profitable opportunities and their ability to quickly redeploy resources in response to those opportunities, thus competing away economic profits especially rapidly. So if we ask only if multimarket contact increases profits, the answer is expected to be no. *On average* there is no such effect. But when we divided markets into those that are concentrated and those that are not (including an accounting for foreign firms' U.S. sales when measuring concentration), we found that, as hypothesized, multimarket contact increases profits in the former and decreases them in the latter. Chapter 5 bolstered the evidence that multimarket contact created by conglomerate mergers may result in higher prices; coordination among diversified oligopolists appears to be more likely when they meet in other markets to a significant extent.

*Can mergers among competitors strengthen competitiveness?* The Reagan administration proposed the Promoting Competition in Distressed Industries Act (U.S. Department of Justice, February 19, 1986), which would have precluded antitrust action against any merger granted exemption because the International Trade Commission had found that an increase in imports had injured, or was likely to injure, an industry. Again, the rationale for the mergers was that they would promote efficiencies and lower costs, thus allowing the injured domestic firms to regain their previous share of the domestic market.

The strong dollar prior to the last years of the Reagan administration helped the United States avoid inflation even while running a huge federal deficit, but the competitiveness, in domestic and foreign markets, of U.S. industrial products consequently suffered. The lack of international competitiveness of U.S. industrial products induced some policy-makers to urge changes in policy toward competition in our industrial markets. The overall thrust of such recommendations was quite wrong. A microeconomic policy was proposed to remedy problems caused in large measure by unsound macroeconomic policy. True, under some circumstances market power in an export industry could improve the exporting country's position vis-à-vis other countries – for example, by converting foreign consumers' surplus into domestic producers' surplus. However, exploiting such possibilities could, because of retaliation, ultimately undermine international trade or prove the first step in undermining the static and dynamic efficiency of the industries in the country promoting market power.

An essential problem was one of macroeconomic distortions stemming from the federal deficit and to some extent from the trade policies of our international trading partners. It needed macroeconomic remedies. The available evidence (which includes the impact of foreign sellers' U.S. sales on seller concentration) suggests that the microeconomic merger policy championed as a response to the "globalization of markets" would make U.S. industry less competitive, not more competitive. The combination of firms in the name of efficiency might not significantly reduce costs but just reduce the number of leading competitors, including foreign firms, in U.S. industries. The reduction in competition could make U.S. industrial products more expensive and less innovative.

### 13.3 R&D cooperation and the extent of innovation

Firms competing in R&D are for many important cases undoubtedly unable to appropriate all of the social returns to their innovative investments. Appropriability of returns is especially likely to be difficult for basic research and generic applied research (Nelson, 1959). If the private marginal value of research is less than its social marginal value, then the private sector will invest too little in research, and there is reason to believe that "co-operative industry research organizations" (Nelson, 1959, pp. 303–304) and government support for basic and generic research is appropriate (Nelson, 1959, pp. 304–306; Nelson, 1982a, pp. 463–466). Indeed, in explaining strategies to revive U.S. productivity growth, Link and

Tassey (1987) emphasize the importance of joint ventures and government support for generating and capitalizing on generic research.

On the other hand, under some circumstances industry may, even without joint ventures, willingly support basic and generic research that is difficult to appropriate, because all firms share in the public knowledge and benefit from the process when successfully exploiting the knowledge for proprietary projects (Nelson, 1982b, pp. 466–468). Further, although it is often reasonable to assume that the total private value of research falls short of its social value, even then it is not obvious that private marginal value is strictly less than social marginal value (Baldwin and Scott, 1987, chapter 2). As Nelson (1982a, p. 480) observes, the situation is complex and competitors may actually spend too much on R&D. Barzel (1968) explains that *incomplete* appropriability in and of itself may lead to too little R&D investment by a monopolist free from the competitive pressure of an R&D race, while competitive pressure given a high enough degree of appropriability may cause too much R&D. Thus, as we have seen in the theory developed in Chapter 8, in a world of *incomplete* appropriability, a monopolist may do too little, while competition may result in roughly the right amount of R&D, especially when in the sense of Nelson (1961) parallel paths are optimal. Thus a firm is discouraged from doing R&D by the prospect that much of the return may go to others who imitate the innovation, but the fear of having a competitor be the first to introduce the innovation is a stimulus to R&D. To the extent that R&D joint ventures allow monopoly power *in R&D,* one can conclude that R&D joint ventures protected by the NCRA may decrease desirable R&D spending.

That possibility is especially likely given Chapter 12's evidence that the cooperative research protected by the NCRA combines R&D across industries in ways similar to the previously existing diversified R&D of individual firms. Joint ventures combining multi-industry research are quite likely to occur in areas where a monopolist of the R&D investment would undertake too little R&D. Consider the ratio of net social value to net private value of innovative investment as the multi-industry nature of the innovation increases. The ratio is expected to increase because of spillovers to consumers and other firms not conducting R&D in the area. The proportion of returns to R&D that are not appropriated by the firm doing the R&D are expected to increase as the multi-industry span – the extent – of the innovation increases, because more areas of technology are involved and the possibilities for applications other than those controlled by the firm increase.[11]

Barzel (1968, p. 352) explains that if the monopolist appropriates a constant fraction of the social return, the innovation is not pursued to the socially optimal extent. Granting that the ratio of net social value to net private value of innovative investment increases, the conclusion that a monopolist will not pursue multi-industry innovations to the socially optimal extent follows a fortiori. Let $z$ measure directly the extent – the multi-industry nature – of the innovation. Net social value $N_s(z)$ is assumed to be greater than net private value $N_p(z)$ because of incomplete appropriability of the returns from innovation. The ratio of net social value to net private value is a function $f(z)$ of the expected value of the measure of the extent of innovation. So, $f(z) = [N_s(z)/N_p(z)]$, and our discussion implies that $f'(z) > 0$.

The optimal extent of innovation from society's standpoint is $z_s^*$ such that $N_s' = 0$ and $N_s'' < 0$, while the optimal level from the private perspective of a monopoly is $z_p^*$ such that $N_p' = 0$ and $N_p'' < 0$. At the monopolist's optimal extent of innovation, $f'(z) = (N_p N_s' - N_s N_p')/N_p^2 = N_p N_s'/N_p^2 > 0$ and thus $N_s' > 0$. Therefore, $z$ is too low; the extent of innovation is less than socially optimal. Conversely, at the socially optimal extent of innovation, $f'(z) = -N_s N_p'/N_p^2 > 0$ and thus $N_p' < 0$. Therefore, from the monopolist's perspective, the extent of innovation is greater than optimal. Thus, if the ratio of net social value to net private value of innovative investment increases as the multi-industry nature of the innovation increases, a monopolist will do too little investment in innovations spanning multiple industries.

Now, it is precisely these innovations that are likely to be pursued by research consorta. As seen in Chapter 12, consortia are putting together R&D efforts that span sets of industries and, further, those sets have been combined previously by individual diversified firms investing on their own. Such consortia then could improve private returns to R&D by eliminating competition that is socially optimal. Competition can stimulate firms to undertake strategies that increase the expected multi-industry span – the extent – of innovation toward socially desirable levels that would not be reached in the absence of competition.

Whether the concern is for the optimal extent of innovation or simply for the optimal expenditure on an innovation particular to a given industry, given that even a consortium would be unable to appropriate all of the returns to its innovative investment, the overbidding (from the private perspective of the firms) of competitors can move R&D investment toward the social optimum. Whether or not it does depends on the extent to which competition entails truly wasteful, duplicative efforts (rather than optimal multiple trials in the context of uncertainty) and the extent to which competition erodes the competitors' appropriation of returns.[12]

### 13.4 Screening cooperative R&D

Congress claims that DOJ and the FTC have "essentially ministerial" duties in processing the notifications of R&D joint ventures. "Neither agency is authorized to 'certify' or 'approve' the conduct described in a notification" (U.S. 98th Congress, September 21, 1984, p. 20). However, under their more general mandates, the enforcement agencies are responsible for screening cooperative R&D to be protected by the NCRA. Yet our discussion of the historical context of the NCRA suggests that DOJ and the FTC are not likely to be objective evaluators. Indeed, the record suggests the Reagan administration's position of advocacy regarding business combinations clouded its scrutiny of the economic consequences of the ventures. DOJ's assessments of cooperative R&D were in fact uncritical.

As documented in Chapter 12, DOJ has said that it wants to preserve competition and will block ventures that lessen it significantly (U.S. Department of Justice, June 26, 1985). But Chapter 12's review of the cooperative R&D granted NCRA protection shows that the projects appear to have quite inclusive memberships, sometimes even when one does not look for a particular niche in the general area of research. The administration had neither developed nor applied a careful, sufficiently complete model within which each actual case could be evaluated.[13]

Our examples in Chapter 12 suggest a willingness on the part of the antitrust enforcement agencies to overlook the possibility that R&D performance would be worse with cooperation than without it, and that willingness can be understood in the historical context that is described in this chapter. Given the historical context, there is reason for concern about the thoroughness and the seriousness of the policy establishment's evaluation of consequences of cooperative R&D. But is there any evidence that the ventures formed are nonetheless of the sort we would want to see? I think not, given the evidence adduced throughout this book. I shall now draw together some of the pertinent evidence and discuss its implications for the usefulness of the NCRA and its newly amended version that extends the act's coverage from R&D ventures to production ventures as well.

### 13.5 Evidence on NCRA cooperative R&D

Championed by the Reagan administration, the NCRA was passed to promote cooperation in research among competitors. The aim is to encourage R&D efforts by overcoming fears of antitrust liability that might inhibit desirable combinations. The combinations can be desirable if they reduce R&D costs by eliminating wasteful duplication of R&D

efforts and allowing realization of scale economies, or if they make it easier for firms to appropriate higher fractions of the returns from their innovative investment, returns that might otherwise be competed away by a host of patentable substitutes.

The Reagan administration actively supported such coordination of competitors' R&D. The support for the NCRA legislation, revealed in the Conference Report[14] on the bill and in the statements of advocacy by DOJ and the Commerce Department, does not persuade me that policymakers appreciate the magnitude of the potential problem arising from the bill. Namely, as explained in Section 13.3, theory suggests that cooperation could worsen performance in the area of technological change. Given the expectation that under monopoly the appropriation of returns to innovative investment will be incomplete, from society's standpoint even a monopolist is likely to underinvest in research and development. Two characteristics of competition in R&D can correct such underinvestment. First, in the uncertain world of innovative investment, some duplication afforded by the parallel paths of competitors can be shown to be optimal. Second, competitors fear preemption and also consider only their individual profits rather than total profits in market. Consequently they have a tendency to overinvest, from a monopolist's private value-maximizing perspective, in innovative investment. That tendency can offset the lessened appropriability in competitive markets. Competition in R&D may bring us closer to the socially optimal level of innovative investment.

There is some evidence to support the a priori reasons for suspecting that combining firms' research efforts may not improve the pace of technological progress. My research causes me to doubt the assertions about the benefits of business combinations in R&D. Earlier research, and some subsequent research using new data but old techniques, finds evidence that, up to a point, R&D intensity increases with seller concentration, but at high levels of concentration, the R&D intensity falls. Such evidence could be used to support the moderate amounts of concentration of resources for research promoted by the new law.

However, in my opinion, there is no general cross-sectional evidence that concentration of research resources matters one way or another. Once the FTC LB data, and the methodology they allowed, were used in Chapters 7 and 10 to control for firm effects as well as the broad industry category effects, seller concentration (the extent to which a few sellers dominate a market, with foreign as well as U.S. sellers' presence measured) had no effect on R&D intensity, although without the controls the effect found by others was clearly present. Some firms, perhaps with better research scientists or with better financial resources, do more R&D than others even when they conduct research in the same industry categories. Some industry categories, such as the pharmaceutical industry, offer more opportunity for R&D than others, regardless of the level of seller concentration. Evidently, differences among firms in the value, cost, and opportunity for R&D, entirely apart from those differences that may arise from differences in the concentration of R&D resources, determine the differences in R&D intensity observed across firms and industries. Whether one looks at "R&D spending" or various elements of that heterogeneous total, the relative importance of opportunity differences and the relative unimportance of seller concentration has been repeatedly documented in a variety of empirical studies (Baldwin and Scott, 1987, chapter 3).

Further, Chapter 12's review of the cooperative R&D projects that have filed for protection under the NCRA suggests that the cooperation fostered by the act may well lower social economic welfare rather than increase it. The cooperative projects are not predominately in unconcentrated industries where joint ventures might be needed to overcome fragmentation of R&D effort. Rather, the ventures are occurring in the more concentrated industries. Neither are the cooperative projects predominately in relatively low-productivity-growth industries, where joint ventures would perhaps improve productivity. Instead, the ventures are occurring in the relatively high-productivity-growth industries. The cooperative projects are not occurring predominately in industries where we have not observed purposive diversification and where the appropriability advantages from such diversification were not able to offset appropriability problems caused by competition in R&D. They are in fact more likely to be found in industry categories combined with others by firms purposively diversifying their R&D activity. Cooperative projects are not occurring predominately in industries where company-financed R&D intensity has been low and where extra stimulus might be needed to get innovative investment, but they are occurring in high-intensity–R&D industries. And as explained in Chapter 12, we are not simply observing that cooperation is most likely where R&D is most likely when we compare old traditional or smokestack industries with high-technology industries. Further, there is no evidence that the cooperative R&D is in categories in which there have been significant appropriability problems. In all, it seems quite likely that the joint ventures will increase the profits of the firms involved but that society will lose because the reduction in competitive pressures was not necessary to get the firms to invest in productive R&D.

Yet based on the optimistic view of these ventures, we have the proposed extensions of the NCRA in order to cover production ventures. My research, in the context of the historical perspective of their uncritical promotion, implies that these laws, contrary to what one might think based on the rhetoric of their proponents, do not offer much prospect for the panacea claimed for them for R & D, for productivity, or for international competitiveness.

### 13.6 Policy to achieve competitive pressure and cooperation simultaneously

When cooperative R & D sacrifices desirable competitive pressure, a new policy that would allow cooperation yet simulate the kind of competitive pressure described in Chapters 8 and 12 could improve social economic welfare. In the next chapter I shall propose that we introduce a new type of taxation that induces desirable competitive responses in R & D behavior in those high-technology industries where coooperation among otherwise competing firms is needed to realize economies of scale and scope, appropriation of returns to innovation, and the mitigation of risk. The taxation policy would be used to simulate the desirable aspect of competitive pressure that is lost because of the cooperation; ideally, the benefits of cooperation can be had without the costs.

I believe there is an urgent need for some movement toward the type of innovation policy I shall propose. The current policy environment is overwhelmingly in favor of promoting cooperation in R & D and production among competing firms. As we have discussed in Chapters 12 and 13, the policy establishment has accepted the arguments that such cooperation is required for the realization of economies of scale and scope, the appropriation of returns from innovative investment, and the mitigation of uncertainties. Jorde and Teece (1988; 1990) have championed the view that has prevailed in the bills extending the provisions of the NCRA from cooperative activities in R & D to joint ventures in production. As we have seen, these laws ignore the potential costs of such cooperation. The cooperation promoted by the laws reduces competitive pressure that may be desirable because, as explained in Chapter 8, it stimulates firms to work harder at innovating to avoid being preempted by rivals, and because, as explained in Chapter 11, it stimulates diversity.

The essence of competition for a firm is the probability that before it innovates a rival will innovate and, by preempting the firm, reduce the value of whatever the firm's R & D investment ultimately produces. Like a sword of Damocles, that constant impending threat can in some circumstances compel the competing firm to strive to innovate rather than lag with a mere imitation. We shall now turn to the task of describing policies that would replace desirable competitive pressure with taxation plans that mimic the effects of such pressure. The policies would theoretically allow desirable competitive pressures to be maintained in those high-technology industries targeted by our new laws that promote cooperative R & D.

# 14

## Damoclean taxation and innovation

Numerous government policies attempt to spur spending for research and development (R&D) in order to achieve socially desirable innovations and productivity growth. Two government policies for promoting industrial R&D that have received a considerable amount of attention recently are the granting of tax reductions in return for increased R&D spending and the lessening of potential antitrust liabilities faced by cooperative R&D ventures. The effectiveness of both policies has been questioned.[1] In this chapter, I use the theory developed in Chapter 8 to show that in circumstances for which the policies have been expected to work they are likely to fail. I then introduce two novel tax policies, either of which can in theory induce socially optimal R&D investment when the conventional policies would fail. The policies are designed to mimic socially desirable competitive pressure in circumstances under which it would otherwise be absent. A policy that would simulate competitive pressures could make an especially important contribution now because of the growing trend toward cooperation among previously rivalrous firms. Thus, I shall consider the practical possibilities for the theoretical taxes proposed.

### 14.1 Introduction

Chapter 12 described circumstances in which cooperation among an industry's firms are conventionally considered socially desirable and for which free-entry noncooperative rivalry is often presumed undesirable. These same circumstances have often been presumed to justify tax breaks in order to stimulate R&D. In the context of those circumstances, Chapter 8 developed a model of industrial R&D rivalry and compared the social economic welfare implications of monopoly or complete cooperation

For helpful comments about the idea of Damoclean taxation, I thank William L. Baldwin, Charles C. Brown, Paul Geroski, Stephen Martin, and Dennis C. Mueller.

with free-entry noncooperative rivalry. Intermediate cases of cooperation among subsets of an industry's firms could be developed from the model, but such development is not important for the purposes of this chapter. Because of the desirable effect of competitive pressure highlighted in the model, the free-entry noncooperative rivalry results in better performance than complete cooperation even though society would, in an ideal world, prefer only one firm. As shown in Chapter 8, although the social optimum would be to have only one firm if that firm could somehow be induced to conduct its R&D spending in the way society would prefer, left to make its own decisions, a monopolist or completely cooperative venture would not do as well as uncooperative rivals. In the present chapter, Section 14.2 discusses government policies in the context of the social economic welfare issues presented in Chapter 8 and focuses in particular on the tax credit. Section 14.3 describes a new policy – the Damoclean tax which is conceptually the same as pure competitive pressure (the pressure alone without any erosion in total private returns). Section 14.4 discusses practical problems and suggests a second tax less directly tied to the concept of competitive pressure yet capable of accomplishing the same result. I show that given the circumstances described in Chapters 8 and 12, the tax credit will not solve the problem of suboptimal behavior by the monopolist or cooperative venture. However, I am able to show that in theory my alternative policies induce socially optimal behavior. Society is able to have the benefits of consolidation and cooperation and yet have the benefits of competitive pressure as well by using either of the proposed policies. Section 14.5 relates the findings in the chapter to the debate about appropriate government policies toward industrial R&D.

## 14.2 Conventional government policies

Conventional policy changes an innovation's private value ($W$ in our model of Chapter 8) or cost by using patent law or tax policy. Additionally, public policy reduces competitive pressure and increases expected profits by fostering cooperative ventures. I shall suggest policies that would allow the benefits of cooperation while maintaining the benefits of competitive pressures. The policies would simulate competitive pressure and could thus be used to bring about the benefits of noncooperative rivalry even when such rivalry is absent.

Of course, at least in the context of our model, the problem of monopoly underinvestment in R&D can be solved by increasing the proportion of the social value of R&D that is appropriated by the monopolist. Patent law and conventional tax breaks for R&D work roughly in this way by trying to increase the proportion of social value appropriated by the innovator.[2] However, these policy instruments yield imperfect results. The

Expected Profits

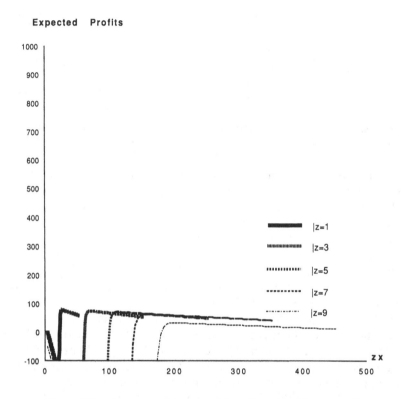

Figure 14.1   A monopoly's expected profits, given the tax credit.

protection afforded by patents is generally quite incomplete and variable.[3] The effectiveness of tax incentives, which typically reduce the after-tax cost of R&D, has often been questioned. Although the effect is in the right direction, it has not usually been considered to be very large and certainly would not be expected to solve the sort of underinvestment problem of concern here and in Chapters 8 and 12.[4]

For example, Figure 14.1 simulates the effect of a tax credit similar to the U.S. R&D tax credit as of 1991 in the context of the model of industrial R&D that we developed in Chapter 8. The law allows the firm to deduct 20 percent of eligible R&D spending from its federal tax bill. Figure 14.1 reproduces Figure 8.9 except that R&D costs are reduced by 20 percent, and the scaling has been changed to make the figure visually directly comparable to Figure 8.8. Thus the reader can see that even the 20 percent tax credit leaves the monopolist in a position far inferior to what would be the case if it appropriated the social value of its innovation. The simulation will overestimate the effect of the actual U.S. credit because only expenditures above a calculated R&D base are eligible. If the project's expenditures are all eligible for the credit, Figure 14.1 (with computer programs behind the scene calculating the optimum that the figure illustrates) shows that with the 20 percent tax credit, the monopolist still (just as in Chapter 8 without the tax credit) chooses only one trial rather than the socially optimal number of five trials. Furthermore, the monopolist's periodic expenditure increases from 22.02 (found in Chapter 8) to only 22.06. The monopolist's expected profits increase from 59.0152 to 65.3662.

Of course, ours is but one parameterization of the R&D problem. I have taken pains to make it a realistic one, though, and as observed in Chapter 8, it is one of an infinitely large set that corresponds to the basic conditions often presumed to require joint ventures and tax breaks. The simulation suggests that the empirical findings of modest effects of the tax credit for R&D spending have a sound theoretical explanation. The simulation certainly provides theoretical support for the U.S. Congressional Budget Office's summary (July 1991, p. 90) of the position of critics of the U.S. tax credit for R&D: "Critics contend that the credit encourages little additional R&D, and so provides a subsidy to firms that would undertake the R&D anyway." The simulation shows that the problem need not be attempts to gain the tax credit by the reclassification of existing expenditures as R&D. Instead, the fundamental problem is that the credit does not provide a strong incentive to increase R&D at the margin even though the credit does increase profits. Basically, the problem is a lack of appropriation on the demand side. Even if we cut R&D costs by 20 percent, to add another trial implies a big jump in R&D costs, and we have done nothing for improving the appropriating of the benefits. With the one trial, the periodic investment had already reached the range where diminishing returns begin, and after the initial range of economies, returns diminish sharply.

Another conventional policy approach is for the government to make direct expenditures for R&D. Once the government gets involved with such expenditures, though, experience shows that avoiding the wasting of the taxpayers' dollars is a delicate matter.[5] The form that government expenditures on R&D should take is the subject of much debate.[6] My purpose here is to propose an alternative instrument for policy – tax policies that simulate pure competitive pressure.

### 14.3 Damoclean taxation

Continuing the example developed in Chapter 8, let us return to the monopoly. Society would prefer one firm, but society wants $z = 5$

R&D units or trials, not the single trial that the monopolist would voluntarily choose. Suppose that the government announced a hazard rate, namely, the conditional probability of taxation – conditional on the tax having not been triggered yet. If the monopoly (or cooperative venture) has not yet introduced the innovation meeting certain specified goals when the tax is triggered, then the full force of the tax will be felt. As long as the targeted innovation had not yet been introduced, the tax would hang over the firm's head like the sword of Damocles. The government, probably in cooperation with the firm, would announce in general terms the goals to be achieved by the innovation. These would typically be general performance goals, not detailed requirements for the form of the specific innovation that achieves the goals.[7]

Then, the government would announce the parameters $s$, $u$, and $v$. The first parameter $s$ is the hazard rate, which would be constant through time. Thus, the probability of taxation being triggered – the sword dropping – by time $t$ is $F_G(t) = 1 - e^{-st}$. The parameter $u$ is the proportion of the innovation's private value $W$ that would be left after taxes if the tax were triggered before the firm or cooperative venture introduced its innovation. If the tax were triggered prior to the introduction of an innovation meeting the preannounced goals, the private value of the innovation to the firm would be $M = uW$. Finally, $v$ is the proportion of the private value that would be left after taxes if the firm did innovate before the tax was triggered. In that case, the private value of the innovation would be $N = vW$. We shall assume throughout our discussion that the government has set $v = 1$, and we continue our simulations with $W = 100$ and now $N = 100$.

The expected value of the innovation for the firm then becomes

$$\int_0^\infty e^{-rt} N(1 - F_G(t)) F_z'(t)\, dt + \int_0^\infty e^{-rt} M F_G(t) F_z'(t)\, dt \qquad (14.1)$$

where the first integral is the value to the firm of innovation before the tax is triggered and the second is the innovation's value if it follows the triggering of the Damoclean tax. $F_G(t) = 1 - e^{-st}$, $F_z(t) = 1 - e^{-zh(x)t}$, and thus the expected revenues for the monopolist are

$$\frac{(N - M)zh(x)}{r + zh(x) + s} + \frac{Mzh(x)}{r + zh(x)}. \qquad (14.2)$$

Expected costs are

$$\frac{zx}{r + zh(x)} + C(z), \qquad (14.3)$$

since the monopolist incurs its periodic costs as long as it has not yet innovated (either by prearranged commitment with the government or because $u$ is high enough to make the continued R&D worthwhile even if the tax has been triggered). The monopolist's expected profits given the Damoclean tax are then

$$p_G(x,z) = \frac{(N-M)zh(x)}{r+zh(x)+s} + \frac{Mzh(x)-zx}{r+zh(x)} - C(z). \qquad (14.4)$$

The government can now select values for $s$ and $u$ such that the monopolist will choose the socially optimal number of trials and periodic expenditure for each. For example, continuing our simulation experiment (without the 20 percent tax credit), one optimal government policy is to set $u = 0.226$ and $s = 6.68$. With these settings, the monopolist will choose the socially optimal investment pattern. It will choose the number of trials $z = 5$, rather than the one trial it chose without the Damoclean tax (or for that matter with the 20 percent tax credit). Furthermore the monopolist will choose periodic expenditure of $x = 22.2$, rather than its choice without the Damoclean tax. Figure 14.2 illustrates the monopolist's expected profits given the Damoclean tax with $u = 0.226$ and $s = 6.68$.

Pairs of $u$ and $s$ that will induce socially optimal behavior are readily found using the following procedure. Letting $x_s$ and $z_s$ denote the socially optimal values for $x$ and $z$, choose a value $u^*$ for $u$ such that $p_G(x = x_s, z = z_s | u^*, s)$ has a maximum value for some $s = s^*$. Thus, $s^*$ is the value for $s$ such that $\partial P_G/\partial x = 0$ at $x = x_s$, $z = z_s$, $u = u^*$, and $s = s^*$ and $P_G$ is at a maximum. In the example of Figure 14.2, given that $x = x_s = 22.2$, $z = z_s = 5$, and $u = u^* = 0.226$, $\partial P_G/\partial x = 0$ at $s = s^* = 6.68$ (the other zero of the function, $s = 3.5$, corresponds to a minimum). Now, since $z$ is integer-valued, we ask what integer value of $z$ maximizes $p_G(x = x_s, z | u^*, s^*)$ or in our example, what integer value of $z$ maximizes $p_G(x = x_s = 22.2, z | u^* = 0.226, s^* = 6.68)$. If that integer value of $z$ is $z_s$, then we have found a policy $\{u = u^*, s = s^*\}$ that will induce socially optimal behavior on the part of the monopolist. In our example,

$$\max_z p_G(x = x_s = 22.2, z | u^* = 0.226, s^* = 6.68)$$

is 4.12823 and occurs for $z = z_s = 5$.

The policy works because given $u^* = 0.226$ and $s^* = 6.68$, the firm chooses $x = 22.2$ and $z = 5$ since it then finds that $\partial P_G/\partial x = 0$ and $P_G$ is maximized in $z$ given $x$. The firm would solve the two simultaneous conditions; successive approximations gets there quickly. Our example is shown in Figure 14.2.

To maximize its expected profits, the monopolist illustrated in Figure 14.2 and facing the Damoclean tax $\{u = 0.226, s = 6.68\}$ would solve simultaneously the conditions $\partial P_G/\partial x = 0$ and $\max_z P_G$. Successive approximations quickly converge to the solution. For example, substituting $z = 1$

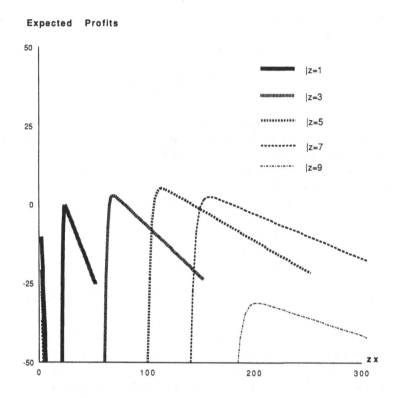

Figure 14.2   Expected profits for the monopolist facing a Damoclean tax.

into $\partial P_G/\partial x = 0$ implies $x = 22.06$, which when substituted into $\max_z P_G$ implies that $z = 5$, which when substituted into $\partial P_G/\partial x = 0$ implies $x = 22.2$, which when substituted into $\max_z P_G$ implies $z = 5$.

Socially optimal $\{u, s\}$ pairs are easy to find with the trial and error technique described above in these situations where competitive pressure is socially desirable, because there is a range of values for $u$ that imply values of $s$ for which $\partial P_G/\partial x$ (at $z = z_s$ and $x = x_s$) equals 0 at a maximum for $P_G$ and for which $\max_z P_G$ occurs for the socially optimal $z = z_s$.

### 14.4  Practical problems and an alternative – The preinnovation periodic tax

Although explaining how a Damoclean tax would work is, I hope, a useful way to explain why pure competitive pressure is desirable to ensure socially optimal innovative investment, the Damoclean tax is no doubt rather impractical. In this section, I shall discuss the practical problems and offer an alternative tax – the preinnovation periodic tax – that Charles C. Brown suggested as a way to meet some of the practical objections to the Damoclean tax and yet retain the desirable effect of the new tax. I believe that Brown's suggestion is particularly likely to be viable as a policy to improve performance of the joint ventures "with a social conscience" that I described in Chapter 12.

*Credibility:* One practical problem with the Damoclean tax is that it might not be a credible policy. That is, the government might, once the tax had been triggered prior to an innovation being introduced, be better off if it reneged on its promise to exact in tax the specified proportion of the innovation's returns once it does appear. The government might typically have an incentive to renegotiate the bargain with the firms investing in R&D. I do not think that credibility would in practice be a problem, though. I believe that the policy would be credible because the government is playing a supergame. It needs to keep its reputation as an enforcer of the tax. In the multiperiod game, the loss from not reneging (in those cases where if there were no future projects reneging would be optimal) is less than the loss from being unable to use the policy in the future.

*Randomness:* Another potential practical problem with the Damoclean tax is that the government's tax authorities and probably the lawmakers and their constituents would balk at introducing such explicit randomness into the tax system. One reader of the earlier version of this chapter even suggested that the tax might be unconstitutional. The solution proposed to me by Charles C. Brown was to use a nonrandom, fixed periodic tax that would be paid in every period up until the innovation was introduced but the tax liability would cease upon introduction of the innovation. With the Damoclean tax, the firms would "hurry up" to beat the triggering of the tax, while with Brown's preinnovation periodic tax the firms would hurry up to hasten the day when they no longer faced the tax liability. Although the preinnovation periodic tax is not as close conceptually to pure competitive pressure, it would accomplish the same thing.

Figure 14.3 simulates the effect of the preinnovation periodic tax and demonstrates that it can be used to induce the technically efficient monopoly or complete joint venture in R&D to invest the socially optimal amount. The algebra of the model is identical to what we have developed carefully earlier, except that now in addition to the flow costs of $zx$, there are additionally flow costs $\phi$ for the periodic tax until the time of the innovation's introduction. Figure 14.3 shows that in our parameterization of the problem, if $\phi = 89.3$ then the venture will choose the socially optimal number of trials ($z = 5$) and the socially optimal periodic investment

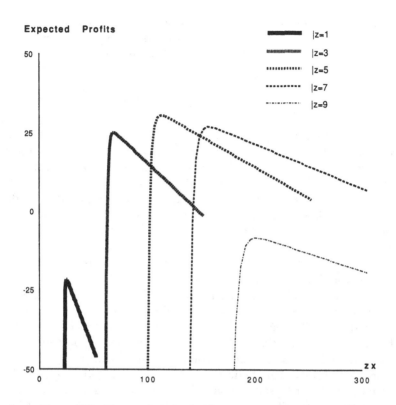

Figure 14.3   Expected profits for the monopolist facing a preinnovation periodic tax.

($x = 22.2$) for each trial. The optimal value for the periodic tax is readily found by choosing a $\phi$ such that expected profits for the venture are maximized at $z = z_s^*$ and $x = x_s^*$. Thus, maximizing expected profits over $\phi$ given the socially optimal choice for $z$ and $x$ yields for our particular parameterization $\phi = 89.3$. Then simulating the venture's behavior using the procedure described in Chapter 8, we find that with $\phi = 89.3$ the venture would maximize its expected profits by setting $z = 5$ and $x = 22.2$. That is, given the optimal preinnovation periodic tax, the venture chooses the socially optimal number of trials and the socially optimal R & D investment.

*Entry:* There are of course additional practical problems that will plague even Brown's tax. For one, given that the socially optimal solution has been engineered, the complete venture will expect profits – in the foregoing example with the periodic tax of $\phi = 89.3$, the expected profits are 29.65. Because expected profits are in general positive, as we have seen in the development of the free-entry Nash noncooperative equilibrium, it will typically be profitable for firms to enter. The government would have to be aware of any attempts to enter and prevent them if the carefully engineered socially optimal solutions are to work.

*Information:* These theoretical tax policies in their most complete forms require more information than will typically be available. First, to be completely implemented, the policies require the knowledge of the underlying technical uncertainty – the relationship between R&D expenditures and the probability of success by any given time. In many circumstances, it might be possible to formulate good estimates of the parameterization of the R&D problem, but such knowledge would not typically be readily available. Perhaps in certain cases where society had a clear mandate to help steer industry toward an R&D solution, the legitimacy of the government's role would make it possible for a successful collaboration between the government and industry in order to establish the necessary information. Nelson (1982a, p. 460) has observed that a "recognized governmental need lends legitimacy to government attempts to stimulate and guide the evolution of the relevant technologies." In such circumstances, the legitimacy of the government's role might make it possible to develop the necessary information and to win acceptance and support for one of the novel policies. The preinnovation periodic tax might be especially appropriate for ensuring optimal investment in technologies designed to solve environmental problems such as those addressed by the numerous joint ventures described in Chapter 12. Industry and government have already joined in these R&D joint ventures. Implementation of the preinnovation periodic tax would be a logical step to ensure timely research, and in addition to inducing efficient R&D investment, the periodic tax could be seen as "just" in the sense that it is paid as long as the environmental problem persists.

Some information problems might be too difficult to solve successfully. For example, Dennis Mueller (personal correspondence) points up that firms would have an incentive to claim that they had in fact innovated even when the developments that are claimed to be innovations do not perform properly or do not sell well. The Department of Defense of course has to solve similar problems in determining when a development contract has been fulfilled. Mueller observes that the taxation authority (the Internal Revenue Service in the U.S.) would have an almost regulatory posture toward firms. The tax authority would have to determine when an innovation had been successfully completed and then check later on to ensure that the technical or market success claimed for an innovation had been realized. Again, perhaps in cases of great importance to society, the recognition of the legitimacy of the government's role would make it possible to surmount such information problems.

With the foregoing problems in mind, perhaps a cautious summary is in order. We can say that in any event the presentation has demonstrated the inherent suboptimality of the existing tax and subsidy policy, *even if existing criticisms are met.* Further, we have seen that a theoretically optimal policy can be designed. Perhaps something approximating it more closely than the present policy could conceivably be implemented, especially in cases where the legitimacy of the government's role is clearly defined.

## 14.5 Conclusion

In the last decade, economists have developed new understanding about Schumpeter's vision (Schumpeter, 1942; Baldwin and Scott, 1987, pp. 1–4) of the importance of rivalry in R&D. At the same time, there has been a broad movement toward cooperation in R&D. Strong advocates for cooperative R&D have emerged among industrialists, policymakers, and academics.[8] The policy establishments of many nations have supported the sensibleness of cooperative research ventures, but the cooperative ventures in the United States have received special attention because of the National Cooperative Research Act of 1984 (NCRA), which lessened any potential antitrust liabilities for those ventures that notified the U.S. Federal Trade Commission and the U.S. Department of Justice of their formation, basic purpose, and members.[9]

There have been concerns that cooperative R&D sacrifices desirable competition in R&D,[10] but the bulk of the commentary has emphasized the benefits of cooperation. Those benefits include realization of economies of scale for research units and economies of scope across research units, greater ability to appropriate the returns from the R&D investments, mitigation of uncertainty, and elimination of wasteful duplication. Proponents of cooperation emphasize these benefits and assume that cooperation will increase desirable innovative investment and that society will benefit. Katz and Ordover (1990) provide an especially balanced assessment of the pros and cons of cooperative R&D and conclude that it is too simple by far to assume that the benefits emphasized by proponents will mean that society will benefit from the cooperation. Yet notifications under the NCRA proceed apace, and the policy establishment gives no evidence of seriously considering the possibility that cooperative R&D will cost society more because of the lost competitive pressures than it gains because cooperation achieves economies of scale and scope, lessens uncertainty, and increases appropriation of returns for the investors. Somewhat similarly, the tax credit for R&D may not always produce a very large effect, yet among policies it has been a bellwether.

In this chapter I have attacked the nonchalance about lost competitive pressure directly. I do so by using theory to point up that even in those joint ventures where at first blush there appears to be the least likelihood that the cost of lost competitive pressure outweighs the gain from cooperation in R&D, it is quite reasonable to expect that cooperative R&D will decrease social economic welfare. Further, I show that the tax credit does not solve the problem. I then suggest new policies – the Damoclean tax and the more practical preinnovation periodic tax – that would allow cooperation to achieve its benefits while preserving the desirable effects of noncooperative rivalry. Like the tax credit and policies making cooperation more attractive, my proposed policies leave the detailed decision making and the solution to the R&D problem to the private sector.

My simulations make clear that even when cooperation in R&D among an industry's firms lessens social economic welfare, the cooperation is likely to be privately profitable. Similarly, even when the tax credit does not significantly improve R&D investment, the credit is privately profitable. It is then not only unsurprising to find that industry urges public support of cooperation among competitors.[11] Heeding industry's cries may lessen social economic welfare. That is because in many cases society would like parallel paths to speed an innovation's development; and yet, a monopolist or cooperative venture would not find parallel paths profitable because just a small portion of the innovation's social value is appropriated privately. If intellectual property rights are insufficient to overcome the appropriability problem, tax credits are unlikely to improve performance significantly. Given conventional policies, free-entry noncooperative R&D rivalry might well be the best market structure from society's standpoint. However, the unconventional Damoclean tax or the preinnovation periodic tax can allow cooperation while preserving desirable competitive pressure. These novel taxes can theoretically induce socially optimal R&D investment, and if their essential ideas could be effected by new practical policies, perhaps society could induce better R&D investment and performance.

AFTERWORD: PERSPECTIVES THROUGH TIME
AND ACROSS COUNTRIES

The findings about industrial diversification described in previous chapters suggest some broad lessons about what it takes for a country's manufacturers to be competitive in international markets. Since the results for U.S. manufacturers are broadly consistent with and complementary to findings in the literature about the manufacturers of other countries, I shall venture some conclusions about the archetypal successful international competitor. Those conclusions also suggest new policies; recall that the declining effectiveness of U.S. manufacturers in international trade provided important motivation for the NCRA policy toward cooperative research and development (R&D) and for the R&D tax credit. Further, the policy initiatives suggested by the research in this book that uses U.S. data are potentially applicable to the policies of many countries because the U.S. approach to antitrust policy is increasingly being applied throughout the world. For example, one prominent antitrust policy publication reports that "For the first time in the history of modern Japan, antitrust enforcement officials in 1991 displayed visible clout and achieved visible results, and they expect to increase their role in the economy during 1992."[1] Antitrust enforcement activity is not only increasing in Japan, but in Canada, the European Community, the United Kingdom, Germany, France, and Italy as well.[2] Further, with grants from the Agency for International Development, the U.S. Department of Justice and the Federal Trade Commission are assisting the nations of Eastern Europe to develop antitrust enforcement programs.[3]

To relate the book's findings to ideas about how private business strategies and public policies affect international competitiveness of firms, I shall need to talk about many of the dimensions of "purposive diversification." Purposive diversification can occur for many reasons. It could be intended to facilitate multimarket contact in order to enhance market

215

power *without* increasing concentration in specific markets, or it could be to internalize competitive spillovers and reduce R&D pressures. It could be intended to obtain static economies of scope, or it could be to internalize positive R&D spillovers. Indeed, it could be intended to achieve the wholly "innocent" static and dynamic efficiencies and yet have as its unintended consequence the increase in market power and the reduction in competitive R&D pressures. One of my arguments in this Afterword is that the historical setting, including Japan's trade policy and policy toward cooperative ventures, may in some industries have favored Japan with a more productive combination of the foregoing possible reasons for purposive diversification. Another of my arguments is that sensible policy toward diversifying behavior can be devised despite the obvious tension between the static and dynamic inefficiencies and efficiencies that can result because of purposive diversification. The tension may be resolved by designing policies that distinguish certain types of diversifying behavior (e.g., internal expansion versus conglomerate merger) and certain types of R&D investment (e.g., generic research versus proprietary applied research) and certain types of spillovers (e.g., negative "competitive" spillovers versus positive "technological" spillovers).

*Success in international competition:* My findings about the efficiency implications of purposive diversification suggest that part of the reason for the success of Japan's manufacturers and the contrasting lackluster performance of U.S. firms in a number of industries during the last quarter century may be traced to two policies. First, the typical U.S. business strategy of rather pure conglomerate diversification leading to a decrease in purposive diversification contrasts with the strategy of Japan's *keiretsu* that link complementary activities among several firms joined in a network of cooperation. Second, the U.S. public policy that encourages joint venture activity by U.S. firms contrasts with the more long-standing public policy in Japan through which government nurtures cooperative activity among an industry's competitors. The nature of Japan's cooperative ventures differs from those in the United States for many reasons. I shall focus on differences directly related to my theoretical and empirical findings. In particular, some evidence suggests that Japan's cooperative ventures are more likely than their U.S. counterparts to develop truly generic research results which the individual firms then incorporate in their proprietary products that benefit not only from the cooperative generic research, but also from the purposive diversification of R&D through the *keiretsu* groups. The Japanese firms then compete with one another and with foreign firms in the sale of those products that use the generic knowledge that was developed cooperatively. In contrast, my evidence suggests that the U.S. NCRA joint ventures may be eliminating competition among purposively diversified firms in the development of proprietary technologies.

I shall focus on the foregoing differences between the cooperation among firms in Japan as contrasted with the cooperation among firms in the United States. There are important additional differences between Japan and the United States in institutional practices and culture; many are discussed by Mueller (1987, pp. 82–86) and Scherer (1992, pp. 1428–1429, 1430). Japanese firms may, for example, take a long-run perspective on investments because of the lifetime tenure of their employees. Mueller (p. 85) cites Itami's (1985, pp. 71–72) observation that Japanese firms typically rely on an internal labor market and an external capital market, yet, as Mueller emphasizes, just the opposite has often been true in the United States. Japan's internal labor market may allow a long-term investment perspective. Further, the external capital market may have imposed discipline that prevented the U.S. pattern of internally financed acquisitions that arguably diverted resources from R&D investments (Adams and Brock, 1991b, pp. 96–112). For the *keiretsu* groups, the external capital market argument must rely on the fact that the parts of a group – in particular, a bank and the manufacturing firms – are independent in the relevant sense. Odagiri (1992, p. 34) supports that interpretation; arguably a bank's membership in a business group allows better information about the quality of loans rather than encouraging unsound banking practices.

I shall focus, though, on the two possible differences which, for reasons understandable in terms of my research, could help further explain the relative success of Japan's international competitors. The two differences are, first, the extent to which industrial size has been attained with purposive diversification and, second, the extent to which cooperation has focused on generic research. As Scherer observes (p. 1426), "successful growth has made Japan's leading enterprises large in an absolute sense, whether size is measured in terms of individual operating units or the more encompassing multiindustry *keiretsu* groups." Further, Scherer observes (p. 1427) that "Japanese companies have also led the way in cooperative research and development ventures."

Scherer believes that taken together, the size and cooperative ventures of Japan's successful international competitors have suggested to many observers that the Schumpeter of *Capitalism, Socialism, and Democracy* may have been right – size and market power may be necessary for good performance despite the wealth of evidence to the contrary in scholarly works. Scherer reviews the prominent differences in institutions and culture and concludes (p. 1429) that "to the extent that organizational cultures do differ, the Schumpeterian large firm–innovator paradigm may apply with greater force in Japan than in America. Merely increasing U.S. company size without changing the underlying culture might fail to spur innovativeness, or even degrade it." Reflecting on these views in the context of my findings about purposive diversification, I believe that without modifications the U.S. cooperative R&D ventures and especially the movement to extend the NCRA to cover production ventures are quite likely to lessen economic performance, even though the Japanese experience with cooperation has brought good results.

*Parallels across countries:* My findings about diversification in the United States are consistent with the findings of others who have studied the manufacturing firms of other countries. Further, as Scherer (1992, p. 1425) observes, the economic policies of France, England, and West Germany have reflected views similar to the Reagan administration's view, reviewed in Chapter 13, that a relaxation of U.S. merger laws would allow U.S. manufacturers to merge and, by becoming larger, to be more capable competitors in international markets. Thus, I believe that the general conclusions about the effectiveness of purposive diversification are quite likely to be valid in many different countries and to be useful, given an understanding of pertinent country-specific factors, for predicting the potential for success of various private and public policies designed to improve both static and dynamic industrial performance in those different settings.

Regarding the effect of rivalry on R&D intensity, the most fundamental finding with U.S. data has been that in conventional tests, differences in the opportunity for R&D explain far more of the variation in R&D behavior and ensuing performance across manufacturing firms than do differences in market structure. Geroski's (1990) work turns up the same basic result with U.K. data that come from the same era as U.S. data studied in Chapters 7 and 10. It would seem reasonable, then, to assume that Chapter 9's findings about purposive diversification and R&D spending and industry productivity, and Chapter 11's findings about rivalry and R&D diversity would show up in similar experiments with U.K. data and, I would venture, with the data from other industrial countries. Review of empirical findings about R&D and market structure does not suggest fundamentally different relationships across countries (Baldwin and Scott, 1987).

My hypothesis that purposive diversification underlies the strong company effects in profits and R&D intensity is certainly consistent with the studies reported in Mueller (1990) for the economies of Canada, France, Japan, Sweden, West Germany, the United Kingdom, and the United States. Although there are differences across the countries in the extent to which individual-company profits diverge from the average and persist over time, there is a "common pattern of permanent departures from average profits across countries" (p. 189). The basic finding that company profitability can diverge from the average and persist over time shows up for all of these economies. Here, as in other international comparisons, there is support for the idea that basic knowledge about industrial economics that is acquired with the study of a single country's manufacturers may be useful in understanding the performance of other countries' manufacturers. Even when differences across countries emerge, they can often be comprehended within a single model of the behavior and performance in question. Most important, the persistence of profits discovered in the studies of the firms of these several countries is consistent with my cross-sectional findings in Parts II and III of firm (i.e., company) effects in profits and R & D intensity. From the cross-country study in Mueller (1990, p. 193), the authors conclude that a "main conclusion to be drawn from the country studies is that firm characteristics are more important than industry characteristics in accounting for differences in long run profit levels." I then conclude that when I find evidence that the U.S. firm effects reflect differences among firms in their purposive diversification, I have at least established a presumption that purposive diversification may underlie the firm effects discovered in the data for other countries.

*Contrasts between the United States and Japan:* The comparison of the United States and Japan provides a particularly provocative set of speculations. I focus on two closely related possibilities for the relative success of Japan's manufacturers in international competition. First, during the period of Japan's ascendancy in international trade, U.S. manufacturers became much more diversified and much less purposively diversified. At the same time, Japanese manufacturers linked complementary activities with *keiretsu*. Second, Japanese manufacturers and the Japanese government developed successful cooperative R & D programs long before the U.S. government tried to encourage such ventures with the NCRA. The success of Japan's exporters in world competition relative to the performance of many leading U.S. firms may well be related to the interaction of these two differences between Japan and the United States.

The *keiretsu* (see Odagiri, 1992, for detailed description of the various forms) promote efficiency by sharing information about production, marketing, and distribution and by coordinating those activities among the firms in the group. The *keiretsu* also coordinate vertical resource flows from upstream suppliers to downstream producers. Some of the information that is shared within a *keiretsu* group in order to make its members more efficient competitors could of course be information that was developed with the precompetitive, generic research of a cooperative research venture supported by the Japanese government and firms from different *keiretsu* groups. Cooperative research may be used to produce generic information that is then used by rivalrous firms from different *keiretsu* who are able to make the most of the information because of the purposive diversification effected by their own *keiretsu*.

Ravenscraft and Scherer (1987) document the increase in U.S. conglomerate diversification by comparing the extent of diversification for U.S. manufacturers in 1950 and in the mid-1970s. They use the same two sources of information that I have juxtaposed in Chapter 3 and used separately in other parts of this book. For 1950 they use the Corporate Patterns data (U.S. FTC, 1972) and for the mid-1970s they use the Federal Trade Commission Line of Business (FTC LB) data. Ravenscraft and Scherer demonstrate that conglomerate diversification for U.S. manufacturers increased dramatically from 1950 to the mid-1970s, when the productivity crisis began to hit hard and concerns about the international competitiveness of U.S. manufacturers took hold. Ravenscraft and Scherer, Mueller (1987), Porter (1987), and others have demonstrated that most U.S. conglomerates did not perform well. Further, Caves and Barton (1990) and Lichtenberg (1990) find that U.S. firms' diversification lowered their productivity.

A major finding of my research has been that firms that *purposively* diversify appear to have advantages that may, given other structural conditions that are favorable, show up in their profits, R&D, and productivity. The increase in pure conglomerateness for U.S. firms implies that the purposive diversification on which I have focused surely declined during the period preceding U.S. difficulties in international competition. Firms facing similar opportunities would be expected to diversify into largely the same set of industries if they were purposively pursuing economies of scope or market power. In fact, using the methodology and information developed in Part I, the significance of the multimarket contact for the leading manufacturing firms in the mid-1970s is typically less than the significance of multimarket contact for the leading firms in 1950. By the mid-1970s, the leading manufacturing firms were typically more scattered, and probably less purposive, in their diversification.[4] When from each manufacturing industry a pair of firms in the 1950 Corporate Patterns data (U.S. FTC, 1972) was drawn randomly, multimarket contact was significant at the 10 percent level for 54 percent of the pairs. When from each manufacturing industry a pair of firms in the 1974 FTC LB sample was drawn randomly, 35 percent of the pairs exhibited multimarket contact significant at the 10 percent level. Thus, as one would guess, given the findings about conglomerateness conventionally defined, *purposive* diversification appears to have declined for the leading U.S. manufacturers during the period from 1950 to the mid-1970s.[5]

In contrast, Japan's manufacturers combined complementary activities in their *keiretsu* groups (Odagiri, 1992, pp. 98–99, p. 134, p. 161). Odagiri's (1992) evaluation and Scherer's (1992) review of the literature suggests that these groups have had positive effects similar to those that I have found for purposive diversification in the United States. My evidence is consistent with the idea that purposively diversified firms are better able to deploy resources to take advantage of profitable opportunities in current markets and in R&D investments. For Japan's *keiretsu,* Scherer observes (p. 1428):

Masahiko Aoki (1990, p. 3) reports that "Japanese firms have cultivated an ability for rapid response by developing an internal scheme in which emergent information is utilized effectively on-site and in which operating activities are coordinated among related operating units on the basis of information sharing." He attributes Japanese *keiretsu* members' innovative successes to their rich in-house information networks and to the growth orientation shared by owner and employee interests because of corporate stock cross-holdings and employees' lifetime tenure.

There is increasing evidence that U.S. firms are striving to create their own imitation of Japanese *keiretsu.* Kelly and Port (1992) suggest that U.S. firms are forming such groups, although because of U.S. banking laws the groups do not have their own banks. Port and Carey (1992, p. 58) even suggest that signs of success for the pioneering U.S. research consortium, Microelectronics & Computer Technology Corporation (MCC), are the result of "blurring the difference between a consortium that does precompetitive research and a *keiretsu* that competes in the marketplace."

I turn now to Japan's relatively early reliance on cooperative ventures. Although cultural differences between Japan and the United States appear to be quite important, even at the basic level of the willingness of independent firms to join in a common effort (Scherer, 1992, p. 1429), I want here to focus on a different issue. The issue is quite pertinent to my findings in Chapter 12 that U.S. cooperative R&D protected by the NCRA may be cooperation that will reduce desirable R&D investment because it serves to internalize what Katz and Ordover (1990) have called "competitive spillovers" – the negative externalities imposed on rivals by individual R&D efforts – rather than "technological spillovers" – the positive externalities caused by appropriability difficulties of the type in which the lost value of the individual R&D is appropriated by the individual firm's rivals. Such "technological spillover" is different from the incomplete appropriability of research efforts that results (1) because the individual firm's R&D efforts reduce the probability of rivals' success and reduce the expected value of their innovations because of postinnovation competition among competing substitutes or (2) because an innovator cannot perfectly price-discriminate and therefore society gains consumer surplus that the firm will not count as a benefit in reaching its investment decision. While "competitive spillovers" cause the individual firms to over-invest from the private perspective of maximizing the joint private profits in the industry, with "technological spillovers" the individual firms under-invest. A cooperative venture in the latter case would then increase the collective R&D investment, since individually each firm stops investing where its own marginal benefit has fallen to marginal cost, yet collective marginal net benefit is positive.

There is good qualitative evidence to suggest that Katz and Ordover's "technological spillovers" are quite likely to be very important in many of the successful cooperative R&D ventures in Japan. Audretsch (1989) describes government support for cooperative ventures with an emphasis on developing generic information and sharing nonproprietary information. He considers the policies of Japan's Ministry of International Trade and Industry (MITI) and observes (pp. 109–110) that MITI's "policy towards patents suggests that the ultimate emphasis is on disseminating scientific knowledge while still preserving competition among firms." Further, Audretsch's analysis suggests (p. 122) that "there appears to be at least some evidence that the Japanese export performance tended to be stronger in industries in which government R&D policy, including the support of cooperative R&D programs, played a major role."

Audretsch does not believe that MITI's policy was *necessarily* the cause of the success in international competition, because there is also ample evidence that MITI may simply have been targeting those industries that were likely to succeed in international competition anyway (p. 122). The positive results of Japanese cooperative R&D projects and Audretsch's description do suggest that the Japanese may have succeeded in using joint ventures to internalize the positive externalities that individual firms would create for their industry if they did substantial generic research that produced results that spilled over to their competitors and increased the productivity of their competitors' research. The cooperative venture would then, other things being equal, increase R&D investment in the generic research beyond the point at which the individual firms would stop.

In Chapter 8, I have developed the theoretical argument that the U.S. cooperative ventures are more likely to internalize privately negative externalities than positive ones; Chapter 12 provides some supporting evidence. The U.S. ventures combine firms whose own, individual purposive diversification of R&D may have been creating private negative externalities because their research reduced the probability of their rivals' success and lowered the value of any innovations that their rivals would introduce. Thus I have argued that the U.S. cooperative ventures that have filed for protection under the NCRA are more likely to be privately profitable because they internalize the Katz and Ordover (1990) "competitive spillovers" rather than "technological spillovers." As a result, given the appropriability problems stemming from the innovator failing to capture consumer surplus and from competitors eroding expected postinnovation profitability, I have suggested that the U.S. ventures are likely to reduce social economic welfare and move R&D investment away from the socially optimal level.

There is of course another very different dimension to the success of Japan's leading firms as international competitors. Many believe that the Japanese success has been the result of unfair trade practices rather than because of the efficiencies of large size and of cooperative ventures. Among the supporters of this thesis were most of the candidates for the U.S. presidency during the campaign of 1992. They claimed that Japan systematically blocks U.S. imports. Thus, as the playing field for international competition widened, several factors other than efficiency may have worked together to tilt it in favor of the Japanese producers.

The supporters of the trade-practices explanation for Japan's success argue as follows. First, the Japanese often block imports into Japan while promoting their own exports. Second, macroeconomic policies have favored Japan's exporters at crucial times (for example during the period that Japan first overtook and then replaced U.S. DRAM chip producers). U.S. macroeconomic policy (in conjunction with Japan's) resulted in an extraordinarily strong dollar. Third, asymmetry in antitrust laws and the awkwardness of the applications of the law have favored Japanese producers. The Matsushita case is an example; it did not involve predatory pricing, but instead, the proponents of the trade practices theory would argue, the use of exporting as a "facilitating practice." Scherer and Ross (1990, pp. 469–471) tell a very convincing story suggesting that the firms in a Japanese domestic oligopoly can spread their fixed costs and yet avoid undercutting the domestic price by selling in the United States and other foreign markets any production in excess of the domestic oligopolistic consensus output.[6] This third point works quite well in conjunction with the first two points, and indeed Scherer and Ross (p. 469) observe that MITI was instrumental in establishing the export cartel formed by makers of Japanese consumer electronic goods. A repercussion of these rather negative views about the relative success of Japan's exporters has been increased antitrust activity in Japan. The antitrust activity has picked up in large measure because of U.S. pressure on Japan to change its policies.[7]

*New policies:* Obviously the forces contributing to Japan's success in international trade are complex, but certain aspects of that success seem especially interesting in the light of my study of purposive diversification. My study is broadly consistent with Porter (1990), because it suggests that society will benefit from purposive diversification in the context of healthy competition. In the context of competition, purposive diversification promotes static efficiencies – the gains from economies of scope and from internal capital markets reallocating capital with good information and minimum transactions costs. Further, in the context of competition, purposive diversification can allow sensibly diversified firms to realize efficiencies of size and scope in R&D investment and allow the benefits of R&D rivalry among several independent firms and yet allow sufficient appropriability of returns to make socially optimal R&D investment possible. Cooperative R&D activity may be socially optimal when there are spillovers from the individual firm's R&D effort that improve the productivity of its rivals' R&D investments. For cooperation to be socially optimal, such technological spillovers must dominate other spillovers that cause society to value the rivalry that cooperation eliminates – i.e., that either increase consumer surplus or reduce the probability of rivals' success or the value of their innovations. Technological spillovers are most likely to dominate when the research is generic and precompetitive. Setting aside the complaints about unfair trade practices that were voiced by the U.S. presidential candidates in 1992, one can make a sound argument that Japan's success stems directly from its firms' purposive diversification (effected by *keiretsu* groups) in the context of intense competition – with each other as well as foreign firms (Ohmae, 1981; Baldwin, 1987, p. 496; Elzinga, 1989; Porter, 1990, pp. 117–122; Odagiri, 1992, p. 101, pp. 201–231) – in the arena of international trade, and by cooperative research to provide generic technological knowledge for use by firms that are vigorously rivalrous in their proprietary technologies. The purposive diversification provided by competing *keiretsu* groups allows efficient production and marketing of products incorporating the precompetitive, generic research provided by cooperative R&D.

If my view is correct, the United States could improve the international competitiveness of its manufacturers if U.S. antitrust law would start paying attention to multimarket contact and to the precise nature of cooperative ventures. Merger evaluation under Section 7 of the Clayton Act has ignored multimarket contact. Performance would be improved if the law was enforced in a way that reduced seller concentration and encouraged purposive diversification that was designed to realize economies of scope. Given the track record for mergers (Ravenscraft and Scherer, 1987; Mueller, 1987; and Porter, 1987) and the possibility of internal expansion by manufacturers, the chapters of Part I suggest that static performance would be better (1) if horizontal mergers were more likely to be blocked when multimarket contact among the industry's firms is high and (2) if conglomerate mergers were blocked when they increased the multimarket contact of a concentrated industry's sellers. Neither of these policies has ever been used. Rivalry in unconcentrated markets among firms diversified purposively in pursuit of economies would result in lower costs and prices as compared with the case where markets are concentrated and multimarket contact is high. The evidence suggests that the worst performance in terms of static allocative and static technical efficiency would occur when firms meeting in concentrated markets are diversified and have high multimarket contact because their pure conglomerate activities coincide. The firms would not have diversified purposively to achieve economies of scope but instead to achieve market power.

Parts III and IV develop the idea that *rivalry* among purposively diversified firms would improve not only static performance but dynamic performance as well. Purposively diversified firms may achieve sufficient appropriation of the returns from their innovative investment to allow rivalry to be compatible with socially optimal levels of investment. Yet rivalry is not the choice of the policy establishment. I have described the U.S. policy establishment's largely uncritical acceptance of mergers, cooperative research, and cooperative production as ways to increase the international competitiveness of U.S. manufacturers. Scherer (1992) observes that such faith has parallels in the European policy establishment, and further that Japan's success in international trade has bolstered such faith.

Building on the theoretical possibilities developed in Chapter 8, I suggest that in the United States the research joint ventures protected by the National Cooperative Research Act of 1984 may well reduce socially desirable R&D investment because the loss of competitive pressure may be more important than the gains from cooperation. The goals of the National Cooperative Research Act of 1984 would be much more likely to be attained if government and industry would cooperate to ensure that the benefits from filing for reduced antitrust liability are available only to research ventures that focus on generic research for which positive technological spillovers among the firms to be joined in the venture are more important than negative competitive spillovers that would cause the cooperative effort to reduce R&D investment below the noncooperative level and result in investment further from the socially optimal level.

Of course, even without positive technological spillovers, the cooperative venture could improve social economic welfare because of economies of scale and scope, wasteful duplication, and the severe appropriability difficulties caused by the negative competitive spillovers and consumer surplus not appropriated by the innovators. I have explained, however, that those conditions need not imply that cooperation is socially desirable in the absence of some mechanism that preserves the benefits of competition at the same time that the technological efficiencies of cooperation are attained. I offer the Damoclean tax and the more practical preinnovation periodic tax as potential mechanisms, although means of implementation remain to be worked out. My point is simply that current policy could be improved if methods were developed to preserve desirable competitive pressures. Further, the historical perspective provided by my review of the NCRA suggests that the casual and perfunctory acceptance of joint ventures as a means to static and dynamic efficiency is deeply rooted in a faith in business combinations that may be difficult to shake with theory or evidence. Yet, in terms of Thurow's (1992) vision of "the coming economic battle" of the twenty-first century, I predict that success is most likely to come *not* to the countries promoting size, diversification, and cooperation per se, but rather to those that play upon the complexities of the links from diversification and cooperation to international competitiveness.

Economics offers many insights about such business combinations and about the organization of firms and industries more generally; nonetheless, there is much room for faith to determine private and public policy. Perhaps the important influence of faith is because the evidence (developed in Part II) of systematic differences in firms and industries is very strong, and yet the portion of those differences that we understand is relatively small. I hope that this book's study of purposive diversification and concomitant multimarket contact contributes to the portion that is understood.

# NOTES

### Chapter 1

1. We shall study this sample again in Chapter 4.
2. See U.S. Federal Trade Commission (1980a, pp. 108–109).
3. U.S. Census (1976); U.S. Office of Management and Budget (1972); and U.S. Federal Trade Commission (1985).
4. See U.S. Federal Trade Commission (1985). These FTC four-digit manufacturing categories are on average somewhat more aggregative than SIC four-digit categories, but generally considerably less aggregative than SIC three-digit categories.
5. Clearly, in many cases the group of manufacturing LBs that I have assigned to a wholesaling category are close for other reasons as well as for their shared distribution channels. Many use similar technologies or are vertically related. Flour and bread use the same distribution channels when sold as separate products, but it is also the case that one is an input for the other. Thus, my simple introductory test, used to illustrate the methodology with an obvious example, could be interpreted as a test of purposive behavior more generally.
6. See U.S. Federal Trade Commission (1979) and U.S. Federal Trade Commission (1981a) for thorough discussions of the sample.
7. Note that for our test of a hypothesis about purposive multimarket behavior of firms, the null hypothesis of randomness generates completely the theoretical probability distribution given observable characteristics of a firm. There are no unknown parameters of that distribution to be estimated while testing alternatives to the null hypothesis.
8. Of course, as mentioned earlier, multimarket operations alone need not signify anything purposeful in the firm's behavior other than random discrepancies in buyers' and sellers' valuations of assets (see Gort, 1969). Further, there can be purposive behavior that is purely conglomerate because of risk aversion of managers (Amihud and Lev, 1981) or of stockholders. From the standpoint of stockholders purely conglomerate diversification by firms is desirable if firms can diversify at lower cost than investors (Scott, 1980). I define transactions costs broadly here; in particular, I include the costs of understanding what the opportunity set is and of avoiding fraudulent or incompetently managed investments. On the other hand, to the extent that purposive multimarket behavior concentrates the ownership of capacity in a set of related markets, it also lowers capital costs (Scott, 1981).

### Chapter 2

1. Stocking and Mueller (1957) provide many examples and develop the theory of anticompetitive consequences from reciprocal buying, and they explain why diversification is especially conducive to reciprocity (pp. 76-77).
2. Baldwin (1987, pp. 444-454) provides an excellent discussion of the law on tying in the context of the economics.
3. Scherer (1980, pp. 340-342) provides an excellent discussion and development of Edwards's ideas.
4. The development of the independent choice of the joint net value-maximizing investment by each of the noncooperating firms is the essential idea in Chamberlin (1929).
5. The idea here is the essential idea in Osborne (1976).
6. Stigler (1988) works out several cases around the general theme that price cutting is less likely when it is easier to detect.

### Chapter 3

1. A listing of the 127 groups is available (Scott and Pascoe, 1987, p. 196, footnote 3).
2. Mueller, personal correspondence, June 30, 1988.

### Chapter 4

1. See also Mueller (1979, pp. 816-817). When firms specialize in a single product and there are economies of large size, small firms in an industry are by definition inefficient. That no longer follows given multimarket operations; the smallest firm in an industry may be part of an industrial giant.
2. See *St. John's Law Review* (special edition 44, Spring 1970), and Blair and Lanzilotti (1981).
3. Statistical tests explored the effect of sellers' interdependence across markets on intramarket profits (Strickland, 1980) and stability of market shares (Heggestad and Rhoades, 1978). Strickland did not find evidence supporting spheres of influence, while Heggestad and Rhoades found greater stability in leading firms' shares, the greater their contact in other markets. Strickland also reviewed work of Mueller (1971) and Adams (1974).
4. If resources flow from declining to expanding industries, the result is elimination of profit in industries that expand. Recognized interdependence across markets could lead to coordination of resource withdrawal from declining markets without a corresponding expansion of resource use in markets producing rents. In such an economy, one would predict that response to demand shocks or cost shocks would differ significantly from that in a competitive economy. One might conjecture that shocks to which a competitive economy would respond by reallocating resources among industries would lead to stagflation if sellers interdependent across markets recognize that efficient reallocation of resources is not in their interests. Given Keynesian macroeconomic policy, one could have a Schultze-like theory of stagflation (Scherer, 1980, pp. 353-354) except that the cause of the problem is diversification that results in multimarket contact coinciding with fewness of sellers.
5. A description of the program is available in U.S. Federal Trade Commission (1979 and 1981a).
6. After reading the first version of this chapter, William Long suggested that I compute the measure ADEV to augment my original measure, PMMC. ADEV is the number of standard deviations the observed number of meetings in other markets is from the mean

for the theoretical probability distribution given the null hypothesis. ADEV is perhaps a more conventional and easily grasped variable, but in any case the results were the same as for PMMC.

7. See note to Table 4.2.
8. Stewart, Harris, and Carleton (1980) suggest the idea of measuring contiguity by similarity of advertising intensity and R & D intensity.
9. See Scherer (1980, pp. 288–292) and Ravenscraft (1980).
10. Regressions otherwise identical to those in Table 4.6 but including a measure of import competition had the same qualitative results. Import competition was never significant, as one might expect for 1974, a year of international shortages and disruption of international markets.
11. He used the phrase in personal correspondence in 1981 when commenting on my earliest work on multimarket contact.
12. See Scott (1978) for an example of extreme interdependence reducing nonprice competition.

### Chapter 5

1. See Chapter 2 above. Edwards (1949, 1955) pioneered hypotheses about multimarket contact. See also Adams (1974), Scott (1982, 1989a), Feinberg (1984), Woodward (1989), Bernheim and Whinston (1990), and the overviews provided by Scherer (1980, pp. 340–342) and by Mueller (1988, pp. 304–305; 1989, p. 3).
2. Chapter 4 discussed the idea that diversification with multimarket contact can increase profits when seller concentration is high, yet decrease them when concentration is low.
3. Mueller (1987) explains how the preferences of managers have shaped the growth and diversification of firms.
4. I have excluded industry 399, the miscellaneous category, and I have placed FTC product classes 40112 and 40113 in industry 202, 93320 in 226, 126121 and 126122 in 261, 128980 in 289, 129112 and 129113 and 129117 in 291. My allocation of the FTC's product classes for 1950 follows from their definitions (U.S. FTC, 1972, Appendix B, pp. 5–34, and Supplement).
5. Note that there are only 18 instead of 20 industries for which multimarket contact measures can be formed because Nunn-Bush, one of the only two firms Bain sampled for high-priced men's shoes, is not in the FTC (1972) data, and because for cement both Lehigh Portland and Lone Star produced in one market only and the needed distribution was degenerate. Bain's other two leaders among cement producers (Alpha Portland and Penn Dixie) also produced in just one product market.
6. Bain's sample of firms is clearly special, even for the population of the 1000 largest U.S. manufacturers. For all 20 industries and the 80 (8 for the 8 industries for which Bain sampled just 2 firms, and $12 \times 6 = 72$ for the remaining 12 industries where he sampled 4 firms) possible within-industry pairings of firms, 70 pairs or 87.5 percent exhibited significant multimarket contact.
7. The coefficient for the dummy variable capturing that distinction was not significantly different from zero. The regression was otherwise unchanged qualitatively.
8. That conclusion is consistent with the observations in Chapter 4 – where for the typically diversified firms among the leading U.S. manufacturers, the significant impact of seller concentration was *conditional* on high multimarket contact.
9. There is a very prominent literature that criticizes the profit measures in the profitability studies that I am addressing here. The critics point up all of the potential errors in the accounting profitability which Bain used as a measure of true economic profits. The

critics largely ignore the fact that the theory of statistics has been developed to deal precisely with such errors. Since the description of industry structure is for a firm's primary industry, in the statistics a sensible a priori assumption would be that the variance of the error in the equation explaining the profit variable increases as the proportion of the firm's operations in its primary industry decreases. The necessary proportion can be calculated from the Corporate Patterns data (U.S. FTC, 1972). Another type of information, which I used to describe the quality of an observation, and hence the variance in the error in equation, concerns the multimarket overlap (also available from the Corporate Patterns data) of a leading pair of firms. For example, although the primary industry category for both General Electric and Westinghouse was electric bulbs, the shipments in that category constitute but a small part of those companies' total shipments. However, it turns out that in several other industries where concentration and barriers to entry were high, these two firms were also the leaders. Thus, the *company* profitability should reflect market power to a greater extent than one would think if the electric bulb category were their only line of business subject to high concentration, high barriers to entry, and multimarket contact. To quantify this one can use the information about the proportion of the firm's shipments from industry categories with the characteristics ascribed to the firm's primary industry. Such a priori structure for the equations' disturbances, however, did not appear important, and so I present White's (1980) general method.

10. Note that I assume that once concentration reaches a critical level, profitable oligopoly is possible. I have tried to assemble a sample of industries for which the barriers to entry are great enough that the oligopolistic diversified leaders would earn excess profits if they could in fact coordinate their behavior. However, to the extent that there are important (in the sense that increases beyond a critical level affect profits) differences across the observations in concentration and barriers to entry, if they are correlated with multimarket contact, the differences in concentration and barriers themselves could explain the differences in profitability that are explained by differences in multimarket contact.

11. For the four-digit level with $n = 418$, the 0.95 criterion provides the best fitting equation when compared with the alternative criteria of either 0.90 or 0.99, although those two equations tell essentially the same story as the equation reported in the text. The observations with insignificant contact run the gamut from those with no contact at all to those with a fair amount of statistically insignificant contact.

12. Using the continuous measure, we have the following equation.

$$\pi = 11.06 + 5.05 \,(\text{PMMC})$$
$$(t = 4.06) \qquad (t = 1.75)$$
$$(t^* = 6.11) \qquad (t^* = 2.60)$$

$R^2 = 0.05$, Adjusted $R^2 = 0.03$, degrees of freedom = 62.

13. Personal correspondence (April 1992).

14. There is, of course, still the question of weighing any efficiencies created by the merger. As emphasized throughout this book, cost-reducing efficiencies can result from the very diversification that increases multimarket contact.

15. For example, in considering firm effects in R&D intensity estimated in Scott (1984), Scherer and Ross (1990, p. 647, note 91) observe that "because company diversification occurs largely through merger and high-R&D companies tend to acquire companies with similarly high R&D/sales ratios, such company dummy variables are undoubtedly mirroring complex industry effects." On the one hand, their observation is misleading because a complete set of four-digit dummies were swept out first and company effects

are still significant. Yet, on the other hand, their observation is sound because firm effects probably reflect different patterns of purposive diversification, and purposive diversification may define meaningful "industries" that are particular collections of activities in conventionally defined industries.

### Chapter 6

1. Fellner (1949) provides a classic statement of the behavior of sellers when they are few; Bain (1956) emphasizes the importance of the condition of entry for profitability of recognized mutual interdependence. Spence (1983), in reviewing the work of Baumol, Panzar, and Willig (1982), explains how purely free entry and exit can provide a normative benchmark for optimal industry performance even when sellers are few.
2. For example, this chapter does not add to the literature about the potential for bias in accounting measures of profitability. See Fisher and McGowan (1983), Fisher (1984), Long and Ravenscraft (1984), and Martin (1984). However, in the absence of any compelling reason to believe that the actual biases are correlated with the included variables, we can assume that the biases are randomly distributed and uncorrelated with the included variables. Our conventional statistical methodology then incorporates those biases explicitly in the equation's error term, and they are no problem if our assumption is correct. Mueller (1990, pp. 8–14) reviews the critical literature and analyzes the possibility for bias in the accounting measures and concludes that the accounting measures are useful and that the most vocal critics overstate their case.
3. Martin (1983) explores the use of simultaneous equations models of profitability, and his work suggests that the points we make would not be sensitive to whether or not such methodology were used.
4. The estimable model (i.e., with unique coefficients) that dropped dummies has the same explanatory power as the corresponding singular model with the complete set of dummies, since both can generate the same range of observations on the dependent variable, and the minimum of the sum of squared residuals is unique.
5. The variables are defined in more detail in Scott and Pascoe (1984).
6. That is, with this variable as with the others constructed as ratios in the statistics of this chapter, a proportion rather than a percentage form is used.
7. Scott and Pascoe (1984) describe the sample in detail. The 376 companies are a subset of the over 500 companies that have filed LB data with the FTC in at least 1 year. They were chosen to allow estimation of LB capital costs as a required rate of return for operating income on assets.
8. "At least" is appropriate because in effect our procedure implies that the unidentified variables were fitted last.
9. Personal correspondence (April 1992).
10. This procedure is described in a study of expenditures on research and development (Scott, 1984). Note that since $k$ is defined at the two-digit level, it cannot be included in these specifications. Its effect is captured by the two-digit dummies.
11. See Schmalensee (1985) and Scott (1984) for examples of the importance of controlling for such effects in studies of structure and performance.
12. Although many other studies – e.g., Martin (1983), Ravenscraft (1983), and Scott and Pascoe (1984) – have found firm-level variables significant, the finding here is contrary to Schmalensee's (1985) result which, as here, is for the complete set of firm effects in the general linear model. The sample here consists only of firms that (1) reported to the FTC LB Program in all 3 years (1974, 1975, and 1976) for which data were available and (2) that could be matched to Standard & Poor's Compustat files. Further, all 3

years of data are used here; Schmalensee used only the data for 1975. Scott (1984, table 10.3, note d, p. 237) found that firm effects in the LB data are extremely sensitive to outliers. The sample here is exceptionally clean with regard to coherent firms since it excludes firms disappearing during the sample period because of mergers and firms for which data could not be reconciled with Standard & Poor's. In addition to examining just one (rather odd) year, Schmalensee used a procedure for sample selection that reduced each firm's number of business units entering the statistics. Estimation of firm effects requires a sufficiently large number of business units for each firm.

13. Schmalensee (1985) concludes that because industry effects are so significant, traditional models that explore the variance in industries' performance, given variance in their structures, are sensibly focused. This chapter adds that firm effects cannot be dismissed, that the traditional industry models do not capture all of the industry variance explainable if we did have the complete set of industry-level variables, and that many important effects may depend on neither industrywide nor firmwide characterizations alone.

### Chapter 7

1. See U.S. Federal Trade Commission (1979, 1981a, 1981b) for a description of the program.
2. I tested the sensitivity of the results to the inclusion or exclusion of the observations for which R&D is zero. The results are virtually the same when the model is rerun dropping all observations for which R&D is zero.

### Chapter 8

1. Integration by parts implies

$$\int_0^\infty (t)(h)e^{-ht}dt = t(-e^{-ht})\Big|_0^\infty - \int_0^\infty (-e^{-ht})\,dt = (-t/e^{ht})\Big|_0^\infty - (e^{-ht}/h)\Big|_0^\infty$$
$$= 1/h,$$

applying L'Hospital's rule to evaluate the first term at $t = \infty$.
2. The probability of failure on a single trial is $1 - F(t) = (1 - (1 - e^{-h(x)t})) = e^{-h(x)t}$. Thus, failure on all $z$ trials has probability $e^{-zh(x)t}$.
3. Martin (1991) shows how to model the detailed market interactions among competitors in a postinnovation market when the old and new technologies can compete side-by-side. Such considerations determine consumer and producer surpluses and underlie an innovation's value, but I shall abstract from those details here to focus on the simple essence of competition in the R&D game. As explained carefully in the text immediately following, the simplicity here has absolutely no effect on the points that I want to make.

### Chapter 9

1. Nelson (1959, p. 302), when discussing basic research, emphasizes that the firm more diversified into several product markets is more likely to be able to appropriate research benefits in a postinnovation market since it can more readily convert ideas into patentable innovations. Farjoun (1991) discovers that much industrial diversification exploits similarities in the human expertise needed for operations in the diverse products. Thus, certain "human expertise profiles" for R&D activity may be common to the industry categories combined purposely.

2. For example, after controlling for all FTC four-digit industry effects, Scott (1984, table 10.6, equation 3, p. 243) finds the elasticity of LB R&D expenditures with respect to LB sales to be 0.99.

3. The complete set of 127 groups is available on request.

4. Note, then, that if firm A performs R&D in industries 1 and 2, while firms B and C each do R&D in 1, 2, and 3, and if all meetings are significant, industries 1 and 2 form a group in which all three firms do R&D, while industries 1, 2, and 3 form a separate group in which B and C do R&D. In the estimations below, the construction could in principle allow results to be influenced by a few (outlier) firms that belong to many groups. However, the frequency distribution of the number of firms in one group, two groups, three groups, and so on, shows that most of the firms belonging to one or more groups belong to one or two, and only 5 percent of the R&D performing firms in our sample are members of more than four groups. Further, 69 percent of our R&D performing firms do not belong to any group. Thus, the density of significant cases in Table 9.3, the balanced design of group versus nongroup firms in the individual tests, and the presence of a different set of firms in each test all suggest that the independence assumption in the statistical tests is not a bad approximation and that the pattern of results is not simply because of the behavior of the most diversified firms.

5. Several studies have documented a complementary relationship between government-financed and company-financed R&D expenditures. Scott (1984), at the LB level, and Levin et al. (1985), at the industry level, report such effects using FTC LB data. Levy and Terleckyj (1983) find that government contract R&D performed in industry-induced private R&D expenditure and that the stock of government contract R&D has a discernible effect on private sector productivity.

6. The estimation in Table 9.5 is based on the following conceptualization. Letting $Q = \Phi e^{\lambda t} R^{\delta} K^{\alpha} L^{\beta} M^{\gamma}$, where $Q$, $R$, $K$, $L$, and $M$ denote respectively output, R&D capital, physical capital, labor, and materials, then $\dot{Q}/Q - \alpha(\dot{K}/K) - \beta(\dot{L}/L) - \gamma(\dot{M}/M) = \lambda + \delta(\dot{R}/R)$. As Terleckyj (1974) observed, since $\delta = (\partial Q/\partial R)(R/Q)$, then $\delta \dot{R}/R = (\partial Q/\partial R)(\dot{R}/Q)$. Letting TFP denote total factor productivity, we have $\dot{TFP}/TFP = \lambda + (\partial Q/\partial R)(\dot{R}/Q)$.

7. The productivity growth measure for each group of industries is constructed by weighting the growth measure for each industry category in the group by the relative size (measured by sales) in our sample of the associated industry category (relative to the size of the group in our sample).

8. Many readers will find it intuitively obvious that a random consolidation of data points should yield unbiased coefficients, and a proof is readily constructed.

9. The difference, examined using Table 9.3's method, is highly significant. Diversification was measured by the inverse Herfindahl index for R&D for each firm, IHR. IHR $= 1/\sum_{i=1}^{253} s_i^2$, where $s_i$ is the share of the firm's R&D expenditures in industry category $i$. Thus the measure will increase with the number of industry categories in which the firm has R&D and will decrease as the variation in activity shares increases. When the firm has an equal share of its R&D expenditures in each industry category, the diversification index equals the number of categories in which the firm has R&D expenditures.

### Chapter 10

1. See Baldwin and Scott (1987, pp. 1–4) for quotes from Schumpeter (1939, 1942) with discussion documenting his vision about the type of competition that counts and about the need for large firms with market power if the economy is to perform well with regard to technological change. Baldwin and Scott (1987, pp. 63–113) and Cohen and

Levin (1989) provide reviews of the empirical literature exploring the Schumpeterian hypothesis about firm size and market power.

2. In Chapters 7 and 9 each LB is the operations of a firm in an FTC four-digit industry category. For the present chapter, in which I want to focus on the competition within broad industry categories, each LB is the operations of a firm in an SIC (and equivalently FTC) two-digit industry category.

3. The elasticity of R&D with respect to business unit size was essentially 1.0 (Scott, 1984, p. 243).

4. The previous literature is reviewed in Baldwin and Scott (1987, pp. 63–113) and Cohen and Levin (1989). There is of course the possibility that the insignificant effect of firm size results because the estimated coefficients are biased by the left-out firmwide variables. Such variables are important, since, as we have seen in Chapter 7, differences across firms explain a large and significant amount of the variance in business-unit R&D intensity even after control for industry effects. Yet the only firm-specific variable controlled by Cohen et al. (1987), firm size, appears to be unimportant. Inclusion of the missing variables characterizing firms could change our current understanding of the data.

5. See Baldwin and Scott (1987) for a review of these and other studies examining the relationships between diversification and technological advance.

6. Baldwin and Scott (1987) review the theories predicting such a relationship as well as the empirical studies that have found it.

7. Our work in Chapter 7 eliminated the relation completely. Levin et al. replicate this result in the sense that the significance of the relation between concentration and R&D intensity is dramatically reduced. Again, the lack of control for firm-level variables may be a problem. The Levin et al. (1985) estimation is at the FTC four-digit industry level. Therefore, the coefficients on the appropriability and opportunity variables (as well as on seller concentration) may be reflecting left-out variables describing the firms or business units. This problem has perhaps been best understood in the literature about market structure and profits. The links between industry characteristics and profits which appear in industry-level data look very different once one looks at disaggregated firm- or especially business-unit data and controls for firm- and business-unit effects. See Chapter 6.

8. Using FTC LB data, Scott (1984), at the LB level, and Levin et al. (1985), at the industry level, have documented a complementary relationship between government-financed and company-financed R&D expenditures. Levy and Terleckyj (1983) find that government-contract R&D induced private R&D expenditure and that the stock of government contract R&D has a discernible effect on private sector productivity. Lichtenberg (1987) has noted that the effect of government-financed R&D on company-financed R&D may be in part because along with greater government-financed R&D comes greater sales to the government, and there may be an identifiable component of the company-financed R&D that is associated with such sales. However, the firm and industry dummies in Scott (1984) control for the systematic differences across firms and industries in the proportion of sales to the government. The relevant differences will have been controlled if, after taking out the firm and industry differences, little difference remained at the LB level. If not, though, it is possible that the effect of government-financed R&D on corporate-financed R&D does not reflect spillovers but instead a compartmentalized link between sales to the government and government funding of R&D effort.

9. The industry effects cannot be estimated for the specifications in Table 10.3, because the necessary dummy variables would be completely collinear with the concentration measures.

10. Note that in the results of Table 10.4, where firm *and* industry effects can be controlled because the concentration measures (having been observed for the multi-industry groups) are not perfectly collinear with the industry effects, we have in effect controlled for all relevant firm-level variables, any relevant powers of those variables, and their interactions, as well as all relevant industry-level variables, their powers, and their interactions, assuming only that the true model is linear in the parameters, although not linear in the variables. From the linear algebra and the Gauss–Markov theorem, the expected value of the intercept is the weighted sum of the entire set of coefficients for the true variables characterizing firms and industries, with the weight of each coefficient being the value its associated variable takes for the base firm or base industry. The expected value of the coefficient of the dummy variable for each remaining industry (or firm) is the difference from the intercept of the weighted sum of the entire set of coefficients for the true variables characterizing industries (or firms), with the weight of each coefficient being the value its associated variable takes for that industry (or firm). Chapter 6 provides the simple linear algebra for this interpretation.

11. New ways of observing behavior and framing Schumpeterian hypotheses are needed not only because of the lack of conclusive evidence from existing tests, but additionally because rather special and exacting circumstances, difficult to obtain in practice, are necessary for interpretation of the tests focusing on the relationship between size and R&D intensity (Kohn and Scott, 1982).

12. See also Link and Lunn (1984).

### Chapter 11

1. See Scherer (1984), Glennan (1967), Mansfield (1968), and Mansfield et al. (1977a) for important descriptions of the trial and error process of development. Dosi (1988) and Freeman (1982) provide overarching perspective about the economics of the R&D process.

2. When $Z = C$, the distribution of the sample space over $x$ is crudely bell-shaped with relatively high degrees of component gestalt (low $x$ outcomes) less numerous than relatively low degrees (high $x$ outcomes). The text discusses the case relevant for an industrial R&D problem, where $Z$ is much larger than $C$ and most of the sample space is concentrated at $x = C$.

3. See Scherer (1984, pp. 222–238), Scott (1984), Levin, Cohen, and Mowery (1985), and Cohen, Levin, and Mowery (1987).

4. Although to estimate the firm effects in the following specifications the effects were absorbed to reduce the size of the $\mathbf{X'X}$ matrix, the $F$-values for firm effects (as well as the industry effects) are for the effects when fitted last (see Scott, 1984, p. 244). Significance levels for a one-tailed test are noted as $a = 0.0001$ and $a^*$ is recorded for the $F$-value that I computed as in Scott (1984, p. 244) and for which I did not have a computer-generated probability value. Computing the relevant integral is burdensome given the large numbers of degrees of freedom, but the result is obviously highly significant.

5. Note that although there are 238 industries, 234 rather than 237 industry dummies are controlled here with both firm and industry effects in the model. Consider the special cases where *in the 1819-observation sample* an industry and a company dummy coincide because a single-LB company is the sole producer in its industry category. Then, the number of industry dummies is reduced until no linearly dependent columns are in the $\mathbf{X}$ matrix.

6. Chapter 6 provides a more formal statement of the fact that the effects of firm- (industry-) level variables are nested within the effects of the firm (industry) dummies.

7. However, once seller concentration is controlled, but without control for other industry variables and without control for firm effects, systems developments decline very slightly with LB sales. Further, the small negative effect associated with firm size does appear to be independent of the size of the LB.

8. I have in effect controlled for all relevant firm-level variables, any relevant powers of those variables, and their interactions, as well as all relevant industry-level variables, their powers, and their interactions, and all relevant group-level variables, their powers, and their interactions, assuming only that the true model is linear in the parameters, although not linear in the variables. The linear algebra and the Gauss–Markov theorem imply that the expected value of the intercept is the weighted sum of the entire set of coefficients for the true variables characterizing firms and industries, with the weight of each coefficient being the value its associated variable takes for the base firm or industry. The expected value of the coefficient of the dummy variable for each remaining industry (or firm) is the difference from the intercept of the weighted sum of the entire set of coefficients for the true variables characterizing industries (or firms), with the weight of each coefficient being the value its associated variable takes for that industry (or firm). Not all LBs are in a group, but for those that are, the coefficient of the dummy variable of any relevant group provides an additional effect that is the weighted sum of the entire set of coefficients for the true variables characterizing groups, with the weight of each coefficient being the value its associated variable takes for that group.

9. See the references in note 3.

10. Mansfield et al. (1977b, pp. 236–238) find in a sample of industrial innovations that the gap between social and private rates of return is typically positive and increases, other things being equal, with the significance of the innovation. They measure an innovation's significance by its annual net social benefits. Society might prefer having a choice among innovations that meet a particular need, yet the monopolist might not appropriate the value such choice generates. If consequently the monopolist underinvests in diversity, a competitive environment could be in the social interest because of the competitors' extra incentive to pursue diverse strategies.

### Chapter 12

1. Link and Bauer (1989) and Link and Tassey (1989) provide important perspectives of cooperative R&D and of the NCRA.

2. For detailed exploration of sequential versus parallel research strategies, see Van Cayseele (1986) and Scherer (1984, chapter 4).

3. The venture is reported in *Federal Register,* vol. 56, no. 156, August 13, 1991 (Washington, D.C., U.S. Government Printing Office), pp. 38464–5. The members include ARCO Products Company, BP Oil Company, Chevron U.S.A., Inc., Exxon Company U.S.A., Mobil Oil Corporation, Shell Oil Company, Texaco Refining and Marketing, Tosco Refining Company, Ultramar Inc., Union Oil Company of California, California Air Resources Board, and Western States Petroleum Association.

4. If one just counts the number of NCRA filings during the first 18 months, there were many more than 61. But that is because new filings were made to record changes in the membership of a venture. In many cases there were several filings made, throughout the period, for a single cooperative project.

5. There was, however, one of the 61 ventures to which I did not formally assign industry categories. Guessing about what would be appropriate, it appears to me that I have in fact probably included in the 81 industry categories virtually all of those that would have been relevant to the particular venture. But I am not sure, because the venture's

participants cover such a wide range of industries and because their project description is unusually broad. However, perhaps not much is lost in any case, because the venture in question was formed in 1972, hardly in response to the NCRA of 1984, although it has now filed for protection under the act.

6. The adjusted concentration ratios for the 261 FTC four-digit industries in 1972 were derived in the same manner as the concentration ratios for the SIC industries in Weiss and Pascoe (1986).

7. The total factor productivity growth rates were based on Zvi Griliches's measurements for three-digit SIC manufacturing industries. The three-digit SIC manufacturing industries are more aggregative than the FTC four-digit manufacturing industries, and each FTC four-digit category within a three-digit SIC category is assigned the three-digit SIC category's productivity growth rate.

8. The R&D/sales figure uses the FTC's published LB reports (1981a, 1981b, 1982, and 1985), averaging the figures available for all the years in which data were gathered – namely, 1974, 1975, 1976, and 1977.

9. Hladik (1985), for example, considers a set of ventures not protected by the NCRA. She explores with probit analysis the determinants of whether or not individual international joint ventures did R&D as part of the venture.

10. For the effects of buyer concentration and buyers' power on the incentive to innovate, see Fixler (1983), Kamien and Schwartz (1982, pp. 36–47), and Yamey (1970).

### Chapter 13

1. As explained in Chapter 12, the NCRA codified U.S. public policy toward joint ventures in R&D. It provided, among other things, that the behavior of a research consortium, if challenged under the U.S. antitrust laws, would be judged under a rule of reason asking whether the alleged restraints of trade were ancillary to the pursuit of efficiency. For those research ventures notifying the government of their participants and purposes, any subsequent antitrust violation would be assessed single, not treble, damages.

2. See for example the dissenting opinion in *U.S. v. Von's Grocery Company,* 384 U.S. 270 (1966) and the discussion of the case in Pitofsky (1986).

3. See U.S. Department of Justice, June 14, 1984, and January 23, 1985.

4. Evidently, the new FTC had no trouble finding such cases. For example, despite convincing evidence to the contrary it decided that the costs imposed by its own LB data collection program were greater than any benefits and killed the program. The commission believed that the private sector of the economy would generate the information if it were worthwhile. In addition to reorienting research, the FTC has taken a new view of the mergers on which it rules – emphasizing the potential for efficiencies and for entry of new competitors to mitigate any adverse consequences of market power. For a firsthand account of the changes at the FTC during the Reagan administration, see Miller (1989).

5. Baldwin (1987, p. 371) discusses the origins of the precedent in the *Bethlehem-Youngstown* decision.

6. There has been some resurgence of court challenges to the agencies' decisions. See, for example, *FTC v. Owens-Illinois, Inc. et al. and Brockway, Inc.,* February 18, 1988, in which the U.S. District Court for the District of Columbia denied the FTC's request for a preliminary injunction blocking Owens-Illinois Inc.'s proposed takeover of Brockway, Inc.

7. See (U.S. Department of Justice, February 15, 1984; *Business Week,* April 2, 1984); more generally, the evidence suggests that we are unlikely to gain much in the way of

production efficiencies when we allow mergers of competitors. After all, if two inefficient production facilities (say the plants are too small) are merged, we typically still have two inefficient facilities. There are possibilities such as product run-length economies which could, by rearranging production tasks across plants, allow lower unit production costs than attainable in each plant. Most of the potential efficiencies, though, would be multiplant efficiencies in nonproduction activities – central-office activities such as advertising, R&D, or finance. The evidence does not support the importance of such economies in the cases of the prominent mergers of concern here. Scherer et al. (1975) find that seller concentration in U.S. manufacturing typically far exceeds what is necessary to realize important plant and multiplant scale economies.

8. The Reagan administration's focus on market power (the ability to increase price above competitive levels for significant periods of time) and the extent to which it is offset by lowered costs may not be the most important focus for antitrust. The difficulties posed by what economists call the theory of second best or big-think questions about social and political implications of market concentration are worthy of evaluation. But even if one accepts the administration's premise that policy should consider only economic efficiency and block business combinations only when they lessen efficiency, the new policy toward combinations may be a mistake. In a world of perfect knowledge about the economic implications of merger, the new policy would *not* (using the narrow view of antitrust) be a mistake, but the world is not that perfect. There is surely a potential trade-off that must be addressed: heightened market power versus lower costs. But in the enthusiasm of advocacy, the new policy provides the groundwork for grave problems.

9. The quote is from U.S. Department of Commerce, July 11, 1985.

10. The evidence that market share, not seller concentration, is associated with high profit rates has received widespread publicity. *Business Week* (November 16, 1981) reviewed the evidence and proclaimed: "Ever since Adam Smith, economists have held that when an industry is dominated by a few companies, they will stifle competition, keep prices uncompetitively high, and garner monopoly profits. This view has long been used to justify stringent government limits on mergers. But studies based on new Federal Trade Commission data are beginning to provide some evidence that this tenet may be wrong. The studies will buttress the arguments of a growing number of economists, both liberal and conservative, who are calling for a substantial easing of antitrust laws. And they support the Reagan Administration's decision to liberalize the guidelines the government uses to decide if potential mergers harm competition within an industry."

11. Mansfield et al. (1977b) provide a way to test that expectation. Mansfield et al. find in their sample of industrial innovations that the gap, which is typically positive, between social and private rates of return increases, other things being equal, with the significance of the innovation. They measure the extent to which the innovation is major rather than minor by its annual net social benefits. With a larger sample of innovations that provided adequate variance in the extent to which the innovations spanned multiple industries, one could test whether the ratio of net social to net private value increased with "the extent" of innovation. In such a sample, however, it would be quite difficult to carry out their methodology.

12. Scott (1988) provides a simple graph comparing the investment by competitors and a venture combining them and illustrating the effects of wasteful duplication, overbidding from a private perspective, and appropriability conditions. Chapter 8 above provides a formal model of these possibilities.

13. Katz (1986) holds the promise that models could be developed that would be useful for the analysis of particular cases.

14. See U.S. 98th Congress (September 21, 1984); it does have a lot of material about the need for a sufficient amount of competition in R & D, but taken in the context of the act itself and the behavior of the enforcement agencies, I do not think the language about the need for R & D competition reflects a serious commitment to ensure it.

### Chapter 14

1. In the United States, for example, discussion has focused on the tax credit (which is expected to become a permanent part of the U.S. tax code in 1992) and the cooperative R & D protected by the National Cooperative Research Act of 1984 (NCRA). Both of these policies are discussed subsequently. For papers discussing the cooperative R & D policies of several nations see Link and Tassey (1989).
2. Current U.S. tax provisions to encourage R & D are described in U.S. Congressional Budget Office (July 1991, pp. 88–90).
3. Geroski (1991b) provides a review of the evidence.
4. See the review of the evidence in U.S. Congressional Budget Office (1991, p. 90), which concludes that "Most observers agree that the tax credit has increased private R & D by a modest but measurable amount." Compare Baily and Chakrabarti (1988, pp. 118–129), who agree that the effect of the tax credit has been small, but argue that the credit provided good incentives relative to its cost to the government in lost revenues. However, in recent work, Baily and Lawrence (1992) and Hines (1991) have presented important evidence suggesting that R & D tax credits have had a large positive impact on R & D investment. In this chapter I focus on a realistic scenario in which the R & D tax credit would *not* work and suggest an alternative approach.
5. See Nelson (1982a).
6. For discussion of the issues see U.S. Congressional Budget Office (July 1991, chapter IV, pp. 73–101), Baily and Chakrabarti (1988, chapter 6, pp. 103–130, and Carey (1991).
7. See Glennan (1967) and Klein (1977) for discussion of the problems if the innovations themselves are required to meet predetermined specifications.
8. Many industrialists touting the benefits of cooperative research contributed to the U.S. Department of Commerce series "High Technology Industries: Profiles and Outlooks." The series (available from the U.S. Government Printing Office, Washington, D.C.) published industry overviews and the proceedings of meetings during the 1980s in which leading executives of high-technology industries and high-level representatives of the Reagan administration discussed the challenges facing U.S. industry in high-technology areas such as robotics, computers, semiconductors, telecommunications, and biotechnology. Prominent policymakers at the Department of Justice and the Department of Commerce spoke of the benefits of cooperation. Chapter 13 provides some historical perspective about the advocacy of cooperation by the Reagan administration's leading officials. Academics – see Jorde and Teece (1988) and also Link and Bauer (1989), for example – developed the arguments favoring joint ventures in R & D.
9. Reviews of the NCRA are provided by Scott (1988), Link and Bauer (1989), and Katz and Ordover (1990), among others. For discussion of other countries' policies toward cooperation, see Link and Tassey (1989).
10. Scott (1988) and Katz and Ordover (1990) express such concerns.
11. See Carey (1991) for a list of "What Industry Wants" in U.S. policies to boost U.S. competitiveness. Encouragement of cooperation and joint research plays a prominent role in industry's ideas about new policies. The flurry of legislation – The National Cooperative Production Amendments of 1991 of the U.S. House of Representatives (*Antitrust and Trade Regulation Report,* June 20, 1991, pp. 847–848; June 27, 1991, p. 878) and The National Cooperative Research Act Extension of 1991 of the U.S. Senate (*Antitrust*

*and Trade Regulation Report,* July 4, 1991, p. 4; July 25, 1991, pp. 116–117), for example – designed to extend the NCRA shows that the policymakers are listening to the requests.

### Afterword

1. *Antitrust & Trade Regulation Report* (vol. 62, no. 1550, January 30, 1992, p. 97).
2. *Antitrust & Trade Regulation Report* (vol. 62, no. 1550, January 30, 1992, pp. 97–105).
3. *Antitrust & Trade Regulation Report* (vol. 62, no. 1550, January 30, 1992, p. 104).
4. If firms in the typical industry face similar opportunities at a point in time, then purposive diversification to realize economies of scope or market power would be expected to increase the significance of their multimarket contact. The evidence is of course also consistent with the possibility that by the mid-1970s there were a greater variety of ways to purposively diversify. Nonetheless, in the context of the large literature showing a dramatic rise in conglomerateness for U.S. manufacturers from 1950 to the mid-1970s, it seems sensible to interpret the secular change in the significance of multimarket contact as a change in the extent of purposive diversification. Firms appear to have become more likely to diversify without a clear notion of the potential gains from economies of scope or market power.
5. At first blush, there are two sources of potential bias here, but on closer examination I do not think they are important for the conclusion that purposive diversification has declined. First, the industry definitions are somewhat different; with the Corporate Patterns data the industries are somewhat more inclusive than the FTC LB industry definitions. However, the probability distribution is formulated to take account of differences in the sample space, and the probability statements are accurate. Nonetheless, the notion of "a meeting in an industry category" is slightly different in the two cases. Second, the firms in the Corporate Patterns data for 1950 are 979 of the largest 1000 manufacturers at that time. The firms in the FTC LB data for 1974 are also taken from the largest 1000. Since the 437 firms in the sample include the largest 250 manufacturers at the time, there are relatively more of the very largest firms in the mid-1970s sample than in the sample for 1950. Previous studies (Caves, 1981, p. 290) have shown that the smaller firms are less "conglomerate" in nature, and their diversification *could* be more purposive than that of the larger firms. Therefore, a sample including relatively more of the smaller firms might show a greater amount of significant multimarket contact. However, in the literature a "less conglomerate" manufacturing firm among manufacturers at a single point in time does not imply a "more purposive" firm since conglomerateness has been measured by the number of industries in which a firm operated or at best by notions about the relatedness of those industries where relatedness is greater when activities share the same aggregative industry as a parent. As I have shown, purposive diversification in manufacturing cuts across even the most aggregative (two-digit) SIC boundaries within manufacturing.
6. U.S. antitrust law, as is often the case, was awkwardly applied. The case (*Matsushita v. Zenith,* 475 U.S. 574, 1986) was not in substance a predatory pricing case of a classic sort although it was addressed that way in the litigation. Arguably the case should have been tried as a violation of Section 5 of the Federal Trade Commission Act in the general sense of that statute. The high prices resulting from the (perhaps tacit) conspiracy would of course be felt in Japan, and the foreign sales and the bureaucratic blocks on U.S. sales in Japan (and U.S. macroeconomic policies) would be facilitating practices allowing the alleged conspiracy to succeed.
7. *Antitrust & Trade Regulation Report* (vol. 62, no. 1550, January 30, 1992, p. 97).

# REFERENCES

Abreu, D., "On the Theory of Infinitely Repeated Games with Discounting," *Econometrica*, 56 (1988), pp. 383–396.

Acs, Z. J., and Audretsch, D. B., "Innovation in Large and Small Firms: An Empirical Analysis," *American Economic Review*, 78 (September 1988), pp. 678–690.

Adams, W., and Brock, J. W., "Joint Ventures, Antitrust, and Transnational Cartelization," *Northwestern Journal of International Law and Business*, 11 (Winter 1991a), pp. 433–483.

Adams, W., and Brock, J. W., *Antitrust Economics on Trial* (Princeton: Princeton University Press, 1991b).

Adams, W. J., "Market Structure and Corporate Power: The Horizontal Dominance Hypothesis Reconsidered," *Columbia Law Review*, 74 (October 1974), pp. 1276–1297.

Amato, L., and Wilder, R., "Firm and Industry Effects in Industrial Economics," *Southern Economic Journal*, 57 (July 1990), pp. 93–105.

Amihud, Y., and Lev, B., "Risk Reduction as a Managerial Motive for Conglomerate Mergers," *Bell Journal of Economics*, 12 (Autumn 1981), pp. 605–617.

Aoki, M., *Information, Incentives, and Bargaining in the Japanese Economy* (Cambridge, England: Cambridge University Press, 1988).

Aoki, M., "Toward an Economic Model of the Japanese Firm," *Journal of Economic Literature*, 28 (March 1990), pp. 1–27.

Arrow, K. J., "Economic Welfare and the Allocation of Resources for Invention." In Universities-National Bureau Committee for Economic Research, *The Rate and Direction of Inventive Activity*. Princeton: Princeton University Press, 1962.

Audretsch, D. B., "Joint R&D and Industrial Policy in Japan," in *Cooperative Research and Development: The Industry-University-Government Relationship*, edited by A. N. Link and G. Tassey, pp. 103–125 (Boston: Kluwer, 1989).

Baily, M. N., and Chakrabarti, A. K., *Innovation and the Productivity Crisis* (Washington, D.C.: The Brookings Institution, 1988).

Baily, M. N., and Lawrence, R. Z., "Tax Incentives for R&D: What Do the Data Tell Us?" manuscript, University of Maryland and Harvard University, January 28, 1992.

Bain, J. S., *Barriers to New Competition* (Cambridge, Mass.: Harvard University Press, 1956).

Baldwin, W. L., *Market Power, Competition, and Antitrust Policy* (Homewood, Ill.: Irwin, 1987).

241

Baldwin, W. L., and Scott, J. T., "Market Structure and Technological Change," *Fundamentals of Pure and Applied Economics*, 17 (London; New York: Harwood, 1987).

Barzel, Y., "Optimal Timing of Innovations," *Review of Economics and Statistics*, 50 (1968), 348–355.

Baumol, W. J., Panzar, J. C., and Willig, R. D., *Contestable Markets and the Theory of Industry Structure* (New York: Harcourt, Brace, 1982).

Bernheim, B. D., and Whinston, M. D., "Multimarket Contact and Collusive Behavior," *Rand Journal of Economics*, 21 (Spring 1990), pp. 1–26.

Bernstein, J. I., "Costs of Production, Intra- and Interindustry R&D Spillovers: Canadian Evidence," *Canadian Journal of Economics*, 21 (May 1988), pp. 324–347.

Bernstein, J. I., and Nadiri, M. I., "Interindustry R&D, Rates of Return, and Production in High-Tech Industries," Economic Research Report 88-04, C. V. Starr Center for Applied Economics, New York University, February 1988a.

Bernstein, J. I., and Nadiri, M. I., "Research and Development and Intraindustry Spillovers: An Empirical Application of Dynamic Duality," Economic Research Report 88-06, C. V. Starr Center for Applied Economics, New York University, February 1988b.

Berry, C. H., *Corporate Growth and Diversification* (Princeton: Princeton University Press, 1975).

Blair, R., and Lanzilotti, R., (editors), *The Conglomerate Corporation* (Cambridge, Mass.: Oelgeschlager, Gunn, and Hain, 1981).

Bradburd, R. M., and Caves, R. E., "A Closer Look at the Effect of Market Growth on Industries' Profits," *Review of Economics and Statistics*, 64 (November 1982), pp. 635–645.

Brodley, J. F., "Antitrust Law and Innovation Cooperation," *The Journal of Economic Perspectives*, 4 (Summer 1990), pp. 97–112.

*Business Week*, "An Antitrust About-Face on Republic and LTV" (April 2, 1984), pp. 31–32.

*Business Week*, "Attacking the Test That Curbs So Many Mergers" (November 16, 1981), pp. 151–152.

Carey, J., "Will Uncle Sam Be Dragged Kicking and Screaming into the Lab?" *Business Week*, July 15, 1991, pp. 128–129.

Caves, R. E., "Diversification and Seller Concentration: Evidence from Changes, 1963-72," *The Review of Economics and Statistics*, 63 (May 1981), pp. 289–293.

Caves, R. E., and Barton, D. R., *Efficiency in U.S. Manufacturing Industries* (Cambridge, Mass.: MIT Press, 1990).

Caves, R. E., and Porter, M. E., "From Entry Barriers to Mobility Barriers: Conjectural Decisions and Contrived Deterrence to New Competition," *Quarterly Journal of Economics*, 91 (May 1977), pp. 241–261.

Chamberlin, E. H., "Duopoly: Value Where Sellers Are Few," *Quarterly Journal of Economics* (November 1929), pp. 63–100.

Chamberlin, E. H., *The Theory of Monopolistic Competition* (Cambridge, Mass.: Harvard University Press, 1933).

Chernow, R., *The House of Morgan* (New York: Atlantic Monthly Press, 1990).

Coase, R. H., "The Nature of the Firm," *Economica*, New Series, Vol. IV (1937), pp. 386–405, reprinted in *Readings in Price Theory*, edited by G. J. Stigler and K. E. Boulding (Homewood, Ill.: Irwin, 1952), pp. 331–351.

Cohen, W. M., and Levin, R. C., "Empirical Studies of Innovation and Market Structure," *Handbook of Industrial Organization*, Vol. II, edited by R. Schmalensee and R. D. Willig (Amsterdam: North-Holland, 1989).

Cohen, W. M., Levin, R. C., and Mowery, D. C., "Firm Size and R&D Intensity: A Re-Examination," *Journal of Industrial Economics,* 35 (June 1987), pp. 543-565.

Dasgupta, P., and Stiglitz, J., "Uncertainty, Industrial Structure, and the Speed of R&D," *Bell Journal of Economics,* 11 (Spring 1980), pp. 1-28.

Demsetz, H., "Industry Structure, Market Rivalry, and Public Policy," *Journal of Law and Economics,* 16 (April, 1973), pp. 1-10.

Dosi, G., "Sources, Procedures, and Microeconomic Effects of Innovation," *Journal of Economic Literature,* 26 (September 1988), pp. 1120-1171.

*Economist, The,* "Japanese Technology," December 2, 1989, pp. 3-18.

Edwards, C. D., *Maintaining Competition* (New York: McGraw-Hill, 1949).

Edwards, C. D., "Conglomerate Bigness as a Source of Power," in the National Bureau of Economic Research conference report, *Business Concentration and Price Policy* (Princeton: Princeton University Press, 1955), pp. 331-359.

Elzinga, K. G., "Collusive Predation: *Matsushita v. Zenith,*" in *The Antitrust Revolution,* edited by J. E. Kwoka, Jr., and L. J. White (Glenview, Ill.: Scott, Foresman, 1989), pp. 241-262.

Evans, W. N., and Kessides, I. N., "Living by the 'Golden Rule'. Multimarket Contact in the U.S. Airline Industry," manuscript, January 24, 1991.

Evenson, R. E., and Kislev, Y., "A Stochastic Model of Applied Research," *Journal of Political Economy,* 84 (April 1976), pp. 265-281.

Farjoun, M., "Beyond Industry Boundaries: Human Expertise, Diversification and Resource-Related Industry Groups," University of Illinois at Urbana-Champaign, manuuscript, 1991.

Feinberg, R. M., "Mutual Forebearance as an Extension of Oligopoly Theory," *Journal of Economics and Business,* 36 (1984), pp. 243-249.

Fellner, W., *Competition among the Few* (New York: Knopf, 1949).

Fisher, F. M., "The Misuse of Accounting Rates of Return: Reply," *American Economic Review,* 74 (June 1984), pp. 509-517.

Fisher, F. M., and McGowan, J. J., "On the Misuse of Accounting Rates of Return to Infer Monopoly Profits," *American Economic Review,* 73 (March 1983), pp. 82-97.

Fixler, D. J., "Uncertainty, Market Structure and the Incentive to Invent," *Economica,* 50 (November 1983), pp. 407-423.

Freeman, C., *The Economics of Industrial Innovation,* 2nd Edition (Cambridge, Mass.: MIT Press, 1982).

Friedman, J. W., *Game Theory with Applications to Economics,* 2nd Edition (New York: Oxford University Press, 1990).

Gale, B. T., and Branch, B. S., "Concentration versus Market Share: Which Determines Performance and Why Does It Matter?", *Antitrust Bulletin,* 27 (Spring 1982), pp. 83-106.

Geroski, P. A., "Innovation, Technological Opportunity, and Market Structure," *Oxford Economic Papers,* 42 (1990), pp. 586-602.

Geroski, P. A., *Market Dynamics and Entry* (Oxford: Basil Blackwell, 1991a).

Geroski, P. A., "Technology and Markets," London Business School, July 1991b (forthcoming in P. Stoneman, editor, *Handbook of the Economics of Innovation and Technical Change,* Oxford: Basil Blackwell).

Geroski, P. A., "Innovation and the Sectoral Sources of UK Productivity Growth," *The Economic Journal,* 101 (November 1991c), pp. 1438-1451.

Glennan, T. K., Jr., "Issues in the Choice of Development Policies," in *Strategy for R&D: Studies in the Microeconomics of Development,* edited by T. Marschak, T. K. Glennan, Jr., and R. Summers (New York: Springer-Verlag for the Rand Corporation, 1967).

Gort, M., *Diversification and Integration in American Industry,* National Bureau of Economic Research, Number 77, General Series (Princeton: Princeton University Press, 1962).

Gort, M., "An Economic Disturbance Theory of Mergers," *Quarterly Journal of Economics,* 83 (November 1969), pp. 624–642.

Greer, D., "Advertising and Market Concentration," *Southern Economic Journal,* 38 (July 1971), pp. 19–32.

Griliches, Z., "Issues in Assessing the Contribution of Research and Development to Productivity Growth," *The Bell Journal of Economics,* 10 (Spring 1979), pp. 92–116.

Griliches, Z., and Lichtenberg, F., "Interindustry Technology Flows and Productivity Growth: A Reexamination," *The Review of Economics and Statistics,* 66 (May 1984), pp. 324–329.

Hartwick, J. M., "Patent Races Optimal with Respect to Entry," *International Journal of Industrial Organization,* 9 (1991), pp. 197–207.

Heggestad, A. A., and Rhoades, S. A., "Multi-Market Interdependence and Local Market Competition in Banking," *Review of Economics and Statistics,* 60 (November 1978), pp. 523–532.

Helfat, C. E., "Know-how Complementarities and Knowledge Transfer within Firms: The Case of R&D," Working Paper 92-15, The Wharton School, University of Pennsylvania, September 1992.

Hines, J. R., Jr., "On the Sensitivity of R&D to Delicate Tax Changes: The Behavior of U.S. Multinationals in the 1980s," Working Paper No. 3930, National Bureau of Economic Research, Inc., December 1991.

Hladik, K. J., *International Joint Ventures: An Economic Analysis of U.S.-Foreign Partnerships* (Lexington, Mass.: Lexington Books, 1985).

Holstein, W. J., Treece, J., Crock, S., and Armstrong, L., "Mighty Mitsubishi Is on the Move," *Business Week* (September 24, 1990), pp. 98–107.

Itami, H., "The Firm and the Market in Japan," in *The Management Challenge,* edited by L. C. Thurow, pp. 69–80 (Cambridge: MIT Press, 1985).

Jaffe, A. B., "Technological Opportunity and Spillovers of R&D: Evidence from Firms' Patents, Profits and Market Value," *American Economic Review,* 76 (December 1986), pp. 984–1001.

Jaffe, A. B., "Demand and Supply Influences in R&D Intensity and Productivity Growth," *The Review of Economics and Statistics,* 70 (August 1988), pp. 431–437.

Jewkes, J., Sawers, D., and Stillerman, R., *The Sources of Invention* (London: Macmillan, 1958).

Jorde, T. M., and Teece, D. J., "Innovation, Cooperation, and Antitrust," University of California Berkeley Business School, Business and Public Policy Working Paper No. BPP-37, October 1988.

Jorde, T. M., and Teece, D. J., "Innovation and Cooperation: Implications for Competition and Antitrust," *The Journal of Economic Perspectives,* 4 (Summer 1990), pp. 75–96.

Kamien, M. I., and Schwartz, N. L., *Market Structure and Innovation* (Cambridge, England: Cambridge University Press, 1982).

Katz, M. L., "An Analysis of Cooperative Research and Development," *Rand Journal of Economics,* 17 (Winter 1986), pp. 527–543.

Katz, M. L., and Ordover, J. A., "R&D Cooperation and Competition," *Brookings Papers on Economic Activity: Microeconomics 1990,* edited by M. N. Baily and C. Winston (Washington, D.C.: The Brookings Institution, 1990), pp. 137–203.

Kelly, K., and Port, O., "Learning from Japan," *Business Week,* January 27, 1992, pp. 52–60.

Kim, E. H., and Singal, V., "Mergers and Market Power: Evidence from the Airline Industry," manuscript, University of Michigan, 1991.

Klein, B., *Dynamic Economics* (Cambridge, Mass.: Harvard University Press, 1977).

Kohn, M., and Scott, J. T., "Scale Economies in Research and Development: The Schumpeterian Hypothesis," *Journal of Industrial Economics,* 30 (March 1982), pp. 239–249.

Kreps, D. M., *Game Theory and Economic Modelling* (Oxford: Oxford University Press, 1990).

Lee, T. K., and Wilde, L. L., "Market Structure and Innovation: A Reformulation," *Quarterly Journal of Economics,* 94 (March 1980), pp. 429–436.

Lemelin, A., "Relatedness in the Patterns of Interindustry Diversification," *Review of Economics and Statistics,* 64 (November 1982), pp. 646–657.

Levin, R. C., "Appropriability, R&D Spending and Technological Performance," *American Economic Review,* 78 (1988), pp. 424–428.

Levin, R. C., Cohen, W. M., and Mowery, D. C., "R&D Appropriability, Opportunity, and Market Structure: New Evidence on Some Schumpeterian Hypotheses," *American Economic Review,* 75 (May 1985), pp. 20–24.

Levin, R. C., Klevorick, R. C., Nelson, R. R., and Winter, S. G., "Survey Research on R&D Appropriability and Technological Opportunity: Part 1," Working paper, Yale University (July 1984).

Levin, R. C., and Reiss, P., "Cost Reducing and Demand Creating R&D with Spillovers," *Rand Journal of Economics,* 19 (1988), pp. 538–556.

Levy, D. M., and Terleckyj, N. E., "Effects of Government R&D on Private R&D Investment and Productivity: A Macroeconomic Analysis," *The Bell Journal of Economics,* 14 (Autumn 1983), pp. 551–561.

Lichtenberg, F. R., "The Effect of Government Funding on Private Industrial Research and Development: A Re-Assessment," *Journal of Industrial Economics,* 36 (September 1987), pp. 97–104.

Lichtenberg, F. R., "Industrial De-diversification and Its Consequences for Productivity," National Bureau of Economic Research Working Paper No. 3231 (January 1990).

Link, A. N., *Allocating R&D Resources: A Study of the Determinants of R&D by Character of Use.* Washington, D.C.: U.S. National Science Foundation, 1981.

Link, A. N., "An Analysis of the Composition of R&D Spending," *Southern Economic Journal,* 49 (October 1982), pp. 342–348.

Link, A. N., "Alternative Sources of Technology: An Analysis of Induced Innovations," *Managerial and Decision Economics,* 4 (1983a), pp. 40–43.

Link, A. N., *Measurement & Analysis of Productivity Growth: A Synthesis of Thought,* National Bureau of Standards Special Publication 660, U.S. Department of Commerce (Washington, D.C.: U.S. Government Printing Office, 1983b).

Link, A. N., and Bauer, L. L., *Cooperative Research in U.S. Manufacturing* (Lexington, Mass.: Lexington Books, D. C. Heath and Company, 1989).

Link, A. N., and Long, J. E., "The Simple Economics of Basic Scientific Research: A Test of Nelson's Diversification Hypothesis," *Journal of Industrial Economics,* 30 (1981), pp. 105–109.

Link, A. N., and Lunn, J., "Concentration and the Returns to R&D," *Review of Industrial Organization,* 1 (1984), pp. 232–239.

Link, A. N., and Tassey, G., *Strategies for Technology-based Competition: Meeting the New Global Challenge* (Lexington, Mass.: Lexington Books, Heath, 1987).

Link, A. N., and Tassey, G., *Cooperative Research and Development: The Industry-University-Government Relationship* (Boston: Kluwer, 1989).

Long, W. F., and Ravenscraft, D. J., "The Misuse of Accounting Rates of Return: Comment," *American Economic Review,* 74 (June 1984), pp. 494–500.

Loury, G. C., "Market Structure and Innovation," *Quarterly Journal of Economics,* 93 (August 1979), pp. 395-410.

MacDonald, J. M., "R&D and the Directions of Diversification," *Review of Economics and Statistics,* 67 (November 1985), pp. 583-590.

Mancke, R. B., "Causes of Interfirm Profitability Differences: A New Interpretation of the Evidence," *Quarterly Journal of Economics,* 88 (May 1974), pp. 181-193.

Mann, H. M., "Seller Concentration, Barriers to Entry, and Rates of Return in Thirty Industries, 1950-1960," *Review of Economics and Statistics,* 48 (August 1966), pp. 296-307.

Mansfield, E., *Industrial Research and Technological Innovation* (New York: Norton, 1968).

Mansfield, E., et al., *The Production and Application of New Industrial Technologies* (New York: Norton, 1977a).

Mansfield, E., et al., "Social and Private Rates of Return from Industrial Innovations," *Quarterly Journal of Economics,* 91 (1977b), pp. 221-240.

Martin, S., "Advertising, Concentration, and Profitability: The Simultaneity Problem," *Bell Journal of Economics,* 10 (1979), pp. 639-647.

Martin, S., *Market, Firm, and Economic Performance,* Monograph 1983-1, Monograph Series in Finance and Economics, Saloman Brothers Center for the Study of Financial Institutions, Graduate School of Business Administration, New York University, 1983.

Martin, S., "The Misuse of Accounting Rates of Return: Comment," *American Economic Review,* 74 (June 1984), pp. 501-506.

Martin, S., "Private and Social Incentives to Form R&D Joint Ventures," manuscript, European University Institute, January 1991.

Mester, L., "The Effects of Multimarket Contact on Savings and Loan Behavior," Research Paper No. 85-13, Federal Reserve Bank of Philadelphia, 1985.

Milgrom, P., and Roberts, J., "The Economics of Modern Manufacturing: Technology, Strategy, and Organization," *American Economic Review,* 80 (June 1990), pp. 511-528.

Miller, J. C., III, *The Economist as Reformer: Revamping the FTC, 1981-1985* (Washington, D.C.: American Enterprise Institute for Policy Research, 1989).

Montgomery, C. A., and Wernerfelt, B., "Diversification, Ricardian Rents, and Tobin's q," *Rand Journal of Economics,* 19 (Winter 1988), pp. 623-632.

*Moody's Manual of Investments: American and Foreign* (New York: Moody's Investors Service, 1951).

Mueller, D. C., "The Effects of Conglomerate Mergers: A Survey of the Empirical Evidence," *Journal of Banking and Finance,* 1 (1977a), pp. 315-347.

Mueller, D. C., "The Persistence of Profits above the Norm," *Econometrica,* 44 (November 1977b), pp. 369-380.

Mueller, D. C., "Do We Want a New, Tough Antimerger Law?" *Antitrust Bulletin,* 24 (Winter 1979), pp. 807-836.

Mueller, D. C., "The Case against Conglomerate Mergers," edited by R. Blair and R. Lanzilotti, *The Conglomerate Corporation* (Cambridge, Mass.: Oelgeschlager, Gunn, and Hain, 1981).

Mueller, D. C., "The Corporation: Growth, Diversification and Mergers," *Fundamentals of Pure and Applied Economics,* 16 (London; New York: Harwood Academic Publishers, 1987).

Mueller, D. C., "The Effects of Mergers," in *Economic Analysis and Antitrust Law,* 2nd Edition, edited by T. Calvani and J. Siegfried (Boston: Little, Brown, 1988), pp. 303-321.

Mueller, D. C., "Mergers: Causes, Effects and Policies," *International Journal of Industrial Organization,* 7 (March 1989), pp. 1–10.

Mueller, D. C., editor, *The Dynamics of Company Profits: An International Comparison* (Cambridge, England: Cambridge University Press, 1990).

Mueller, W. F., "The Rising Concentration in America: Reciprocity, Conglomeration, and the New American 'Zaibatsu' System," *Antitrust Law and Economic Review,* 4 (Summer 1971), pp. 91–104.

Mueller, W. F., and Culbertson, J. D., "Inter-Industry Technology Flows in the U.S. Food-Processing Industries," *Managerial and Decision Economics,* 7 (September 1986), pp. 163–168.

Naj, A. K., "Creative Energy," *Wall Street Journal,* vol. 215 (June 14, 1990), pp. A1, A9.

Nelson, R. R., "The Simple Economics of Basic Scientific Research, *Journal of Political Economy,* 67 (June 1959), pp. 297–306.

Nelson, R. R., "Uncertainty, Learning, and the Economics of Parallel Research and Development Efforts," *Review of Economics and Statistics,* 43 (1961), pp. 351–364.

Nelson, R. R., "Government Stimulus of Technological Progress: Lessons from American History," edited by R. R. Nelson, *Government and Technical Progress* (New York: Pergamon, 1982a), pp. 451–482.

Nelson, R. R., "The Role of Knowledge in R&D Efficiency," *Quarterly Journal of Economics,* 97 (1982b), pp. 453–470.

Nelson, R. R., and Winter, S. G., *An Evolutionary Theory of Economic Change* (Cambridge, Mass.: Harvard University Press, 1982).

Odagiri, H., *Growth through Competition, Competition through Growth: Strategic Management and the Economy in Japan* (Oxford: Oxford University Press, 1992).

Ohmae, K., "Japan vs. Japan: Only the Strong Survive," *The Wall Street Journal,* January 26, 1981, p. 20.

Osborne, D. K., "Cartel Problems," *American Economic Review,* 66 (1976), pp. 835–844.

Oster, S. M., *Modern Competitive Analysis* (Oxford: Oxford University Press, 1990).

Penrose, E. T., *The Theory of the Growth of the Firm* (Oxford: Basil Blackwell, 1959).

Pitofsky, R., "Coke and Pepsi Were Going Too Far," *New York Times* (July 27, 1986), p. 2F.

Port, O., and Carey, J., "This Research Consortium Gets Its Research to Market," *Business Week,* January 27, 1992, p. 58.

Porter, M. E., *Competitive Advantage: Creating and Sustaining Superior Performance* (New York: Free Press, 1985).

Porter, M. E., "From Competitive Advantage to Corporate Strategy," *Harvard Business Review,* 65 (May–June 1987), pp. 43–59.

Porter, M. E., *The Competitive Advantage of Nations* (New York: Free Press, 1990).

Ravenscraft, D. J., "Collusion vs. Superiority: A Monte Carlo Analysis," manuscript, December 1980.

Ravenscraft, D. J., "Structure–Profit Relationships at the Line of Business and Industry Level," *Review of Economics and Statistics,* 65 (February 1983), pp. 22–31.

Ravenscraft, D. J., and Scherer, F. M., *Mergers, Sell-Offs, and Economic Efficiency* (Washington, D.C.: The Brookings Institution, 1987).

Rhoades, S. A., and Heggestad, A., "Multimarket Interdependence and Performance in Banking: Two Tests," *The Antitrust Bulletin,* 30 (1985), pp. 975–995.

Rosenberg, N., "Technological Interdependence in the American Economy," *Technology and Culture* (January 1979), pp. 25–50.

Rumelt, R. P., *Strategy, Structure, and Economic Performance,* Division of Research (Boston: Harvard Business School, 1974).

Salop, S. C., "Practices That (Credibly) Facilitate Oligopoly Co-ordination," pp. 265–290, in *New Developments in the Analysis of Market Structure,* edited by J. E. Stiglitz and G. F. Mathewson (Cambridge, Mass.: MIT Press, 1986).

Salop, S. C., and Scheffman, D. T., "Raising Rivals' Costs," *American Economic Review,* 73 (May 1983), pp. 267–271.

Scherer, F. M., "Firm Size, Market Structure, Opportunity, and the Output of Patented Inventions," *American Economic Review,* 55 (December 1965), pp. 1097–1123.

Scherer, F. M., "Market Structure and the Employment of Scientists and Engineers," *American Economic Review,* 57 (June 1967a), pp. 524–531.

Scherer, F. M., "Research and Development Resource Allocation under Rivalry," *Quarterly Journal of Economics,* 81 (August 1967b), pp. 359–394.

Scherer, F. M., *Industrial Market Structure and Economic Performance,* 2nd Edition (Chicago: Rand McNally, 1980).

Scherer, F. M., "Inter-industry Technology Flows and Productivity Growth," *The Review of Economics and Statistics,* 64 (November 1982), pp. 627–634.

Scherer, F. M., "The Propensity to Patent," *International Journal of Industrial Organization,* 1 (1983a), pp. 107–128.

Scherer, F. M., "Concentration, R&D, and Productivity Change," *Southern Economic Journal,* 50 (July 1983b), pp. 221–225.

Scherer, F. M., *Innovation and Growth: Schumpeterian Perspectives* (Cambridge, Mass.: MIT Press, 1984).

Scherer, F. M., "Schumpeter and Plausible Capitalism," *Journal of Economic Literature,* 30 (September 1992), pp. 1416–1433.

Scherer, F. M., et al., *The Economics of Multi-Plant Operation: An International Comparisons Study* (Cambridge, Mass.: Harvard University Press, 1975).

Scherer, F. M., et al., "The Validity of Studies with Line of Business Data: Comment," *American Economic Review,* 77 (March 1987), pp. 205–217.

Scherer, F. M., and Ross, D., *Industrial Market Structure and Economic Performance,* 3rd Edition (Boston: Houghton Mifflin, 1990).

Schmalensee, R., "Do Markets Differ Much?" *American Economic Review,* 75 (June 1985), 341–351.

Schumpeter, J. A., *Business Cycles,* 2 vols. (New York: McGraw-Hill, 1939).

Schumpeter, J. A., *Capitalism, Socialism, and Democracy* (New York: Harper, 1942).

Scott, J. T., "Nonprice Competition in Banking Markets," *Southern Economic Journal,* 44 (January 1978), pp. 594–605.

Scott, J. T., "Corporate Finance and Market Structure," chapter 13 of *Competition in the Open Economy: A Model Applied to Canada,* edited by Richard E. Caves et al. (Cambridge: Harvard University Press, 1980), pp. 325–359.

Scott, J. T., "The Pure Capital-Cost Barrier to Entry," *Review of Economics and Statistics,* 63 (August 1981), pp. 444–446.

Scott, J. T., "Multimarket Contact and Economic Performance," *Review of Economics and Statistics,* 64 (August 1982), pp. 368–375.

Scott, J. T., "Firm versus Industry Variability in R&D Intensity," in *R&D, Patents, and Productivity,* edited by Z. Griliches, chapter 10, pp. 233–245 (Chicago: University of Chicago Press for the National Bureau of Economic Research, 1984).

Scott, J. T., "Component Gestalt and Industrial R&D: Firm Effects and the Sample Space for Industrial R&D," Dartmouth College Working Paper No. 87-7, presented at the 57th annual conference of the Southern Economic Association in Washington, D.C., November 22–24, 1987.

Scott, J. T., "Diversification versus Cooperation in R&D Investment," *Managerial and Decision Economics,* 9 (September 1988), pp. 173–186.

Scott, J. T., "Purposive Diversification as a Motive for Merger," *International Journal of Industrial Organization,* 7 (March 1989a), pp. 35–47.

Scott, J. T., "Historical and Economic Perspectives of the National Cooperative Research Act," in *Cooperative Research and Development: The Industry–University–Government Relationship,* edited by A. N. Link and G. Tassey, pp. 65–84 (Boston: Kluwer, 1989b).

Scott, J. T., "Purposeful Diversification of R&D and Technological Advancement," in *Advances in Applied Micro-economics,* vol. 5, edited by A. N. Link and V. K. Smith, pp. 7–28 (Greenwich; London: JAI Press, 1990).

Scott, J. T., "Research Diversity Induced by Rivalry," in *Innovation and Technological Change,* edited by Z. J. Acs and D. B. Audretsch (New York; London: Harvester-Wheatsheaf, 1991a).

Scott, J. T., "Multimarket Contact among Diversified Oligopolists," *International Journal of Industrial Organization,* 9 (June 1991b), pp. 225–238.

Scott, J. T., and Pascoe, G., "Capital Costs and Profitability," *International Journal of Industrial Organization,* 2 (September 1984), pp. 217–233.

Scott, J. T., and Pascoe, G., "Beyond Firm and Industry Effects on Profitability in Imperfect Markets," *Review of Economics and Statistics,* 68 (May 1986), pp. 284–292.

Scott, J. T., and Pascoe, G., "Purposive Diversification of R&D in Manufacturing," *The Journal of Industrial Economics,* 36 (December 1987), 193–205.

Shapiro, C., and Willig, R. D., "On the Antitrust Treatment of Production Joint Ventures," *The Journal of Economic Perspectives,* 4 (Summer 1990), pp. 113–130.

Shepherd, W. G., "The Elements of Market Structure," *Review of Economics and Statistics,* 54 (February 1972), pp. 25–37.

Shepherd, W. G., "Causes of Increased Competition in the U.S. Economy, 1939–1980," *Review of Economics and Statistics,* 64 (November 1982), pp. 613–636.

Singh, H., and Montgomery, C. A., "Corporate Acquisition Strategies and Economic Performance," *Strategic Management Journal,* 8 (July–August, 1987), pp. 377–386.

Spence, M., "Contestable Markets and the Theory of Industry Structure: A Review Article," *Journal of Economic Literature,* 21 (September 1983), pp. 981–990.

Stewart, J. F., Harris, R. S., and Carleton, W. T., "The Role of Acquired and Acquiring Firm Product Market Characteristics in Merger Behavior," manuscript and seminar presentation, September 1980.

Stewart, M. B., "Noncooperative Oligopoly and Preemptive Innovation without Winner-Take-All," *Quarterly Journal of Economics,* 98 (November 1983), pp. 681–694.

Stigler, G. J., "A Theory of Oligopoly," in *Economic Analysis and Antitrust Law,* 2nd Edition, edited by T. Calvani and J. Siegfried (Boston; Toronto: Little, Brown, 1988), pp. 148–159.

Stocking, G. W., and Mueller, W. F., "Business Reciprocity and the Size of Firms," *The Journal of Business,* 30 (April 1957), pp. 73–95.

Strickland, A. D., "Conglomerate Mergers, Mutual Forbearance Behavior and Price Competition," manuscript, George Washington University (1980).

Strickland, A. D., and Weiss, L. W., "Advertising, Concentration, and Price–Cost Margins," *Journal of Political Economy,* 84 (1976), pp. 1109–1121.

Tandon, P., "Rivalry and Excessive Allocation of Resources to Research," *Bell Journal of Economics,* 14 (Spring 1983), pp. 152–165.

Taylor, R. E., "A Talk with Antitrust Chief William Baxter," *Wall Street Journal* (March 4, 1982), p. 28.

Teece, D. J., "Economies of Scope and the Scope of the Enterprise," *Journal of Economic Behavior and Organization,* 1 (September 1980), pp. 223–247.

Terleckyj, N. E., *Effects of R&D on the Productivity Growth of Industries: An Explora-tory Study* (National Planning Association, Washington, D.C., 1974).

Terleckyj, N. E., "Output of Industrial Research and Development Measured as Increments to Production of Economic Sectors." Paper given at the 15th Conference of the Inter-national Association for Research in Income and Wealth, York, England, 1977.

Terleckyj, N. E., "Direct and Indirect Effects of Industrial Research and Development on the Productivity Growth of Industries," edited by Kendrick, J. W., and Vaccara, B. N., *New Developments in Productivity, Measurement and Analysis* (Chicago: University of Chicago Press for the National Bureau of Economic Research, 1980).

Thurow, L., *Head to Head: The Coming Economic Battle among Japan, Europe, and America* (New York: Morrow 1992).

U.S. Bureau of the Census, Census of Wholesale Trade, 1972, *Volume I. Summary and Subject Statistics,* Appendix E. "Industry Product Codes and Descriptions – Manu-facturers' Sales Branches and Sales Offices," U.S. Government Printing Office, Wash-ington, D.C., 1976, pp. E1–E10.

U.S. Congressional Budget Office, *Federal Financial Support for High-Technology Indus-tries* (Washington, D.C., June 1985).

U.S. Congressional Budget Office, *How Federal Spending for Infrastructure and Other Public Investments Affects the Economy,* July 1991.

U.S. Department of Commerce, "Remarks of Malcolm Baldrige, Secretary of Commerce, before the American Bar Association, Section of Antitrust Law," (July 11, 1985).

U.S. Department of Justice, Statement of J. Paul McGrath about the proposed merger of LTV Corporation and Republic Steel Corporation, News release, February 15, 1984.

U.S. Department of Justice, News release and *Merger Guidelines,* June 14, 1984.

U.S. Department of Justice, *Vertical Restraints Guidelines,* January 23, 1985.

U.S. Department of Justice, News release of June 26, 1985, with accompanying letter of June 25, 1985 by Charles F. Rule, Acting Assistant Attorney General, Antitrust Divi-sion, U.S. Department of Justice, to counsel for CAM-I.

U.S. Department of Justice, News release with the Reagan Administration's five proposed new antitrust laws with statements by the Attorney General and the Secretary of Com-merce, fact sheets, and the proposed bills (February 19, 1986).

U.S. Department of Justice, Statement of Douglas H. Ginsburg before the Committee on the Judiciary, U.S. House of Representatives, March 5, 1986.

U.S. Department of Justice and U.S. Federal Trade Commission, Press Release, Joint Statement, and *Horizontal Merger Guidelines,* April 2, 1992.

U.S. Federal Trade Commission, *Statistical Report, Value of Shipments Data by Product Class for the 1,000 Largest Manufacturing Companies of 1950* (Washington, D.C.: U.S. Government Printing Office, January 1972).

U.S. Federal Trade Commission, *Statistical Report: Annual Line of Business Report, 1973,* Report of the Bureau of Economics (Washington, D.C.: U.S. Government Printing Office, 1979).

U.S. Federal Trade Commission, *Statistical Report on Mergers and Acquisitions, 1978,* Bureau of Economics (Washington, D.C.: U.S. Government Printing Office, August 1980a).

U.S. Federal Trade Commission, *Statistical Report on Mergers and Acquisitions, 1978,* Bureau of Economics, table 26: "List of Manufacturing and Mining Companies Ac-quired with Assets of $10.0 Million or More, 1948–1978," pp. 128–218 (Washington, D.C.: U.S. Government Printing Office, August 1980b).

U.S. Federal Trade Commission, *Statistical Report: Annual Line of Business Report, 1974,* Report of the Bureau of Economics (Washington, D.C.: U.S. Government Printing Office, September 1981a).

U.S. Federal Trade Commmission, *Statistical Report: Annual Line of Business Report, 1975,* Report of the Bureau of Economics (Washington, D.C.: U.S. Government Printing Office, 1981b).

U.S. Federal Trade Commission, *Statistical Report: Annual Line of Business Report, 1976* (Washington, D.C.: U.S. Government Printing Office, May 1982).

U.S. Federal Trade Commission, "Industry Category List for FTC Form LB, 1977," Appendix E, pp. 309–319, *Statistical Report: Annual Line of Business Report: 1977,* Report of the Bureau of Economics (Washington, D.C., U.S. Government Printing Office, April 1985).

U.S. General Services Administration, *Federal Register,* 50 (Washington, D.C.: U.S. Government Printing Office, 1985).

U.S. General Services Administration, *Federal Register,* 51 (Washington, D.C.: U.S. Government Printing Office, 1986).

U.S. 98th Congress, *National Cooperative Research Act of 1984* (October 1984) Public Law 98-462.

U.S. 98th Congress, *National Cooperative Research Act of 1984: Conference Report* (September 21, 1984) House of Representatives Report 98-1044.

U.S. House of Representatives, 101st Congress, 2d Session, Report 101-516, "National Cooperative Production Amendments of 1990," Report by the House Judiciary Committee on H. R. 4611, which was amended and passed by the House on June 5, 1990, reported in *Trade Regulation Reports,* no. 109, June 12, 1990, Part II.

U.S. Office of Management and Budget, *Standard Industrial Classification Manual, 1972,* "Wholesale Trade," Washington, D.C.: U.S. Government Printing Office, pp. 241–257.

Van Cayseele, P., "Spillovers and the Cost of Multiproject R&D," *Managerial and Decision Economics,* 7 (June 1986), pp. 133–139.

Weiss, L. W., "The Concentration–Profits Relationship and Antitrust," edited by H. J. Goldschmid et al., *Industrial Concentration: The New Learning* (Boston: Little, Brown, 1974), pp. 184–233.

Weiss, L. W., and Pascoe, G., "Adjusted Concentration Ratios in Manufacturing – 1972," manuscript, Line of Business Program, Federal Trade Commission, July 1982.

Weiss, L. W., and Pascoe, G. A., Jr., *Adjusted Concentration Ratios in Manufacturing, 1972 and 1977,* Statistical Report of the Bureau of Economics (Washington, D.C., Federal Trade Commission, 1986).

Weston, J. F., "The Nature and Significance of Conglomerate Firms," *St. John's Law Review,* special edition 44 (Spring 1970), pp. 66–80.

Whinston, M. D., "Tying, Foreclosure, and Exclusion," *American Economic Review,* 80 (September 1990), pp. 837–859.

White, H., "A Heteroskedasticity-Consistent Covariance Matrix Estimator and a Direct Test for Heteroskedasticity," *Econometrica,* 48 (May 1980), pp. 817–838.

Williamson, O. E., *Conglomerate Control and Business Behavior: An Inquiry into the Effects of Organization Form on Enterprise Behavior* (New York: Prentice-Hall, 1970).

Williamson, O. E., "The Modern Corporation: Origins, Evolution, Attributes," *Journal of Economic Literature,* 19 (December 1981), pp. 1537–1568.

Wilson, T. A., "An Analysis of the Profitability of Businesses of Diversified Companies," *Review of Industrial Organization,* 7 (1992), pp. 151–185.

Woodward, P., "Tacit Collusion by Conglomerates Operating under Imperfect Monitoring," Ph.D. Dissertation, University of Wisconsin-Madison, 1989.

Yamey, B.S., "Monopoly, Competition and the Incentive to Invent: A Comment," *Journal of Law and Economics,* 13 (1970), pp. 253–256.

# INDEX

Abreu, D., 22-3
accounting: data, 51; procedures, 52, 63; profits, 51, 229, 231
acquisitions, *see* merger
Acs, Z. J., 6, 135
Adams, Walter, 7, 217
Adams, William James, 13, 55, 228, 229
adjusted concentration ratio, *see* concentration
advertising, 28, 51, 55, 85-6; game, 49; intensity, 47-50, 52, 75, 229-30; traceable, 47-50; *see also* barriers to entry; nonprice competition
aerospace: firms, 184; industry, 184; *see also* aircraft
Agency for International Development, 215
aggregate concentration, *see* concentration
aircraft, hypersonic trans-atmospheric, 150-1
Alcoa case, 191
allocative efficiency, *see* efficiency
Alpha Portland, 229
Amato, L., 84
American Car & Foundry Company, 35
American Distilling Company, 36-7
Amihud, Y., 11, 227
anticompetitive behavior or performance, 20-1; *see also* market power; merger; predatory pricing; reciprocal buying
antitrust, 7, 223, 238; enforcement, 19, 21, 65-6, 188-9, 215; enforcement agencies, 20-1, 40, 188, 190, 194, 199, 239; guidelines, 189, *see also Merger Guidelines;* law, 3, 6-7, 56, 187-9, 191, 223, 237, 238, 240; liability, 199, 203, 225, *see also* damages; policy, 6, 21, 41,

43, 56, 65-6, 215, 223-5; reorientation of, 6-7, 187-202, 237, 238; violations, 7, 237; *see also* Assistant Attorney General for Antitrust; merger
Aoki, M., 3, 221
applied research and development, *see* research and development
appropriability conditions, 6, 113, 116, 117, 121, 122, 126, 128, 137, 180-1, 234; and appropriation of returns to R&D, 7, 111, 113, 117, 119, 121, 170-7, 180-1, 183, 196-8, 200-2, 204-5, 213, 221, 223-5, 238; and competition in the post-innovation market, 6, 85, 104-5, 135-7, 142, 149, 153-6, 161, 221, 223, 232; and R&D in the preinnovation market, 135-7, 143, 197; measures of, 126, 180; *see also* spillovers
ARCO Products Company, 236
arms-length trading, 18, 39, 42, 114; *see also* market
Armstrong, L., 3
Arrow, K. J., 113
assets: indivisible, 114; LB, 74-5, 231; physical, 114; valuation of, 11, 57, 227; *see also* common assets; value
assets/sales, *see* capital intensity
Assistant Attorney General for Antitrust, 7, 21, 189, 191, 194
asymmetry, 22, 25-7, 29-30, 162-3
Audretsch, D. B., 6, 135, 222

BP Oil Company, 236
Baily, M. N., 6, 239
Bain, J. S., 56-66, 229, 231; *see also* sample, Bain's
Baldrige, M., 192, 193